PRACTICAL
DIRECTORSHIP

PRACTICAL
DIRECTORSHIP

A GUIDE TO THE DUTIES
OF A COMPANY DIRECTOR

BY

HENRY E. COLESWORTHY
A.C.A., A.S.A.A.

CHARTERED AND INCORPORATED ACCOUNTANT

GOLD MEDALLIST OF THE SOCIETY OF INCORPORATED
ACCOUNTANTS AND AUDITORS

AUTHOR OF
" SECRETARIAL BOOK-KEEPING AND ACCOUNTS "

SECOND EDITION

LONDON
SIR ISAAC PITMAN & SONS, LTD.
PARKER STREET, KINGSWAY, W.C.2
BATH, MELBOURNE, TORONTO, NEW YORK
1931

First Edition   .   .   1924
Second Edition   .   .   1931

PRINTED IN GREAT BRITAIN
AT THE PITMAN PRESS, BATH

PREFACE
TO THE SECOND EDITION

SINCE the publication of the first edition of this volume two events of the greatest importance to directors have taken place. The first is the passing of the Companies Act, 1929, and the second is the collapse of the Stock Markets following on the unhealthy "boom-issue" period of 1928.

The general effect of the Companies Act, 1929, as regards directorship was the tightening-up of the legislative aspect of the duties of Boards of Directors. In addition, many items of directorial conduct which owed their existence to custom alone were given the force of statutory obligation under the new Act. In the following pages will be found set out the practical effect both of the old duties as amplified by the 1929 Act and of the new obligations which had no counterpart in the Companies Consolidation Act of 1908.

The second important happening quoted above, viz., the collapse of the Stock Markets, will have to be referred to on several occasions throughout the book. The reason for this is to be found in a statement made recently to the effect that inefficient directorship—more than any other cause—had been responsible for the period of mad finance which led to the crash of 1929–30. Coupled with the statement was a rider that capable directorship could, if directors so wished, become the principal factor in the rehabilitation of British finance and the resuscitation of industrial prosperity.

To ascribe the principal portion of the blame to the

delinquencies of directors may possibly appear un-
justifiable. But when the more outstanding abuses of
recent Joint Stock Company administration are examined, it will be found that whilst directors may not
always have been solely or even primarily to blame,
they had the remedies in their own hands in every
case. It is to be hoped that the revival of trade, which
is already overdue at the time these lines are written,
will be helped forward by efficient and practical
directorship. This entails the earnest endeavour on
the part of every director to assist in the complete
abolition of the dishonest and unsound issuing house,
to render the misleading prospectus a thing of the
past, and to oppose resolutely the committing of the
entire management—and consequently the fortunes—
of their companies to the mercy of one man. In addition, the practical director will help to eliminate the
guinea-pig finally and completely; he will insist upon
the reduction of unwieldy boards; he will combat the
scandals usually attendant on the payment of directors'
compensation; and, lastly, he will refuse to be a party
to that most grievous clog to the whole system of Joint
Stock enterprise—the thwarting of shareholders by
any unfair use of proxy-voting, and their subjugation
by means of the poll. It is safe to say that the return
of confidence to the investing public after every slump
is retarded to a regrettable degree by the memory of
sharp, and almost criminal, treatment which has been
meted out to investors by their own servants in Annual
General Meetings.

The particular thanks of the author are due to Mr.
A. E. Langton, who contributed largely to the revision
of the second edition.

H. E. C.

1931

CONTENTS

CONTENTS

PART II

THE DIRECTOR AND FINANCIAL CONTROL

CHAPTER IV

The director and accounts—The simplicity of accounts—
Modern accountancy—The meaning of double entry—
Debits and credits—A rule with no exceptions—The
identification of accounts—The classification of accounts
—The profit and loss account—Stock-in-trade—Balance
sheet—The difference between balance sheet and profit
and loss account—The composition of the balance sheet.

CHAPTER V

Depreciation—Wear and tear, fluctuation, and obsolescence—Ascertainment of depreciation—Amortization of
leases — Machinery — Residual value — Revaluation of
assets—Other methods—The board and depreciation.

CHAPTER VI

Manufacturing account—Trading account—Profit and
loss account—The appropriation account.

CHAPTER VII

The issued capital—Issue of shares—Issue of shares at a
discount—Writing off discount on shares—Commission
on shares—Preference shares—Redeemable preference
shares—Alterations of capital—Reduction of capital—
Reduction of paid-up capital out of profits—Return of
excess capital—Cancellation of uncalled capital—Debentures—Issue of debentures—Writing off discount—Repayment of debentures at a premium—Reissue of redeemed
debentures—Conversion of debentures—The capital account in the balance sheet.

CHAPTER VIII

Fixed and working capital—Classification of assets—
Classification of liabilities—Composition of control statements—Examples of statements—Alternative forms—
Working capital statements—Monthly profit and loss
accounts—Gauging capital requirements—Initial working
capital — Sources of capital — Seasonal or emergency
capital.

CHAPTER IX

Danger of elaboration—Presentation of statistics—Useless returns—Essential returns—(1) Return of total sales
or business done—Accumulation of stocks—(2) Return of
production or output—(3) Return of outstanding orders—
(4) Return of working capital—(5) Monthly profit and
loss accounts.

CHAPTER X

Issued share capital—Secured debentures or loans—
Open loans—Supply of goods on credit—Legal meaning
of subsidiary—The parent company—Losses of subsidiary companies—Auditors' report on subsidiary companies—The parent company's accounts.

PART III

THE DIRECTOR AND CONTROL OF PRODUCTION

CHAPTER XI

Comparison of cost—Class of stock produced—Shortage
of orders—Production in economic quantities—Danger of
over-production—The director and production.

CHAPTER XII

Costing personnel—The objects of costing—Constituents
of cost—The benefits of costing—Wages—Oncost.

CHAPTER XXII

The purchase of small businesses—Business agencies—
Absorption of companies—Fixing a purchase price—Purchase of a going concern—Valuation of assets—Past profits
and goodwill—Valuation of goodwill—Average normal
past profits—Stock exchange rules—Payment for goodwill otherwise than in cash—The ascertainment of liabilities—The future of the purchased business.

APPENDIX

PRACTICAL DIRECTORSHIP

PART I
The Director and Administration

CHAPTER I

THE QUALITIES OF DIRECTORSHIP

THE quality or office of directorship differs from the professions and commercial callings in the very important point that it is what each and every holder makes it. It is not bounded by any set code of duties and is subject to no control beyond that provided by the Companies Act of 1929. It follows, therefore, that perfunctory attention to a company's business, even if limited to the task of endorsing cheques for fees in respect of theoretical services, is termed "directorship" in business terminology just as the same term is correctly applied to real control and practical direction.

Directors have been variously described as managers, managing partners, trustees, and by a hundred and one descriptions, differing but slightly in their import. In any consideration of the full duty of a director no term is more apt than that of trustee. The term is not used to imply that a director is a trustee in the strict legal sense of the word, but that he is holding his post with the confidence of the proprietors and that he has their trust to conserve and guard ; it is used to indicate that the office is even more important than that of "managing partner appointed to fill that post by a mutual arrangement between all the shareholders."[1] Statute law and legal opinions have rarely impressed the office of directorship with a status much higher than that of agency and this definition provides a striking analogy between the present conception of directorship and the full connotation of trusteeship. There has been an unmistakable movement during recent years to render the difference between the two classes of responsibility less marked, but unfortunately the movement has been directed towards the alleviation of the burden on the trustee. Such a step is to be regretted, and one can only hope that recent events will bring about a reaction. Joint-stock enterprise cannot possibly be on a perfectly sound footing until the responsibility of directors in respect of a company's property is made real as well as apparent. At the moment there has only been one sign of a movement in the right direction. The Companies Act of 1929 made illegal, as from a date not later than May, 1930, all clauses in the Articles of Association of Companies purporting to indemnify directors and other officers from the consequences of their "negligence, default, breach of duty, or breach of trust." The insertion of this provision in the Act (Sect. 152) was a direct result of the "City Equitable" case, in which it was found that the articles contained a clause relieving its officers from any liability for negligence or breach of their duty.

This circumstance brought to an abrupt conclusion an action which that particular company had opened against certain of its officers.

Sect. 152 of the Companies Act, 1929, which renders void all such clauses in future, reads as follows—

Sect. 152. Subject as hereinafter provided, *any provision, whether contained in the articles of a company or in any contract* with

[1] *Automatic Self-Cleansing Filter Co.* v. *Cunningham,* 1906.

a company or otherwise, *for exempting any director*, manager, or officer of the company, or any person (whether an officer of the company or not) employed by the company as auditor from, *or indemnifying him against, any liability* which by virtue of any rule of law would otherwise attach to him *in respect of any negligence, default, breach of duty, or breach of trust* of which he may be guilty in relation to the company *shall be void—*

Provided that—
(a) in relation to any such provision which is in force at the date of the commencement of this Act, this section shall have effect only on the expiration of a period of six months from that date; and
(b) nothing in this section shall operate to deprive any person of any exemption or right to be indemnified in respect of anything done or omitted to be done by him while any such provision was in force; and
(c) notwithstanding anything in this section, a company may, in pursuance of any such provision as aforesaid, indemnify any such director, manager, officer, or auditor against any liability incurred by him in defending any proceedings, whether civil or criminal, in which judgment is given in his favour or in which he is acquitted or in connection with any application under section three hundred and seventy-two of this Act in which relief is granted to him by the court.

Nominal and Active Directors.

It is difficult to define the distinction between nominal and active directorship, but if, as is prophesied, the day of the "guinea-pig director" will shortly be over, the point may not be of great consequence. Whether this opinion, which appears to be held by the majority of our leading financial writers, will be borne out by the event remains to be seen. Reluctantly, the writer is unable to share in their optimistic forecast. It is agreed that public confidence has received rude shocks from misplaced confidence in the supposed ability of directors whose sole qualification was a title or a naval or military rank. But the public memory is very short, and custom dies hard. The inexplicable delusion that non-commercial peers, half-pay generals, and retired admirals are essential to the commercial prosperity of a public company will be difficult to eradicate entirely from the public mind. And in any event the third and fourth rank issuing houses will still seek the use of " names " to give an air of respectability and security to the flagrantly dishonest issues which are always in the immediate wake of the next favourable turn in the trade cycle.

There is a final point which prevents one from joining in the enthusiastic cry that the financial disasters of 1928–30 marked definitely the end of the nominal director's career. It is that no nominal director considers the strictures passed by the public and by the press to be applicable to himself. In no case does he realize that he is a totally uneconomic unit in the joint-stock structure. He never stops to reflect that his fees constitute neither payment for labour, wages of management, nor regard for organization. On the contrary, it remains the pathetic truth that the incompetent and superfluous nominal director frequently regards himself as one of the mainstays of his company. It seems to follow that he will not disappear until the appointment of original directors passes from the hands of promoters and until shareholders are given a real share in the filling of vacancies. This means that little improvement can be expected until the capability and experience of a director are taken into consideration ' before the property of the investor is committed to his care.

The Aim for a Higher Status.

There is a good deal of support for the view that every successful effort towards the improvement of the status of directorship will be an individual one only. Such efforts are more likely to attain the desired object than either legislation or combination for advancement in the form of a directors' learned society. Directorship does not lend itself to a course of study punctuated by examinations. It is rather a career in which an innate ability to lead and control is required. This first qualification is of the greatest importance and is absolutely indispensable. But it must be supported by a sound business training and by a thorough grasp of the principles of joint-stock finance. Under no circumstances must an appointment to a directorship be regarded as conferring the status of " giant of finance " upon the unequipped and inexperienced aspirant. In any case that status is one which may easily be a delusion. As Mr. Justice Coleridge once said : " I derive some consolation from the reflection that these giants of finance, upon closer investigation, dwindle down to very ordinary proportions. They usually transact business with each other involving millions in a most unbusinesslike way." Remarks similar to these occur with unfailing regularity in the course of every case, civil and criminal, brought before the courts. A study of the judgments in such cases as *Lagunas Nitrate Co.* v. *Lagunas Syndicate*, 1899, *Oxford Benefit Building Society*, 1887, and *Coventry and Dixon's case*, 1880, will prove clearly that the appointment to a directorship does not automatically transform the holder into a complete captain of industry. The office is one to be approached cautiously and with a sense of responsibility not unmixed with a certain degree of humility.

Efficiency in Directorship.

It is the view of one of our leading city editors that efficiency in directorship will be achieved when a standard of training in the principles of business comes to be regarded as equally essential in the case of a director as it is a condition precedent to the appointment of any subordinate officer. This is indeed a sound suggestion. It does not mean that every director should submit himself to an elementary course in commercial procedure or that he should pass through long periods of erudite study. When it is remembered that the majority of directors are either men who have taken seats on boards after years spent in production or salesmanship, or men who have had long experience in the control of a sole trader's business, it is apparent that an extensive theoretical training is impracticable. And yet in these cases, just as much as in the case of young men who assume directorships straight from the university, there seems no reason why a standard of efficiency should not be expected when such a condition is imperative in the case of every officer of the company of lower grade. The case of the young man direct from the university is of greater importance than the other. It is unfortunate that " directorship " is marked down by parents as a profession for their offspring, requiring no exact qualification beyond a pecuniary one. Happily this practice, so rife during the immediate post-War period, is dying out. Nowadays such candidates wisely proceed to the board by way of the practical training required for the commerce degrees, or submit themselves to a period of training in subordinate posts.

Amateur Directors.

Professor Dicksee, the eminent accountant, once stated that whereas one inefficient doctor may imperil the lives of but comparatively few people, the incompetence of an amateur auditor may encompass the ruin of thousands and entail the self-destruction of a great number. It has always been thought that this stricture was intentionally exaggerated, and that its purpose was to bring home the grave responsibility resting upon the shoulders of auditors. But the events of recent years show that had it been applied to amateur directors it would have been entirely and literally correct.

What Practical Directorship Means.

The director will then ask what practical director-ship entails and what is expected of him in order that his company may feel the benefit of his services. *In the first place he must be well acquainted with his legal responsibilities and obligations. On the practical side, every director should be able to appreciate the general principles of joint-stock finance, he should know how to control the working capital of his company, understand the organization of its staff, be in a position to offer constructive criticism on finance and policy, and be able to preserve a spirit of independence and a power of judging for himself. Lastly, he must be acquainted with accounting principles, be able to read a balance sheet, and be competent to grasp the information conveyed by periodical returns.* In case of doubt he should know to whom he must turn for information on any point affecting the welfare of the concern whose destiny is committed to his charge.

The Application of Knowledge.

The ability to apply the principles of practical directorship must vary in individual cases, but the need of every company for whole-hearted application remains constant. The director must therefore ensure that his company receives the benefit of his direction as well as his control. In later chapters will be found an explanation of the manner in which financial data are usually prepared, together with appropriate ex-planations of the information conveyed. The con-clusions drawn by each director may be applied either through the medium of board meetings or by personal contact with the company's officers. Unless the know-ledge gained is put to practical use, then the control exercised by the director is nominal only and does not constitute direction. It is unfair to leave the formulation of policy to the officers, and that is what occurs when the members of a board grasp the meaning and effect of information laid before them, but either neglect or shirk the application of their knowledge.

One-Man Control.

This need for real direction is equally important whether the decisions of a board are carried out by a managing director or by the company's staff. Unless the board expresses its views on the actual conduct and progress of the business its meetings resolve into a series of reports of the past work of one or two executive officers who receive no real assistance and are left to their own devices. This is an instance of excessive delegation of authority and is one of the reasons why many a company proceeds along a path mapped out by one man, until the peaceful security into which it has been lulled is rudely shattered by some disturbing incident revealing a very much less happy state of affairs than was imagined. Such occurrences can be obviated only by whole-hearted interest and direction by each and every member of the board. If any director is content to acquiesce in the decisions of one or more strong, yet perhaps misguided, spirits, then he becomes a nonentity whose personal immunity from statutory penalties is seriously threatened. He is completely unfitted to guide any company.

Multiple Directorships.

Except in the case of the managing director or managing directors, the office of director is rarely one calling for full-time services. It is natural then that most part-time directors accept seats on more than one board. As long as this practice does not preclude the devotion of sufficient time to each company as set out above, little can be said against it. It is inadvisable, however, for an aspirant to directorship to join in the competition for holding the record number of appointments recorded in the " Directory of Directors " or in the " Official Intelligence." To term this practice an abuse is perhaps too hard a term, but it is indeed difficult to believe that the division of a director's attention between fifty companies—and instances of such multiple appointments do exist—can be conducive to the best interests of each and every company whose assets are entrusted to his care. It goes without saying that such a director, if he has his finger on the pulse of every one of his companies, is nothing short of a genius.

Weighing the Responsibilities.

Before accepting a post on any board it is everyone's bounden duty to weigh thoroughly the responsibilities involved. If the company is already established, then its past history must be known to the intending director. If he is assuming a seat on the inception of the company then his responsibility dates from the time he is named as a director by the signatories to the Memorandum of Association, elected by the shareholders, or appointed to his post by the Articles themselves. If he is appointed by the Articles he must file with the Registrar of Joint Stock Companies a consent in writing to act as a director and sign the Memorandum agreeing to take up shares at least to the number required for qualification. Alternatively, he must file a contract with the Registrar stating that he will take and pay for the required number of shares. These duties are prescribed by Sec. 140 of the Act of 1929, which further forbids the publication of a prospectus naming a director who has not previously carried out these provisions. It follows that the responsibility of the director who joins a board on the incorporation of the company commences immediately, and he must consider the burden resting upon him from the day the prospectus is handed to him for approval. His trust will take effect from the time the public are invited to join as shareholders; his responsibility will continue throughout the time he remains on the board and for certain purposes even after the dissolution of the company or after his own resignation or disqualification.

Statutory and Moral Responsibility.

A director's responsibility should not be regarded as a duty bounded by the letter of the statute but as a duty which can be carried out successfully if carried out conscientiously. It will appear from succeeding chapters that some duties may legally be performed in a manner not consistent with the spirit of the law. Certain provisions are made for the protection of the shareholders which may be avoided by devious and yet legal manipulation. It is possible to ride roughshod over Sects. 35 and 38 of the Companies Act, 1929, which seek to ensure that the public shall be given specific information in prospectuses. There is also a method of avoiding the consequences of Sect. 37, which provides remedies for misled subscribers. Numerous instances could be given of loopholes in the 1929 Act, but they will not be quoted or explained in this book except to emphasize that practical directorship is successful directorship. Practical directorship is incompatible with any attempt, no matter how apparently justifiable, to drive a coach and four through any section of an Act which has for its purpose the protection of the public. The investor treats the director as a trustee, places his capital under his charge, and honours him with his unqualified confidence. The successful director then will be the one who regards his duty in this light and who recalls his stewardship if in doubt as to the extent to which he should, for instance, disclose his interest in property to be purchased (Sec. 35), or if tempted to follow the common yet illegal practice of taking qualification shares from a promoter and executing blank transfers. The practical director will be in word and in deed, the warden of his employers' chattels and the guardian of their interests.

Nominee Companies.

We conclude the chapter with a reference to the ever-growing uses, and, incidentally, abuses, of nominee companies. Originally, these companies were used by the principal joint-stock banks for the purpose of holding registered shares in companies, which shares were pledged to them as security for loans granted. By degrees the practice spread to the minor banking and financial houses and discount companies; finally, nominee companies were formed specifically for a purpose which was entirely alien to that for which they were introduced. This new purpose was the concealment of movements of shares belonging to certain of the shareholders, from the main body of the members.

The reason for the new subterfuge is readily apparent when it is considered that heavy falls in the Stock Exchange quotations of shares are followed immediately by frantic inspections of the register at Somerset House. One of the first questions the public asks is, "Have the directors unloaded?" If the shares of a director are registered in the name of a nominee company the search is fruitless.

The practical director is urged not to be a party to the abuse of what is intended to be a useful custom; in the hands of the joint-stock banks it is a convenient method of securing loans and overdrafts. In the hands of unscrupulous directors it could develop into an outstanding scandal of company administration.

CHAPTER II

THE organization of the staff of joint-stock companies differs from that of partnership businesses and sole trading concerns in so many ways that it is necessary to explain in detail the principles followed. Slight variations occur in different companies, but a knowledge of the usual channels through which authority is delegated step by step from a board of directors will enable the reader to apply the principles to any company irrespective of the class of trade carried on. In the first place the directors, and not the subordinate officers, are responsible to the shareholders for every matter affecting their property. It is true that the secretary is liable to penalties for omissions of duty under the Act, and that all officers, including auditors, are liable for the contravention of the particular sections affecting them. Nevertheless the board is in fact the accounting party to the shareholders and not the managing director, the secretary, the accountant, the auditor, or the solicitor. Authority is therefore traced downwards from the directors in every case. An outline of the channels of delegation is given on page 14. It represents the chain of authority of a manufacturing and selling company owning subsidiary companies.

The Preparation of a Chart.

It will be realized that the chart is intended only as an illustration and that the order of delegation is not applicable to any given company. A practical point which has proved of great use to many directors relates to this chart. Each newly appointed director should ask the secretary to prepare for him a list of the names of all principal officials of the company. From this the director should draw up a chart similar to that set out on page 14, with the addition of the full name of the holder of each post. The chart will then be found of great value during the course of the director's appointment, particularly at board or committee meetings.

The Board of Directors.

The organization of a Board of Directors does not vary greatly in English companies. There is usually a chairman, who is supported by a deputy chairman. The orders of the board are usually put into effect by a managing director who spends his whole time with the company. The directors, whether ordinary members of the board or whether acting as chairman or managing director, are appointed in various ways, depending to a great extent on the Articles of Association, which are rules for the internal government of a company. The Articles often provide that the first appointments shall be made by the signatories to the Memorandum or that the signatories themselves shall become the first directors, and that later vacancies shall be filled by the board subject to confirmation at a general meeting. The appointment is therefore entirely subject to the rules set down by the company for its own management, and it is quite possible to arrange that the directors shall have absolute power to recruit other directors to fill vacancies ; in that case the shareholders have no voice in the matter unless there exists such dissension on the board that new directors cannot be elected. Vacancies will then be filled by the shareholders. On the other hand, the Articles may

DELEGATION OF AUTHORITY IN A MANUFACTURING COMPANY

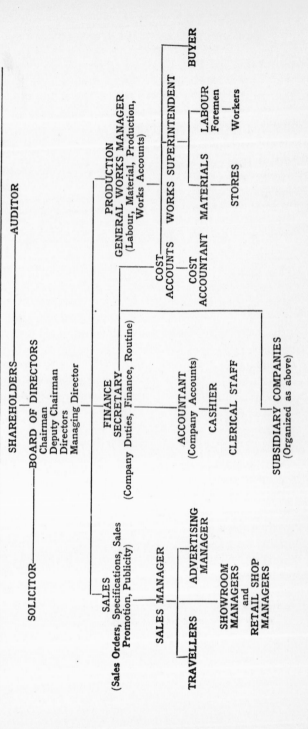

be framed in such a way that the shareholders only may appoint directors or that appointments made by the board shall be confirmed by the members at the next annual general meeting. It is the duty of every director to study the Articles of Association, and to ascertain whether his own appointment and the constitution of the board are valid. It is not sufficient to leave these matters to the company's solicitor or secretary.

Qualification Shares.

If the Articles are silent as to the number of qualification shares to be held, Table " A " applies. This provides that one share only need be taken up by each director. If the Articles stipulate that qualification shares must be acquired, and set forth the manner of acquiring them, then the directors must follow the exact provisions laid down by the Articles. In any case the shares must be acquired within two months of appointment (Sect. 141). It is a grave breach of trust on the part of a director to accept qualification shares as a gift from a promoter or to put the shares at the disposal of a promoter by means of a blank transfer. This latter custom cannot be too rigidly condemned; it is an act in the nature of a misfeasance.[1]

An instance of the grave effects of this practice occurred recently in a finance company floated in 1928. None of the directors paid for his qualification shares, which were held, with blank transfers, by the company. After a time the concern came under the control of an undischarged bankrupt, who proceeded to play fast and loose with the assets. One of the directors, and one only, realized the true state of affairs, and at once endeavoured to arouse his fellow-directors from their lethargy which was aiding the unprincipled manager.

[1] *London and South Western Canal Case,* 1911.

He failed to do so, and succeeded only in alienating the sympathy of his chairman. At once the manager induced the board to disqualify the director by having his blank transfer completed and his qualification shares registered in another name. There was a sequel which does not bear directly on the point under discussion, but which may be mentioned for the sake of interest. The company survived for a period of eight months only, its demise resulting in a total loss to the shareholders.

The Chairman, Deputy Chairman, and Managing Director.

The chairman and deputy chairman are ordinarily chosen by the directors from among their own number. The posts carry higher fees than those payable to the other members and in most cases the chairman is given a casting vote. On the matter of fees, it should be observed that no director is entitled to fees by a statutory right, and that if he carries out duties for a time and resigns from the board, he has no right to payment *quantum meruit* if the Articles contain no provisions for the payment of fees. Whether directors are entitled to fees or not depends entirely on the Articles. If the Articles are silent on the matter then any sum voted by the shareholders in general meeting is of the nature of a gratuity only. If the Articles do not provide for the payment of fees, and the shareholders do not vote a payment, then a director has no agreed claim to remuneration. The position of the managing director is rather different. In his case there is usually an agreement for service under the seal of the company, providing for payment of a salary. The managing director in that case is an employee of the company, with rights to remuneration in the terms of his contract.

Chairmanship and Continuity.

From time to time there arises a cry for " limited-period chairmanship." It is impossible to form any definite opinion on this matter until one has had an opportunity of gauging the acumen and efficiency of the chairman in power at the time. Every director should, therefore, form his own opinion after taking into consideration all the circumstances peculiar to his own company. It is important that the custom be kept in mind in order that its adoption may be suggested if the control of the board appears to be devolving into one-man administration to the evident detriment of the company's interests. The argument in favour of limited-period chairmanships is that they lead to increased efficiency. It is true that many insurance companies and banking houses follow the practice with undoubted success. As against this there is, of course, the case of the late Sir Edward Holden. One is often tempted to ask whether the Midland Bank would be in its position to-day if Sir Edward had held the office only during broken periods. That the bank grew from a tiny concern in one office to a place in the " Big Five " is perhaps the most striking tribute to continuous control one could find. In the case of industrial companies everything will depend on the circumstances. Generally speaking, it is advisable that continuity should be preserved on account of the difficulty which arises whenever a stranger chairman takes office. The fact that he requires some months to acquire a knowledge of the company's business must be kept constantly in mind.

In the case of public finance companies a change of chairman is often a profitable course to follow. Particularly is this so if the chairman is also the managing director and if the company or group tends to be regarded as his proprietary concern. The history of many of the financial groups which have been linked with the names of one or other of the pseudo-financiers makes depressing reading. One cannot help recalling in this connection the words of Mr. Alfred Salmon, of Lyons & Co., Ltd.: "I have a great dread of a large undertaking with a great deal of money involved where the whole of the activities depend upon the inventive genius of one individual."

The Secretary.

The office of secretary is perhaps the most onerous and important in every company organization. In some companies the secretary's duties are segregated from pure accountancy work and the latter is delegated to an accountant. In other cases it is the custom for the secretary to combine the duties of accountant with his own. This is due in no small measure to the training in accountancy prescribed for members of the Chartered Institute of Secretaries. This body has successfully raised the professional status of the secretary by insistence on the acquirement of full knowledge of accounting as well as secretarial work. Members of the principal accountancy bodies, on the other hand, also receive adequate training in secretarial practice. Whether or not the practice of combining the two offices obtains in his company must be ascertained by the director on joining the board. A distinction between an *accountant* and an *auditor*, which will be explained at greater length under the heading "Auditors," must be noted at this point.

The Secretary's Office.

The dignity and importance attaching to the office of secretary cannot be over-emphasized. The secretary is the agent of the company through whom practically all the important business of the company is carried out. The Articles frequently provide that all deeds sealed by the company shall be countersigned by him, and it is his duty to bring all matters of consequence before the board, to deal with their orders, and to control the clerical work and staff. On these grounds the director should always endeavour to preserve the dignity of the secretary's post and to avoid belittling his authority or control in any way. The whole of the clerical staff should be subject to this officer, in whose discretion all rules relating to the discipline of subordinates should remain. It is inadvisable for a managing director to arrange that his own clerical staff—including his private secretary—should be placed outside the jurisdiction of the secretary. If the secretary sees fit to formulate instructions as to the times of attendance of the staff and similar matters which may not, perhaps, quite coincide with the views of certain directors, then the matter should be rectified by a private talk with the secretary. He can then adjust the rules without loss of dignity. It is a deplorable practice—but, unfortunately, common—for a director to lessen the authority of the company's premier officer in any way.

In the chart given on page 14 the secretary forms the link not only between his own accounting offices and the board, but also between the works, the sales department, the purchasing department, and the subsidiary companies. Strictly speaking, therefore, all inquiries should be directed to the secretary, who will obtain the requisite information from the proper sources. In practice it will be found possible, and satisfactory, to proceed to the heads of departments direct.

The responsibilities of the secretary for clerical work in the company's factories will vary according to circumstances. It is desirable that he should be left in charge of all clerical staff, whether employed in the works offices or in the central accounting office. The reason for this principle is that the works manager should be free to concentrate his attention on production instead of having to spend considerable time in the supervision of the clerks. In any case the works clerical staff should be subject to the secretary for discipline. On the other hand, it is usual for the secretary to pass his directions as to accounting returns and requirements through the works manager. Whatever arrangements of detail are found necessary for co-ordination between the factory and the counting-house, the principle of control by the chief officer of the company, the secretary, should be observed. He alone is capable of judging the efficiency of the clerical staff and of economizing in, or adding to, the expenditure under this heading.

The Sales Department.

The sales department is controlled by a sales manager, who concentrates entirely on the disposal of the company's products, conducts its advertising and governs its salesmen. The sales manager directs the company's travellers and showroom managers. He plans the travellers' journeys and receives from them at frequent intervals reports concerning their work.

The sales department does not keep any books of account; the ledgers relating to customers' accounts are kept in the counting-house under the secretary or the accountant. Liaison is therefore necessary between the two departments at all times. All orders from customers are passed through the accounts office immediately upon receipt. They are marked by the secretary's staff with a note to the sales department as to the state of the customer's account with the company or as to his known status with other concerns. The sales department then approves the order and passes it forward to the works or the stores for execution, or files it until the customer either settles his previous account or provides cash against a *pro forma* invoice. Another matter demands the maintenance of co-operation between the accounts department and the sales department, namely, the provision of lists of outstanding accounts to be carried by the travellers on their journeys. The lists, which are prepared by the counting-house, assist the travellers to judge the advisability or otherwise of booking large orders from dilatory retailers. This form of liaison helps the Accounts Department$\frac{7}{2}$ in the collection of their old accounts.

It will assist the director to know that the Sales Department should be in a position to give the sales results for different territories, for different classes of goods, and from different travellers. On the other hand the Accounts Department should be able to give the total amount of goods invoiced from day to day, and from month to month, and the amount of goods not paid for at any date. This matter is referred to in a later chapter, but it is introduced at this point to draw attention to the real function of the sales department and to emphasize that it is not directly concerned with any financial records or accounting.

The Purchasing Department.

The purchasing department is controlled by a head buyer. It is his duty to supervise the purchases of his company and to direct the energies of the subordinate buyers. The importance of this department varies according to the type of business. A merchanting company importing finished goods from abroad or buying finished goods from manufacturers at home will have a purchasing department whose chief will, in a way, be subordinate to the sales manager. The sales manager in such a business often sells his goods before they have been purchased, and he therefore orders from the purchasing department the goods he requires to fulfil his sales. Purchases for stock are usually arranged at conferences between the sales manager, the managing director, and the head buyer.

In the case of a manufacturing business the procedure is rather the reverse. Once the board or the managing director has mapped out a production policy for the factory, the purchasing department proceeds to buy the raw material or the finished parts required for the programme adopted. Goods for manufacture are then taken into store under the control of the stores manager or chief store-keeper and issued to the works against requisition.

The Works Manager.

The works manager is subject to the board through the managing director, although matters of routine are carried out through the secretary. His production policy is dictated to him by the board as soon as they have formulated their programme. This programme is based upon the reports of the sales department and the finance department in manner to be explained in a later portion of this book. It is essential that the director should have a sound knowledge of the company's products and processes of manufacture. For this reason he will be well advised to become acquainted with the works manager by paying frequent visits to the works, and studying, with him, the production possibilities and limitations. Much time and money is lost by enforcing a policy on the works manager which is incapable of economic fulfilment. Directors should be acquainted with the type of plant employed; they should know its life and functions, and understand absolutely the conditions of labour existing in each department of the factory. Unless this knowledge is acquired it is impossible to comment to advantage on the manufacturing accounts when they are laid before the board, or to furnish practical advice on matters of policy such as rates of pay, the replacement of plant, and so on.

Subsidiary Companies.

When a parent company owns as much of the issued share capital of other companies as can legally be held by one individual then the organization of those sub-sidiaries generally follows that applied to the chief company. Variations suited to the particular requirements of each are, of course, introduced, and when practicable, the clerical work is committed to the parent company's staff, thus effecting great economies.

With regard to the directors of subsidiary companies, it is customary to appoint a board of nominees for each company, the nominees usually being members of the parent company's own board. In addition, it is usual to co-opt officials of the subsidiary or its former managers as additional directors. In the case of a subsidiary formerly conducted under partnership guidance and now absorbed by a holding company, it is common to retain the former partners as directors of the newly incorporated subsidiary company in addition to a majority of nominee directors of the main body. The case of the subsidiary company not wholly owned is a difficult one and will be discussed separately. In the case of the subsidiaries wholly owned, however, it is possible to give some general advice as to the director's conduct in connection therewith.

Subsidiary Directorships.

The practice of placing members of the parent board in charge of subsidiaries is a good one provided the directors appointed realize the dual nature of their trust. It sometimes happens that directors placed in charge of subsidiaries fail to realize that the policy of the smaller companies must accord with the policy of the parent company. It is useless, for instance, to embark upon heavy expenditure in order to ensure the illusory success of the subsidiary, if foresight plainly reveals that the capital burden will fall heavily on the parent company. The satisfaction of declaring a paper dividend to the parent company should be ignored if the ultimate benefit of the whole concern is likely to be reduced by such a course. This difficulty arises more frequently in cases where the boards of subsidiaries are not composed entirely of members of the parent board. The outside directors naturally desire to present as favourable a report of their work as possible and they are apt to resent the imposition of a policy which, though benefiting the parent company, may do so at the expense of the subsidiary. In order to obviate this trouble it is recommended that no outside directors be appointed to the boards of the companies wholly owned.

If the practice is at all possible, it is further recommended that all members of the parent board be appointed to seats on the boards of the subsidiary companies. The reason for this may not be quite clear and a word of explanation may not be out of place. It is a maxim of successful direction that all actual execution should be delegated. Unfortunately, the dividing line between direction and execution is not always recognized and some directors are apt to delegate duties which should be carried out by themselves. The existence of a subsidiary board furnishes a temptation to excessive delegation whenever the directors having power to delegate do not happen to have seats on the smaller concern's board.

Matters of the highest importance are brought forward by the technical officers of the subsidiary company for decision by the directors and the responsibility is shirked by the simple expedient of referring the question to the board of the subsidiary. The same objection may be raised to the unbusinesslike method of referring matters of policy to committees of subordinate officers. It may be advanced that this practice is sound on account of the fact that the business of the subsidiary is often quite alien to that of the parent company and that the principal directors have no practical knowledge of the manufactures or processes of the subsidiaries. But this is not an argument against the practice of making the directors of one company members of the boards of all the companies; it is an argument against the practice of forming huge amalgamations of companies between the products of which there is no connection.

Vertical and Horizontal Trusts.

The experience of the past few years has proved conclusively that combines realize the benefits for which they are organized only when the business of the subsidiary is identical with or ancillary to the main business. The amalgamation of the engineering company with the shipping company, the plantation company and the boot-making company rarely succeeds. No oncost saving is effected, for the staff of the various companies know nothing of the business of the others in the group. Huge headquarters and composite boards are formed and complete disintegration sets in after the outlay of no inconsiderable portion of the main company's liquid assets. The only cases in which amalgamations succeed are those in which the various boards and officers are cognizant in some measure of the practical side of all the associated businesses. The absorption of companies producing raw materials for the main manufacture is not open to the same condemnation, for the soap manufacturer, for instance, must always have some practical knowledge of the merchanting of the oils, derived from his previous dealings with independent suppliers. It is the case of the shoemaker refusing to stick to his last that leads to disaster. This matter has been dealt with at some length in order to illustrate the difficulties besetting combines when the divergence between the nature of goods manufactured by the constituent companies is such as to preclude the appointment of all the chief directors to seats on the boards of all the subsidiaries.

Subsidiaries Not Wholly Owned.

Directors must be particularly careful to differentiate between the subsidiary wholly owned and the subsidiary in which the parent company owns the majority of the shares. In the latter case it is undesirable to control the policy of the subsidiary without full regard to the rights of outside shareholders. The will of the majority cannot be forced upon the minority to the detriment of the latter's interest.

This matter is one of extreme importance and it is essential that the director should see the whole issue in correct perspective.

It may be accepted firstly that the internal management of a company concerns none but the shareholders. As a general principle it may be taken that it is in order for the majority to dictate the policy of the company. This first principle was laid down in the case of *Foss* v. *Harbottle* (1843), in which it was held that individual shareholders could not proceed against directors. Only a majority of the members could sustain an action, and only the general body of shareholders could bring an action to redress a wrong committed by members of the board. At the same time it is well established that the majority will always be restrained from imposing or causing loss to the minority. In addition, the danger of injuring the minority *without intent to do so* should be so constantly present that the director cannot do better than refrain from any act which even resembles harshness to the minority.

It is perhaps hardly necessary to warn the director of a parent company which holds a majority of shares in a subsidiary that the majority cannot practise fraud—as distinct from harsh treatment—upon the outside shareholders. In this connection it must be remembered that certain acts may be fraudulent upon a minority in their early stages and yet possible of ratification by the majority at a subsequent general meeting. Such acts are equally illegal.

Then there is the case in which the parent company may attempt an imposition which is not fraudulent but which is inequitable. In this case the rule in *Foss* v. *Harbottle* is laid aside, and the court will certainly interfere to prevent the wrong.

The next case is that in which the consent of the minority is obtained by trick or without disclosure by the majority of material facts which would cause the minority to withhold its agreement. The minority is able to prevent the parent company from acting upon any resolution obtained in this way.[1]

The last case, and perhaps the most important of all, is that in which the majority of the shareholders attempt to alter the Articles. In one instance which came before the Courts,[2] the proposed alteration was designed to force a minority to part with its shares,

---

[1] *Baillie* v. *Oriental Telephone & Electric Co.*, 1915.
[2] *Brown* v. *British Abrasive Wheel Co.*, 1919, 1 Ch. 290.

but it is probable that the doctrine will extend to any effort to alter Articles to the detriment of a minority.[1]

The Auditors.

The position of the auditor or auditors in the organization of the company should be grasped thoroughly by all directors. Every company must employ an auditor or auditors, to whose inspection the books and accounts of the company must be open at all reasonable times. The auditor is an officer of the company and is subject to the provisions of Sect. 276, which reads as follows—

276.—(1) If in the course of winding-up a company it appears that any person who has taken part in the formation or promotion of the company, *or any past or present director*, manager or liquidator, or *any officer of the company*, has misapplied or retained or become liable or accountable for any money or property of the company, or *been guilty of any misfeasance or breach of trust* in relation to the company, the court may, on the application of the official receiver, or of the liquidator, or of any creditor or contributory, examine into the conduct of the promoter, director, manager, liquidator, or officer, and compel him to repay or restore the money or property or any part thereof respectively with interest at such rate as the court thinks just, or to contribute such sum to the assets of the company by way of compensation in respect of the misapplication, retainer, misfeasance or breach of trust as the court thinks just.

(2) The provisions of this section shall have effect notwithstanding that the offence is one for which the offender may be criminally liable.

(3) Where in the case of a winding-up in England an order for payment of money is made under this section, the order shall be deemed to be a final judgment within the meaning of paragraph (g) of subsection (1) of section one of the Bankruptcy Act, 1914.

The case which lays down that the auditor is an officer of the company [2] is noteworthy also on account of the remarks made by Mr. Justice Lopes in the course of his judgment—

It is the duty of an auditor to bring to bear on the work

[1] The point must not be confused with the statutory provision under which dissentients to a scheme of transfer of shares to another company are forced to accept a price for their shares as fixed by the Court. (Companies Act, 1929, Sec. 155.) This provision which has been characterized as a " legal injustice crying aloud for repeal " is referred to in greater detail later.

[2] *Kingston Cotton Mills, Co.*, 1896 (1 Ch. 6).

he has to perform that skill, care, and caution which a reasonably competent, careful and cautious auditor would use. What is reasonable skill, care, and caution must depend on the particular circumstances of each case. An auditor is not bound to be a detective or, as was said, to approach his work with suspicion or with a foregone conclusion that there is something wrong. He is a watchdog but *not a bloodhound*.

The last sentence is particularly important and must be noted by every director. As a matter of fact it is impossible for an auditor to carry out duties approximating to those of a watchdog or of a bloodhound unless he is in attendance at the company's offices throughout the year. A great portion of the watchdog's duty must therefore remain with the directors, and they should prevent themselves from being lulled into false security by thinking that sufficient check is placed on the company's funds by visits of the auditor once or twice a year. The installation of an efficient *internal* audit, which will be explained in due course, is a duty resting upon the directors and not upon the company's auditors.

There is no fixed scale of remuneration for auditors. It is usual for the directors and the auditor to agree upon a fee, either fixed or based upon time spent, in spite of the fact that Sect. 132 (s.s. 6) provides that the remuneration of auditors shall be fixed by the company in general meeting. In this case everyday practice carries out satisfactorily what an indefinite and scarcely practical sub-section could not bring about.

Distinction Between the Auditor and the Accountant.

Many companies employ an official known as the Accountant and charge him with the supervision of the accounting work, which is in such cases separated from the secretary's department. Whether the accountant is a full-time employee or a practising accountant, his work consists in the accounting for, and the recording of, the company's business as a *servant* of the company. He actually writes up, or causes to be written up, all the financial records, and he prepares the directors' accounts for presentation to the shareholders. The auditor, on the other hand, is appointed by the shareholders (Sect. 132, s.s. 1). He is entirely independent of the board and his independence should be observed rigidly at all times by the directors. He does not write up the books or prepare the accounts. He audits the *directors'* accounts and reports upon them to the shareholders in general meeting. Stress is laid upon the expression " directors' accounts " because it is sometimes imagined that it is the duty of the auditor to prepare the accounts and to present them for the directors' approval. This is not so ; the directors themselves are responsible for the preparation of the accounts and they do it personally or through their servants, usually the secretary or the accountant. They then present their accounts to the auditor, who examines them and reports upon them to the proprietors.

Among the many deplorable phases of the clearing up of the 1928–9 debacle a noticeable feature was the readiness to blame auditors for delay in the presentation of accounts. Particularly was this the case with companies falling within the category described picturesquely and appropriately by Mr. Arthur Wade of the *Evening Standard* as " dirt-track issues." The directors, who were generally inept if they were not actually rogues, were much disturbed by the constant inquiries made by city editors as to the delay in presentation of their accounts. It was then that one bright genius hit upon the excuse that " the auditors had not yet made up the accounts," apparently oblivious of the fact that he was thereby condemning his own incompetence as a director. He was not alone, however, and before long the specious excuse was takeñ up, with variations, on all sides. Some went so far as to say that the board had no idea whether a profit or a loss had been made because the auditors had not written up the company's books.

In small private companies the auditor does, on occasion, make entries in the books, but it must always be borne in mind that whilst so acting he is an accountant and the agent of the directors.[1]

Auditors' Reports.

The auditor is free to make any report on directors' actions in any terms his discretion dictates, and he cannot be tied by instructions from any board or by any set of Articles. This independence was emphasized in the case of *Newton* v. *B.S.A., Ltd.*, in which it was held that a company could not adopt Articles preventing the auditor from reporting on a company's secret reserves if he thought fit to do so. In order that the independence of the auditor may be maintained the Act provides (Sect. 132, s.s. 3) that no person other than the retiring auditor may be re-elected for another year unless notice of the intention to propose some other person has been served at the company's office at least fourteen days before the annual general meeting. This notice must also be communicated to the auditor and to the shareholders at least seven days before the meeting.

The Solicitor.

The relation between the solicitor and the company is different from the relation existing between the auditor and the company. The relation is no more

[1] *Western Counties Steam Bakeries*, 1897 (1 Ch. 617).

than that subsisting between a solicitor and an ordinary client. The solicitor is appointed by the directors and usually charges scale fees for work done. He may be replaced by another solicitor without the sanction of the shareholders and without notice to the members. He is not ordinarily subject to the provisions of Sect. 276 (*supra*), and is not an officer of the company. It may happen, however, that where a solicitor acts in a capacity other than that of a solicitor he may render himself liable to misfeasance proceedings, and he may be regarded as a promoter if his actions with regard to a flotation or prospectus exceed those ordinarily required of a solicitor as such in these matters.

Subordinate Officers.

The other officers of a company vary in number, salary and authority according to the size and business of the company It is unnecessary to tabulate the usual appointments here, for a director must appreciate the particular scheme of administration adopted by his company before he can gauge the relative importance of subordinates. In addition to the secretary, accountant, managing director, sales manager and head buyer there may be works managers, technical advisers, general managers, cost accountants, and a thousand and one minor officials to whom authority is in greater or less degree delegated. Except as indicated above, however, these officials are not officers of the company within the usual meaning of the Act, and their responsibilities are bounded by the decisions of the board on the matter. A director cannot make any serious mistake if he follows the rough test of responsibility provided by the Act. He will not then be guilty of the error of allowing a technical adviser, for instance, to dictate to, or to assume any of the responsibilities of the board. Pitfalls of this kind may be avoided by insisting that all officials, no matter how high-sounding their descriptions, should approach the board and take their orders from the board through the medium of the secretary.

Harmonious Organization.

Harmony in company organization is often subject to the onslaught of a disturbing factor for which the remedy is in the hands of the directors alone. Officials with a grievance are prone to air their complaints by means of communications made direct to individual members of a board. Any tendencies of this sort should be stamped out ruthlessly and the communications treated as they would be if they were anonymous. Even where a complaint appears to have grounds of justification, the recipient should make it clear that he will not be a party to a departure from the adopted routine of administration. Officials with complaints must not be allowed to cause a rift by passing over the heads of their superior officers, and the directors should regard it as their duty to put an end to the practice. Efficient administration needs harmony, and demands a fixed routine in every matter affecting the business of the company and the duties of its officials.

CHAPTER III

THE ADMINISTRATION OF JOINT-STOCK COMPANIES

THE success or failure of joint-stock enterprise probably depends upon efficient administration to a far greater extent than upon any other factor. Capable administration can steer a company successfully through times of deepest trade depression whilst ignorant administration can often ruin another company at a time when trade could offer its brightest hopes of success. Administration depends firstly upon correct organization. It is useless to attempt to administer unless the machinery for the execution of the board's instructions is efficient and able to cope with the demands made upon it. It follows, as a natural corollary, that a well-organized company cannot work efficiently unless the administration of the board is sound, logical, and practical.

The chief essential of administration is that it should be definite and unequivocal. The board cannot vacillate or give ambiguous directions, blaming subordinates for inefficiency when half-hearted plans miscarry. Policy in all matters must be clear cut and the directors must accept full responsibility for their decisions.

Use of Board Meetings.

The decisions of the directors are arrived at through deliberations at periodical meetings, each of which it is the duty of every director to attend. The actual decisions upon each particular point are recorded in minutes written up by the secretary from his own notes or those of the chairman. The views of each director must be obtained by putting the resolution to the meeting and objection should be made if a director is not satisfied that the decision is being correctly recorded.

A great deal depends upon the methods of the chairman. Occasionally chairmen neglect to put resolutions forward in a manner embodying the various views of members of the board. The secretary is then caused considerable trouble when numerous objections are made to the minutes he has framed from the chairman's declarations. Other chairmen are apt to declare their own views on particular matters with such vehemence and authority that their words are taken as the unanimous opinion of the whole board.

Any tendency to turn the board into a one-man concern must be strongly resisted. No director should allow his judgment to be overruled by any other members unless they have convinced him that he is in the wrong. Directors should not arrive at meetings with only a hazy idea of the general state of affairs, or of the matters which arose at previous meetings. It is the general practice for the secretary to circulate draft copies of the minutes of each meeting prior to entering them in the minute book. The director should examine the draft, prepare any objections he may have and notify the secretary as soon as possible. At the next subsequent meeting he should voice his objection as soon as the chairman asks the directors whether it is their pleasure that he sign the minutes as circulated as a correct record of the previous proceedings.

Should it happen that a director was absent from a meeting he should not gloss over any points in the circulated draft which he cannot fully understand. He should make it his business to have the questions raised afresh in order that he may obtain the context and grasp the full effect of the decision. Too often do directors allow emergency meetings to decide upon important matters and permit the draft of the decisions of meetings, at which they were not present, to receive their tacit consent.

Filing Minutes.

All drafts of minutes should be filed and indexed by the director's private secretary. He will then be in possession of a copy of the minute book together with a record of the names of the directors present at any particular meeting. It is practically impossible for a director to trust to his memory to recall every decision of the board without the aid of his draft. He should refresh his memory from time to time, particularly just before meetings at which agreements and financial documents are to be brought forward for sanction. Agreements relating to bank overdraft guarantees, agreements with servants, and officers, and agreements for purchase of assets, are matters to which a director should give his assent only when he has carefully examined the previous commitments and policy of the company as outlined in the minutes.

The Memorandum and Articles.

A director should always be acquainted with the main objects clause of the company's Memorandum and with the principal Articles of Association. It is indeed advisable for him to carry his copy of the Memorandum with him to each board meeting, for he is often bound to consider whether any act of administration in which he participates is *ultra vires* or not. A company is not allowed to carry out acts which are *ultra vires* or not sanctioned by the Memorandum.

Should a director acquiesce in the employment of the company's funds outside the scope of the Memorandum he may render himself personally liable for the moneys if they prove to have been misapplied. It is true that the court has power to grant relief, but the director should not rely on this doubtful protection.

Administration Through a Managing Director.

Administration through a managing director is sometimes very successful and, strangely enough, sometimes disastrous. Everything depends upon the quality and personality of the managing director himself. Occasionally it is found possible to communicate the decisions of a board to the managing director at board meetings and to leave the administration entirely to him. This practice may be successful in many cases, but it is unwise for the directors to make this autocracy complete or to allow the managing director to constitute himself a committee of one under such circumstances as are permissible by Clause 85 of Table " A."

This mistake was committed recently by the board of a public company. The directors decided to acquiesce in the suggestion of the managing director that he should be constituted a " Finance Committee " under Clause 85, which reads as follows—

TABLE " A "—85. The directors may delegate any of their powers to committees consisting of *such member* or *members* of their body as they think fit; any committee so formed shall in the exercise of the powers so delegated conform to any regulations that may be imposed on it by the directors.

As the Finance " Committee " proceeded to sell the company's quoted investments and to reinvest the cash in concerns which ultimately proved worthless, the danger of the policy was well illustrated.

Table " A " is a model set of Articles applying to companies which do not adopt special Articles. Any clauses of Table "A" which are not specifically excluded by special Articles apply to all companies. Unfortunately several of its clauses tend to facilitate errors of judgment similar to that quoted above. For this reason every director should keep a careful record of the clauses which are not excluded from his company's own articles of association. These non-excluded clauses are often as important as the provisions which have been incorporated specifically by the company's lawyers.

Control Over Managing Director.

There are many ways in which a board may exercise control over the managing director whenever he is entrusted with the administration. Full use should be made of the check provided by the financial and production reports of the secretary and works managers, and by the selling and purchasing returns of the sales manager and head buyer. These reports should reach the board direct through the secretary. It is unwise to allow the managing director to incorporate them in his own reports, though naturally he will approve them before they are circulated.

Management Committees.

Occasional attempts are made to form management committees consisting of the sales manager, the head buyer and the managing director or general manager. These three officials must always be in touch with each other, but it will rarely be found to lead to efficient administration to form them into a committee with equal powers. This practice almost invariably leads to dissension and to slack administration. One man only, either the managing director or the secretary, should transmit the policy of the board to the various officers concerned. Committees usually endeavour to dictate their own policy, and at times the individual members usurp the powers of the board. It is not the duty of a managing director or any other officer to dictate his own policy. He must only carry out the administration decided upon by the directors. If he fails in the administration then his responsibility is fixed. It is almost impossible to fix responsibility for failure on a management committee when its members are at variance with one another.

Co-ordination.

The appointment of management committees must not be confused with the establishment of co-ordination among officers. Co-ordination is absolutely essential throughout. Financial administration may be delegated to the secretary and general administration to the general or managing director, but there must be the closest liaison between these two officers and also between them and all principal officials. The presence of senior officials at board meetings is a practice which might be adopted more widely with advantage. It ensures the elimination of the disadvantages of one-man control, and the directors are enabled to obtain information on matters of detail direct from departmental managers. It is necessary, even in that case, to cause the decisions of the board to be recorded in the usual manner, and for the secretary to circulate memoranda of the decisions arrived at by the directors. This routine must be followed in spite of the fact that the managers may have taken their own notes at the meeting.

Working Directors.

From time to time one encounters boards composed entirely of working directors. They meet in board meetings for the purpose of recording their

decisions officially. Usually each takes charge of a
section of the administration, and their efforts are
co-ordinated by means of frequent unofficial conferences. Such conferences differ from the meetings of
management committees appointed by a board because
the members of the conferences are directors and are
directly responsible to the shareholders instead of
through a board. Dissensions are only likely to arise
under the circumstances in which they arise in partnership businesses. A majority of the directors could
then resort to methods similar to those adopted in
partnerships in dealing with recalcitrant partners.
The aggrieved director has of course the remedy of
ascertaining the feeling of the proprietors in general
meeting. This method of administration is the most
successful but the one least frequently possible of
adoption.

Administration Through a General Manager.

Certain classes of business are of such a nature that
although the control must be in the hands of a strong
board, the business is actually in the hands of a general
manager. Instances of this class of business will be
found in the investment and trust companies. There
is a secretary and perhaps an accountant, but no sales
managers, works managers or buyers. In these companies—though the fact is not always appreciated—
the responsibility of the board is far greater than in
the industrial company. The power of the manager
must necessarily be so wide that the board may find
itself in danger of becoming the administered body.
In order to maintain as strict a control as possible
the board should meet far oftener than in the case of
a commercial company. The books of the company
should be examined by the board, and every member
should understand the principles of a finance company's

accounting. The board should insist upon a monthly audit by a firm of professional auditors, who should report direct to the board after each examination. Every transaction should be recorded in the minutes and the unwise practice of allowing financial transactions up to a stated limit to be carried through without previous or subsequent report to the board should be discountenanced.

It must be realized that companies of this class are largely at the mercy of the manager, and that any director taking a seat on a board of such companies is playing with fire unless he makes it his business to control the shareholders' money efficiently and continuously. It is only necessary to remind the reader that most of the company failures which have brought out the danger of inefficient directorship have been non-manufacturing companies. This emphasizes the danger awaiting the weak, ignorant, careless or amateur director. He cannot fail to be fair game to the captain of finance, whose wits, sharpened by years of city experience, permit him to deal successfully with the gentlemen who " direct," " control," and " advise " him in his work.

Directors and Detail.

If the organization of a company has been planned on sound lines, then the administration will flow smoothly through the channels of delegation. It should be unnecessary for directors to follow their administrative directions through the company. They should decide upon their policy, give their orders, accept or reject quotations, and then await the result of their work. Delving into detail is as great a fault with some directors as glossing over principles is with others. This may be illustrated by an example. Let us suppose that the technical officers have drawn up a scheme for the installation of new plant, or for the erection of new shops, and that the scheme has received the approval of the sales department. It is then laid before the board. The directors have to weigh the pros and cons, examine the financial aspect of the matter with the aid of a report from the secretary, and finally reach and record a definite decision. If it is resolved to adopt the scheme, all that is necessary is to pass a minute to that effect and allow the officials to proceed. It is no part of the directors' work to usurp the subordinate duties of the works manager, for instance, and to insist on the installation of the plant in any manner other than that which seems best to the man on the spot and his associates. There is nothing to prevent any director from tendering practical advice he may have to offer, but he should not interfere with detail.

Similarly it is wrong for directors, collectively or individually, to engage subordinate staff and foist them upon the secretary or works executives. The secretary is responsible for his department to the board, and interference with the personnel with which he must work is not likely to preserve harmony in administration. It is quite out of place for a director to give directions to a subordinate over the head of superior officers.

In short, the directors should direct only, and allow the manager to manage his works and the secretary to work his own department. If any officer cannot control his department successfully, then the only duty devolving on the directors is to remove him.

On the matter of staff it is most important that directors should avoid any suggestion of nepotism. To engage staff from among personal acquaintances, either directly or by exercising influence over the officers, is a cause of dissatisfaction rife in joint-stock companies to-day.   It makes the chief officers at one with the lower grades in the feeling of injustice which is experienced by the latter whenever directors exert an influence contrary to the spirit of their trust.

PART II

The Director and Financial Control

CHAPTER IV

AN OUTLINE OF COMPANY ACCOUNTING

The Director and Accounts.

IN this section we propose to deal with the director's duty in connection with his company's accounts. Many directors profess a profound contempt for the book-keeping and accountancy aspects of the activities of the organization they direct. So well-known and widespread is this tendency that a critical—and perhaps cynical—observer was once led to observe: "*This pose is a clever one. He maintains persistently that he never had, and never would, understand accounts ; at other times he repeats some fallacious but dangerous tag such as—'figures can be made to prove anything !' He is then assured of the endorsement of his equally incompetent confrères.*"

Unfortunately there is a great deal of truth in this stricture. It is a well-known but regrettable fact that there are public directors who endeavour to conceal the fact that they do not know a debit from a credit by simulating scorn for the "book-keeper and all his works." The pity is that there is not the slightest need for this dissimulation. If only those directors would recognize that the amount of accountancy knowledge they need is easily acquired, the benefit to joint-stock enterprise would be almost incalculable.

We propose to lay before the reader as simple an exposition as possible of the minimum amount of the art of accountancy with which every director should be familiar.   But lest he fear that he is in danger of being drawn into a morass from which he has so far kept himself free, we hasten to add that we shall avoid every technical expression and every semblance of abstruseness.

The Simplicity of Accounts.

The aim of every director with regard to accounts should be the acquisition of an ability to read and understand his company's balance sheet and profit and loss account.   Unless he can do this there is no doubt that he is completely incapable of real direction. To equip himself with the requisite knowledge he need only grasp a few simple rules which will be explained in this chapter and which cannot possibly impose an undue task upon the aspirant director.

Modern Accountancy.

There is only one system of accountancy in use to-day in England, and that is the "Double Entry" system.   The identity of its inventor is unknown, but a monk of the name of Pacioli, who lived in the fifteenth century, is believed to be its principal sponsor.   It is modern in the sense that no other system has been found to supersede it over its course of five hundred years.

The Meaning of Double Entry.

Every director should acquaint himself with the meaning of the term "Double Entry" and with the principle which underlies it.   The principle is the recognition of the fact that in every possible commercial transaction there is a double aspect ; no matter what the dealing may be, there is always a "giving" and a "receiving" aspect.   There is always a giver and a receiver.   It is the "Double-entry" system, and no other, which records this twofold aspect by entering in separate accounts in the books the "giving" and also the "receiving." The result is that there is a "complete" record of every transaction and not merely a record of a part of each dealing. If, for example, the company buys raw material from a supplier named George Jones, a full record is made, not only in George Jones's account, but also in a "Raw Materials" account. Turning now to the books in which this twofold aspect of every transaction is recorded, we may perhaps be permitted to surprise the director by telling him that there is only one essential book of account—the ledger. No matter how elaborate the company's system of book-keeping may be, the key to the situation is concentrated in one book. As a rule this book is broken up into several parts for the sake of convenience, but this does not alter the fact that the several parts constitute one ledger.

Debits and Credits.

In order to distinguish between the entries relating to the receiving and those relating to the giving aspects, a very simple yet ingenious procedure is adopted. Each ledger account is ruled down the centre so as to divide it into two equal parts. The left-hand side is then allocated to the receiving aspect of every transaction affecting any particular account, whilst the right-hand side is devoted to the giving aspect. The left-hand side is referred to as the "Debit," and the right-hand side is known as the "Credit."

A Rule with No Exceptions.

This very simple rule is unalterable and it has no exceptions. It may therefore be committed to memory, a task which should not occupy many minutes. As soon as this has been done the director should commence to practise the art of distinguishing between debits and credits at sight. He should not be content until he is able to tell instantly whether any given item should be credited or debited in his company's books. Conversely, he should be able, when inspecting the ledgers, to understand what any given debit or credit represents. A simple method of acquiring this ability is to set down, in the form of a table, as many commercial transactions as can be called to mind. Next, an attempt should be made to identify the "receiving account" and the "giving account." Finally, from this identification the debits and the credits should be classified. If this advice is followed, the director will find that his understanding of the annual or periodical accounts is increased many times over; in addition, he will experience a feeling that he is at least equal to the accountant when discussing the annual accounts.

The Identifications of Accounts.

In order to demonstrate the simplicity of the rule discussed above we will consider, for a moment, the identification of a number of ledger accounts. The importance of this matter cannot be over-emphasized, and the aspirant director is urged to master the point under discussion at the very outset of his career. It may be said, without fear of contradiction, that the inability to distinguish between a debit and credit lies at the bottom of many a director's incompetence to grasp the true state of his company's affairs.

The example we take is that of the Success Company, Ltd., which raises £500,000 from the public for the purpose of establishing a factory to produce furniture. In the following table will be found the successive steps in the history of the company during the early period of its existence. It will be seen that the "giving account" and the "receiving account" almost assert themselves and that the classification of the debits and credits is practically automatic—

	DEBIT	CREDIT
1. The receipt of cash from the public in respect of shares	Cash Account	Shareholders' Account
2. The purchase of a freehold factory site for cash	Freehold Land Account	Cash
3. A contract is made with the X Building Co., Ltd., for the erection of a factory	Buildings Account	X Building Co., Ltd.
4. A payment is made to the X Co. by way of deposit	X Building Co., Ltd.	Cash
5. The building is completed and paid for	X Building Co., Ltd.	Cash
6. The fittings and furniture are bought for cash	Furniture and Fixtures Account	Cash
7. The plant and machinery are bought on credit from the Y Co., Ltd.	Plant and Machinery Account	Y Co., Ltd.
8. A consignment of timber is bought for cash	Purchases Account	Cash
9. The first week's wages are paid	Wages	Cash
10. The salaries are paid	Salaries	Cash
11. Trade expenses of various kinds are paid	Trade Expenses	Cash
12. Goods are sold to Stores, Ltd., on credit	Stores, Ltd.	Sales
13. Goods are sold to B & Co. for cash	Cash	Sales
14. Goods are sold to F & Co. on credit	F & Co.	Sales
15. Stores, Ltd., make a payment on account	Cash	Stores, Ltd.
16. F & Co. are made bankrupt and cannot pay for their goods	Bad Debts	F & Co.
17. Stores, Ltd., give a bill of exchange in payment of their account	Bills Receivable	Stores, Ltd.
18. Timber is bought from Z Ltd.	Purchases	Z Ltd.
19. A bill is given to Z Ltd. in payment	Z Ltd.	Bills Payable
20. Stores, Ltd.'s bill is met	Cash	Bills Receivable
21. The bill given to Z Ltd. matures	Bills Payable	Cash

The Classification of Accounts.

We now come to the last elementary rule with which we need bother the director. And again, in regard to this last rule, we are in the happy position of saying that it is an extremely simple one, and that it is subject to no exception. The rule is that every debit balance or account appearing in the company's books represents either an asset or a loss (i.e. an expense), and that every credit balance is either a profit (i.e. an item of income) or a liability. The value which lies in the memorizing of this rule is too obvious to be stressed. Once it is grasped the director is in a position to differentiate at a glance between assets and liabilities, between profits and losses. He is able to understand the nature of every item appearing in the balance sheet and to join, usefully, in any discussion concerning the board's treatment of any doubtful item.

The fact that there is no exception to the rule may be demonstrated by applying it to the table given above—and to any similar table which can be compiled from a company's books. Taking the debits first, it can be seen that they fall under the sub-heading of Assets or Expenses almost automatically, thus—

ASSETS	EXPENSES
1. Cash	8. Purchases Account
2. Freehold land	9. Wages
3. Buildings	10. Salaries
6. Furniture and fixtures	11. Trade expenses
7. Plant and machinery	16. Bad debts
12. Stores, Ltd. (a debtor)	
14. F & Co. (a debtor)	
17. Bills receivable	

The credits may be classified with equal facility, thus—

LIABILITIES	INCOME
1. Shareholders' Account	12. Sales
3. X Building Co., Ltd. (a creditor)	
7. Y Co., Ltd.	
19. Bills payable	

We may now take it that the reader is in a position to classify, mentally, every entry in his company's books, firstly as a debit or a credit, and then to classify the debits as assets or losses and the credits as liabilities or profits. That being so, we are able to explain the extreme simplicity which underlies the preparation of a company's profit and loss account and balance sheet.

This is a matter which often causes great difficulty to inexperienced directors. Their difficulty is one for which they must blame themselves, however; if they had first equipped themselves with a knowledge of the simple rules set out in the foregoing paragraphs, they would never experience the slightest trouble with the annual or periodical accounts of their companies.

The Profit and Loss Account.

The object of the profit and loss account is indicated clearly and fully by its name. It shows the profit or the loss which has been made or sustained by the company over a given period. It achieves this by setting the debit accounts relating to expenses against the credit accounts representing profits or income. This "setting-against" is conveniently arranged in the form of a debit and a credit. Thus, all the expense items are shown as debits in the profit and loss account, and all the income items are shown as credits. In this way we get an account in which the purchases, the wages, the factory expenses, the salaries, the rent, and the selling expenses (all debits), are set down against the sales, the discounts received, the interest, and the income from investments. The difference between the two sides represents the profit or the loss. And in accordance with the immutable rule already explained, a debit difference is a loss and a credit difference is a profit.

Stock-in-Trade.

There is one minor point to be discussed at this juncture—it scarcely deserves the term "complication" —and that is stock-in-trade. It would obviously be misleading to set the purchases against the sales unless account were taken of the stock of raw material and finished goods. For this reason we debit the profit and loss account with the stock-in-hand at the commencement, on the assumption that it has been used during the period under review, and that it therefore constitutes an "expense" or outlay, and we credit the closing stock to the profit and loss account on the grounds that we are so much better off, i.e. that the value is equivalent to an item of "income." Then in accordance with our earlier rule, which is also unchangeable, we pay full regard to the debit which must appear in our accounts in respect of the credit value of the stock entered in the profit and loss account. The debit, which must be an asset, "Stock-in-trade," is therefore noted for insertion in the balance sheet, which we now proceed to study.

Balance Sheet.

The title of the Balance Sheet is not quite so self-explanatory as is the title of the profit and loss account; nevertheless, its composition is just as simple. It "balances" the assets against the liabilities and tells the director whether the possessions of the company, at a given date, exceed the amounts due to creditors and shareholders, or *vice versa*. The assets are set out on the right-hand side and the liabilities on the left. This may seem a little confusing, as one would expect to see the order reversed. In American balance sheets the assets and liabilities do, in fact, appear on the sides on which they might be expected to be shown. The apparent confusion can only be excused by saying that the Balance Sheet is not in truth an "account" but merely a statement. The reversal of sides is, therefore, not a departure from the rule we have committed to memory, but an instance of the national perverseness for which we are noted.

A little reflection serves to show that if the assets exceed the liabilities, the difference must be equal to the accumulated profits appearing in the profit and loss account. Conversely, if the liabilities are greater, the difference must represent a debit balance in the profit and loss account. The link between the two "accounts" is therefore made perfectly apparent. Finally, it is demonstrated that all debits representing losses or expenses find their way into the profit and loss account, and that all debits representing assets are included in the balance sheet. Of the credits, those representing profits or income are entered in the profit and loss account, and those representing liabilities are set out in the balance sheet.

The Difference between Balance Sheet and Profit and Loss Account.

The importance, for the director, of grasping the difference between the profit and loss account and the balance sheet cannot be exaggerated. As mentioned in the first edition of this volume—

Many directors will persist in looking for wages or other revenue items which happen to be under discussion, in the Balance Sheet, or endeavour to join in a parley on intangible assets with the Profit and Loss Account before them—utterly failing to grasp the points at issue. Such farcical procedure can only be obviated if the director has a clear idea of what a Balance Sheet really is, and is able to follow the principles involved when resolutions are passed affecting the company's accounts.

This paragraph would have been omitted from this present edition but for the fact that it was quoted and confirmed as a common occurrence by no less an authority than Mr. Hartley Withers in his popular work *The Quicksands of the City.*

The Composition of the Balance Sheet.

The composition of a balance sheet may be grasped easily by taking an extremely simple case and then proceeding, by steps, in the gradual compilation of a public company's more involved annual account. The first step is to take the balance sheet of a public company which has just made an issue of, say, 350,000 shares of £1 each to the public at a cost of £25,000 in preliminary expenses. The balance sheet of such a company, immediately after the issue, would appear as follows—

THE X Y COMPANY, LTD.
BALANCE SHEET AS AT 31ST DECEMBER, 1931

Liabilities	£	Assets	£
Authorized and Issued Capital—		Cash at bankers .	325,000
350,000 shares of £1		Preliminary expenses	25,000
each, fully paid .	350,000		
	£350,000		£350,000

At the end of the first year it has not carried on any trading, but it has acquired freehold land for £10,000 and has erected a factory at a cost of £150,000. This outlay has been paid for except for a sum of £5,500 which is still due to the building contractors. The balance of the cash resources has been invested in first-class securities. The draft balance sheet at 31st December, 1932, therefore, appears somewhat as follows—

THE X Y COMPANY, LTD.
BALANCE SHEET AS AT 31ST DECEMBER, 1932

Liabilities	£	Assets	£
Authorized and Issued Capital—			
350,000 shares of £1		Freehold land . .	10,000
each, fully paid .	350,000	Factory buildings .	150,000
Sundry Creditors .	5,500	Investments . .	170,500
		Preliminary expenses	25,000
	£355,500		£355,500

At the end of the second year we will assume that manufacturing and trading operations have been carried on successfully and the balances standing on the various accounts on the ledger are as under—

	Dr.	Cr.
	£	£
Share capital		350,000
Preliminary expenses	25,000	
Freehold land	10,000	
Factory buildings.	150,000	
Plant and machinery	90,000	
Sundry debtors	45,000	
Sundry creditors		25,500
Cash at bankers	12,500	
Sales		129,500
Directors' fees	2,500	
Purchases	92,300	
Wages	32,700	
Salaries	5,000	
Closing stock in trade	30,000	30,000
Factory expenses	7,500	
Office expenses	13,500	
General expenses	2,500	
Interest and dividends received . . .		5,500
Bills receivable	22,000	
	£540,500	£540,500

The statement of ledger balances set out above is known as the "Trial Balance," which must not be confused with the balance sheet or the draft balance

THE X Y Z CO., LTD.
Balance Sheet as at 31st December, 1933

Liabilities	£	Assets	£
Share capital . .	350,000	Freehold land . .	10,000
Sundry creditors .	25,500	Factory buildings .	150,000
Profit and Loss Acc.—		Plant and machinery	90,000
Profit per annexed		Sundry debtors .	45,000
account . .	9,000	Cash at bankers .	12,500
		Bills receivable .	22,000
		Stock in trade . .	30,000
		Preliminary expenses	25,000
	£384,500		£384,500

sheet. From the trial balance we proceed to compile the balance sheet as at the close of the second financial year of the X Y Z Company, Ltd.; and, because the company is now trading, we also build up, from the same source, the profit and loss account.

THE X Y Z CO., LTD.

PROFIT AND LOSS ACCOUNT FOR THE YEAR ENDED
31ST DECEMBER, 1933

	£		£
To Purchases . .	92,300	By Sales . . .	129,500
,, Factory expenses.	7,500	,, Interest and divi-	
,, Wages . .	32,700	dends . .	5,500
,, Salaries . .	5,000	,, Stock in trade at	
,, Office expenses .	13,500	close of year .	30,000
,, General expenses.	2,500		
,, Directors' fees .	2,500		
,, Profit carried to			
Balance Sheet .	9,000		
	£165,000		£165,000

Published Balance Sheets.

It will be appreciated, of course, that the accounts given above are intended merely to explain general principles. The published balance sheets of companies are subject to a great number of rules and regulations, and are naturally presented in very different form from the *pro forma* drafts we have used. The consideration of actual accounts is, however, deferred to later chapters.

CHAPTER V

Depreciation.

IN addition to the charges and expenses which are met in cash the directors must debit profit and loss account with the periodical loss suffered by the company in the form of depreciation. Certain of the assets, such as Plant and Machinery, wear away through use, and becomes less and less valuable as time goes on. Others, such as Leases, depreciate in value by the effluxion of time, not by wear and tear. Others, such as Investments, fluctuate in value from year to year according to their market value. Lastly, there are assets which lose their value through becoming obsolete or out of date.

Wear and Tear, Fluctuation, and Obsolescence.

It will be found that the terms used to denote depreciation vary considerably, according to the asset or class of asset concerned. The more common of these terms are as follows—

I. WEAR AND TEAR. This term is applied to the wear and tear of such assets as plant, machinery, furniture, etc. It is not commonly used commercially, but is always applied to the allowance granted by the Inland Revenue Authorities to cover depreciation.

2. FLUCTUATION. This term is rarely included in accounts, but is used colloquially. Fluctuation in the value of investments is generally referred to in accounts as "Depreciation of Investments," or "Amount written-off Investments," in the case of a fall in value; appreciation might be referred to as "increase in value of

investments." In practice, however, it is unusual and unwise to take credit for unrealized profit represented by appreciation of investments.

3. OBSOLESCENCE. Obsolescence is also a term which is used colloquially. Where it occurs it will usually be found that the obsolete plant has been sold, and that the proceeds have been credited to the asset account. The balance remaining to the debit represents the obsolescence, but it is generally described in the accounts as "Loss on Sale of Plant."

4. AMORTIZATION. This term is applied to the depreciation of such assets as leases, patents, copyrights, etc. These assets do not suffer wear and tear, but amortize by effluxion of time. In this case the loss is actually described as amortization, e.g. "Amortization of Lease."

Ascertainment of Depreciation.

Whilst we know that the loss called "Depreciation" is an actual loss, we have not yet considered the means of ascertaining the extent to which it should be charged to profit and loss account to cover the annual loss in value. If each asset is considered separately, however, the director will find that a method of measuring the loss presents itself to him readily. The case of leases may be taken first.

Amortization of Leases.

As a lease becomes valueless at the end of a given period of years, it is clear that its value expires at a rate represented by its cost divided by its total life. This annual amortization, being the amount lost each year, is the amount to be charged to profit and loss account. This is the simplest form of depreciation; it consists of nothing more than debiting the accounts with a fixed annual instalment. The instalment is arrived at by dividing the cost by the number of years of the lease's life. Unfortunately, this simple form of depreciation is given an impressive title. It is known as the "Fixed Instalment Method of Depreciation."

Machinery.

Whereas a lease may be supposed to give equal annual service, the same is not always true as regards other assets, such as machinery. Apart from wear and tear, the profit and loss accounts will always have to bear a charge in respect of repairs and renewals. These repairs are generally light during the early years of the machinery's life, and heavy in the later years. The directors of a company are therefore forced to discover a means of apportioning the depreciation charge in such a way as to equalize the total expense of upkeep over the life of the asset. To do this means charging a heavier amount of depreciation in the early years in which the cost of repairs and upkeep will be small, and a lighter amount of depreciation in the later years in which the repairs will be costly.

Such a method is to be found by making a percentage deduction calculated on the diminishing value of the asset. Thus, in the case of a machine costing £100, an annual percentage deduction of 10 per cent would amount to £10 in the first year, £9 in the second year (10 per cent of £100 – £10), £8 2s. in the third year (10 per cent of £100 – £10 – £9), and so on. It will be seen that this method gives what is required, a reducing annual charge to the profit and loss account.

This method of depreciation is known as the "Diminishing Balance Method."

Residual Value.

Certain assets, such as Leases and Patents, have no value whatever at the end of their term of life.

Other assets, however, whilst of no value for their original purpose, possess some value even at the expiration of the term for which they have been usefully employed. Machinery, for example, will generally have a value as scrap after it has become worn out. This scrap value is known as "Residual Value," and should be taken into account when calculating depreciation. A simple way of taking it into account is to estimate its amount and deduct it from the value of the machinery on which depreciation calculations are to be made.

Revaluation of Assets.

There are types of assets which do not lend themselves readily to any of the foregoing methods of depreciation. Such items as casks, loose tools, packages, timber, moulds, and patterns cannot be treated in the same way as fixed machinery. They are, therefore, checked over physically each year, listed and valued. The valuations are then compared with the values appearing in the ledger. The differences are written off to profit and loss account and credited to the various assets concerned, thus reducing the balances on the accounts to agree with the revaluations. This method is known as the "Revaluation Method."

Other Methods.

There are other methods likely to be encountered by the director from time to time, but as their application is highly technical, we need do no more than refer to them briefly. They are as follows—

(a) ANNUITY METHOD. Under this method the asset is regarded as an investment earning a certain amount of interest each year. The interest is added to the asset account, and both are written down by equal annual instalments. This method is applied to such assets as long leases, provided there is no intention of replacing the leases at the end of their period.

(b) DEPRECIATION FUND METHOD. By this method the asset is allowed to remain at its original figure, but depreciation is charged to profit and loss, and credited to a sinking fund. At the same time, an amount of cash equal to the sinking fund instalment is withdrawn from the business and invested in gilt-edged securities. When the asset is worn out, the account is closed off, the securities are realized, and a new asset is purchased to replace the old. This method, is usually adopted whenever it is desired to make provision for the replacement of an asset owned by the company.

(c) INSURANCE POLICY METHOD. The insurance policy method is similar to the depreciation fund method, except that the cash is applied to the purchase of an insurance policy which will provide the funds required for the ultimate replacement of the asset.

The Board and Depreciation.

The decisions as to the amount of depreciation to be charged in a company's accounts rest with the directors. It is essential, therefore, that the following point regarding the treatment of depreciation of machinery should be grasped. The director will then be in a position to give his advice when the question comes before the Board at the end of the year.

As a rule it is impracticable to charge the correct amount of depreciation of machinery in any one year's accounts. To do so would necessitate the separate treatment of each constituent item. The probable life and residual value of every piece of machinery would have to be worked out carefully. The vast amount of work involved in such a procedure in large concerns precludes its adoption and it is general to substitute a flat percentage covering as many items as possible.

From the point of view of financial accounting, there is no alternative to the adoption of a flat rate, but the directors may do much to minimize its errors by dividing the plant into broadly defined classes, and adopting suitable rates for each. Thus a distinction might be drawn between shop fixed plant and motive power plant, and between special process plant and transportation plant.

The cost accounts of the company are designed to charge depreciation more accurately to different shops and departments than is possible in the financial accounts. By following suitable general divisions and adjusting the rates to each one, it is possible for the directors to arrive at a more or less equitable charge which will correspond to the detailed charges of the costing records. The lines of treatment must necessarily be broad on account of the limitations common to all business enterprises, and when the asset accounts are small the Board is quite justified in applying a flat percentage each year.

CHAPTER VI

THE TRADING ACCOUNT, THE MANUFACTURING ACCOUNT, AND THE APPROPRIATION ACCOUNT

In the simple illustrations of company accounts used in Chapter IV we entered the whole of the expense and income items in the profit and loss account. In practice, however, the profit and loss account is split into sections so as to ascertain separately the Gross Profit and the Net Profit; in manufacturing concerns a further subdivision is made with a view to arriving at the Manufacturing Profit. We deal below with each of these sections.

Manufacturing Account.

This section of the profit and loss account contains all the items of expenditure incurred by the works in the actual production of the manufactured article. The chief factory or works items of expenditure are workmen's and foremen's wages, materials used, gas, electricity and water consumed, rent, rates, insurance, etc., of the factory, remuneration of the works manager, his clerical and technical staff, and the general expenses of the works, such as carriage and cartage, labourers' wages, and cleaning charges.

In the case of a factory producing one type of article only, the division of the total charges in the manufacturing account by the number of articles produced, gives the cost of manufacture per unit. This figure of cost is termed the " works cost " or " prime cost " or " production cost."

A specimen manufacturing account is given on the next page.

MANUFACTURING ACCOUNT

Dr.   FOR THE YEAR ENDED 31ST DECEMBER, 193–   *Cr.*

PRODUCTION FOR MONTH: 110,000 UNITS

	£		£
To Stock at 1st Jan., 1934—		By Trade price of 110,000 Units	
Raw material . . .	13,000	manufactured, transferred	
Work in progress . .	16,112	to Trading Account . .	117,962
,, Purchases of raw material .	45,040		
	74,152		
Deduct Stock at 31st Dec., 1934—			
Raw material . £10,050			
Work in progress 20,700			
	30,750		
	43,402		
,, Carriage on raw materials .	850		
,, Manufacturing wages . .	45,500		
Prime Cost .	89,752		
,, Factory Oncost—			
Rent and rates on factory	1,201		
Gas, light, and water .	1,693		
Wages and factory salaries	1,943		
Repairs and renewals .	1,030		
Depreciation . . .	1,100		
Interest on capital . .	2,500		
	99,219		
Deduct: Proportion of Oncost			
on increased work in progress	932		
Total Factory Cost of Produc-			
tion—110,000 Units . .	98,287		
,, Manufacturing profit on works			
production carried to Profit			
and Loss Account . .	19,675		
	£117,962		£117,962

In the above illustration—

(*a*) The manufacturing account is credited with the wholesale price of the articles manufactured during the year and is debited with the manufacturing cost.

(*b*) The production, 110,000 units, divided into the total works cost, gives works cost per unit, namely £·8935.

(*c*) The difference between the total expenses and the value of the production arrived at in a similar manner to that shown above gives works manufacturing profit or loss. The importance of this matter will be appreciated by directors who may not previously have seen a loss tracked to the factory. It is often impossible to trace the point at which losses are incurred from an account in which all sections are combined under the general heading " Profit and Loss Account."

The profit on the above manufacturing account, viz. £19,675, is carried forward to the general profit and loss account, whilst the goods at wholesale price (£117,962) are transferred to the trading account.

Trading Account.

This account sometimes takes the place of the manufacturing account in businesses engaged in merchanting only, i.e. buying and selling completely manufactured articles. In the present instance, however, the account is debited with the wholesale price of goods manufactured, and the expenses of insurance and warehousing. The account is credited with the total sales price of the goods sold during the period and with the value of the stock in hand at the end of the period after deducting the value of the stock at the commencement. The difference between the total debits and credits represents the profit or loss on *trading* and is also transferred to the general profit and loss account.

The following is an example, in a form similar to that in which it should be produced to the board, of the trading account, based upon the manufacturing account already illustrated—

TRADING ACCOUNT

Dr.   FOR THE YEAR ENDED 31ST DECEMBER, 1934   Cr.

	Units	£		Units	£
To Wholesale price of goods manufactured, transferred from Manufacturing Ac.	110,000	117,962	By Sales . .	92,500	143,904
„ Warehousing and insurance . .		1,168	„ Stock— At 1st Jan. 35,600 At 31st Dec. 18,100	17,500	15,636
„ Gross trading profit carried to Profit and Loss Account .		40,410			
	110,000	£159,540		110,000	£159,540

It will be noticed that the compilation of the above account requires the inclusion of two stock figures, the opening and the closing stock. As explained in Chapter IV, the accounts would be useless unless the increase or decrease of stock-in-trade were taken into account.

Stock-taking is usually a lengthy and arduous task, except in the case of single-unit companies. In these companies valuation of the stock on hand may be carried out in a very short space of time from the office records. In the case of companies dealing in many classes of commodities, the valuation of the stock must necessarily be a lengthy procedure even when the office records are relied upon and a physical check is dispensed with. It will be realized from this that whereas a weekly account may be produced by one company, another will find it difficult to produce one at less than three months' intervals. It is a common practice now to estimate the stock for the monthly account by deducting the known average gross profit percentage from the sales. This method is satisfactory when the market selling price is stable, but not otherwise.

Profit and Loss Account.

Into this account is brought the balance of the profit or loss from each of the works or departmental trading accounts. It is then charged with the administrative, establishment, and distributive charges of the company. It contains such items as head office salaries, travellers' expenses and salaries, office expenses, and bad debts, together with directors' fees, bank and other interest payments, and any expense of a revenue nature which has not been charged in either the manufacturing or trading accounts.

This account is credited with any interest or dividends received from investments in subsidiary or outside companies.

The balance of the general profit and loss account represents either the net profit or the net loss for the period. Whether the profit is a profit available for distribution to the shareholders or not depends upon other factors which will be discussed later.

The Appropriation Account.

One of the most important matters to be learnt by the aspirant director is the difference between a charge against profits and an appropriation of profits. As soon as he understands this, the meaning of the appropriation account becomes quite clear to him. Unfortunately there are still many boards of directors who issue their annual accounts in such a way as to show that they confuse the two matters hopelessly. The appropriation account is an adjunct to the profit and loss account. The company's net profit for the year is transferred to it for appropriation in accordance with the decisions of the directors and the shareholders. It should contain no charges against profits, although the mistake is quite commonly made of entering depreciation in it. Depreciation is chargeable to profit and loss account, and profits are not profits until it has been so charged. Income tax, on the other hand, is not an expense but an appropriation of profit, and is rightly debited in the appropriation account. Other appropriations are transfers to reserve accounts, reserve funds, payments of dividends, bonus distributions to shareholders, and so on. Debenture interest is a profit and loss charge, and profits are not profits unless it has been deducted or provided for.

It will be seen from this that the profit and loss contains all debits which have to be met before the balance can be regarded as net profit to be disposed of by the members in general meeting. It is true that income tax has to be met, but it is an appropriation of profit made. It is not levied on losses, although debenture interest may be, and if any doubts existed as to its correct place in a company's accounts, they were set at rest in the decision of the courts in the *Johnston* v. *Chestergate Hat Manufacturing Company's* case.

The practical treatment of the appropriation account will be dealt with fully at a later stage, when we consider the duty of the directors in connection with the published accounts of their companies.

CHAPTER VII

THE share capital of a company consists of the authorized capital upon which a duty of £1 per cent is payable. It is not necessary to issue the whole of the authorized capital, and there is often a difference between the authorized and the issued capital.

The Issued Capital.

The issued capital may consist of shares of one class, in which case the shares are referred to simply as shares, or it may consist of preference shares, redeemable preference shares, ordinary shares, and/or deferred shares. The rights attaching to the various classes are set out in the Memorandum and Articles of Association.

Issue of Shares.

A *newly-formed* company can only issue its shares at par or at a premium. It cannot issue them at a discount. If an issue is made at a price above par the premium does not form part of the capital. It is credited to " Premium on Shares " Account, and carried forward separately in the Balance Sheet. If the company has been in existence for some time, then it is possible, under the circumstances set out below, to issue new shares at a price below par.

Issue of Shares at a Discount.

The Companies Act, 1929, for the first time made legal the issue of shares at a discount. The conditions

attaching to the permission are briefly as under
(Sect. 47)—

1. Shares issued at a discount must be of a class
already issued.

2. The company must pass a resolution in general
meeting on the matter.

3. The issue must be sanctioned by the Court.

4. At least one year must have elapsed since commencement of business.

In addition to the foregoing rules it is stipulated
that any discount on shares issued shall be stated
in every balance sheet until the whole amount is
written off.   This means that it is not enough to
record only the debit in the cash book in respect of
the cash paid in by allottees of shares issued at a
discount. The company must enter in the share
capital account a credit for the full nominal value of
the shares issued and raise a " Discount on Shares "
Account, which will appear as an asset in the balance
sheet.

Writing Off Discount on Shares.

A prudent board of directors loses no time in writing
off discount on shares. There is no recognized rate at
which the writing-off should be effected, and provision
is made according to circumstances. The "amortization" is not treated as a trading expense chargeable
against profits, but as an appropriation. It is therefore
debited to appropriation account, the corresponding
credit being made to "Discount on Shares," thus reducing the amount standing to the debit of that
account.

Commission on Shares.

In addition to allowing discount on shares, it is
possible for a company to grant commission on its

6—(1641)

shares. The regulations governing this matter are contained in Sect. 43 of the Companies Act, 1929, which provides *inter alia* that—

1. The payment must be authorized by the Articles.

2. The amount paid must not exceed 10 per cent of the issue price.

It is laid down in Sect. 44 that commission on shares shall, like discount, be shown separately in the balance sheet until it has been written off.

Preference Shares.

Directors should familiarize themselves with the particular rights attaching to preference shares. Such shares may carry a right to a preferential dividend only or to that preference plus a right to return of capital in priority to other classes of shares. On appointment to the board, therefore, the director should study the company's Articles and ascertain exactly what are the obligations to the preference shareholders. In addition, he should now—in view of the Companies Act of 1929—be aware of the conditions attaching to the issue of redeemable preference shares.

Redeemable Preference Shares.

A company may issue preference shares which "are, or at the option of the company are liable, to be redeemed." The conditions which are set out fully in Sect. 46 of the Companies Act, 1929, include the following—

1. The redemption may be made either out of the cash representing profits available for dividend, or the necessary funds may be provided out of the proceeds of a new issue of shares made for the purpose.

2. Only fully-paid shares may be redeemed.

3. When the shares are redeemed out of profits a

corresponding amount must be transferred to a "Capital Redemption Reserve Fund."

4. The balance sheet must specify what part of the issued capital consists of redeemable shares, and must state the latest date by which such shares are liable to be redeemed.

There are several problems concerning the proper interpretation of this section, but as they are not likely to confront every director, we do not propose to refer to them at length here. Should it happen that the director is concerned with the difficulties attending a redemption of preference shares at a premium or at a discount, he is referred to *Secretarial Book-keeping and Accounts*, published by Sir Isaac Pitman & Sons, Ltd., pages 129 *et seq.*

Alterations of Capital.

The capital accounts of sole traders or partners may be adjusted from year to year by adding profits which have been made or by deducting losses. This is not so in the case of companies. The profits are kept apart from the issued capital in the profit and loss appropriation account. Accumulated losses result in a debit balance on profit and loss account, and this, also, is shown separately—but on the assets side— in the balance sheet.

From time to time the accumulated profits can be capitalized by means of bonus issues of shares, but this is not effected merely by a transfer from appropriation account to issued share capital account. Resolutions of the members in general meeting are required, and the provisions of the Articles must be complied with carefully.

When losses are accumulated to any considerable extent, it becomes necessary for the directors to consider the advisability of writing the issued capital down.

The object of this process is to bring the capital into accordance with the depleted net values of the assets.

Reduction of Capital.

Reduction of capital is governed by Sects. 55 and 56 of the Companies Act, 1929, the terms of which must be closely followed. It is necessary for the company to pass a special resolution, and also to obtain the sanction of the Court. In many cases the consent of creditors is also required. After the reduction the Court may order the words " and reduced " to be added to the name of the company. The text of the sections relating to reduction is given below—

55. (1) *Subject to confirmation by the court*, a company limited by shares or a company limited by guarantee and having a share capital *may, if so authorized by its articles, by special resolution reduce its share capital* in any way, and in particular, without prejudice to the generality of the foregoing power may—

(a) Extinguish or reduce the liability on any of its shares in respect of share capital not paid up; or

(b) either with or without extinguishing or reducing liability on any of its shares, cancel any paid-up share capital which is lost or unrepresented by available assets; or

(c) either with or without extinguishing or reducing liability on any of its shares, pay off any paid-up share capital which is in excess of the wants of the company,

and may, if and so far as is necessary, alter its memorandum by reducing the amount of its share capital and of its shares accordingly.

(2) A special resolution under this section is in this Act referred to as " a resolution for reducing share capital."

56. (1) Where a company has passed a resolution for reducing share capital, it may apply by petition to the court for an order confirming the reduction.

(2) Where the proposed reduction of share capital involves either diminution of liability in respect of unpaid share capital or the payment to any shareholder of any paid-up share capital, and in any other case if the court so directs, the following provisions shall have effect, subject nevertheless to the next following subsection—

(a) Every creditor of the company who at the date fixed by the court is entitled to any debt or claim which, if that date were the commencement of the winding-up of the company, would be admissible in proof against the company, shall be entitled to object to the reduction.

(b) The court shall settle a list of creditors so entitled to object, and for that purpose shall ascertain, as far as possible without requiring an application from any creditor, the names of those creditors and the nature and amount of their debts or claims and may publish notices fixing a day or days within which creditors not entered on the list are to claim to be so entered or are to be excluded from the right of objecting to the reduction.

(c) Where a creditor entered on the list whose debt or claim is not discharged or has not determined does not consent to the reduction, the court may, if it thinks fit, dispense with the consent of that creditor, on the company securing payment of his debt or claim by appropriating, as the court may direct, the following amount—

(i) If the company admits the full amount of the debt or claim, or, though not admitting it, is willing to provide for it, then the full amount of the debt or claim;

(ii) if the company does not admit and is not willing to provide for the full amount of the debt or claim, or if the amount is contingent or not ascertained, then an amount fixed by the court after the like inquiry and adjudication as if the company were being wound up by the court.

Reduction of Paid-up Capital Out of Profits.

Before the passing of the Companies Act, 1929, it was possible to apply accumulated profits in reduction of paid-up share capital. This process was not subject to the approval of the Court, and needed only the sanction of the necessary resolutions of the shareholders. Under the Companies Act, 1929, the procedure is no longer available, and the only method of effecting this type of reduction is by submitting it to the Court for sanction.

Return of Excess Capital.

As distinct from a return of accumulated profits to shareholders, there is a procedure known as " Reduction of Capital by Return of Excess Capital." This form of reduction requires the sanction of the Court, but it is far more likely to be approved than is a scheme for return of profits. The effect, as regards creditors, is practically the same and it is not on their account that a distinction between the two methods is drawn. The real reason for the differentiation is that if profits are applied to a reduction of share capital, there is a loss to the Inland Revenue of super-tax on the dividends which would otherwise be declared.

A scheme for the return of surplus capital in

reduction of share capital may either provide for the extinction of the shareholders' liability or for its retention.

Cancellation of Uncalled Capital.

A further instance of a capital reduction scheme is to be found in the cancellation of uncalled capital. This procedure is specially authorized by Sect. 55 of the Companies Act, 1929. It differs entirely from reduction of capital due to losses. It is adopted, not by companies which have had a chequered career, but by those which are in a position to free their shareholders from the liability to put up further capital. The legal steps to be taken in cancelling uncalled capital are set out on page 72, and should not be overlooked by the director.

Debentures.

A debenture is a document of title held by a creditor in respect of cash advanced to the company. The title may give the holder a fixed charge or mortgage on the fixed assets as security for his advances; or it may confer a floating charge over the assets, which charge will crystallize in case of default.

Debentures may be perpetual or redeemable. In the former case the company retains permanently the cash advanced by the debenture holder. This retention is specifically authorized by Sect. 74 of the Companies Act, 1929, and overrides the old rule that the equity of redemption can never be obstructed. In the case of redeemable debentures there is usually a stated date for redemption, although it is possible to stipulate that redemption shall be at the option of the company.

Issue of Debentures.

The directors may issue debentures at a premium or at a discount. They constitute a debt due by the company—and not capital—and the rules governing the issue of shares at a discount do not, therefore, apply. If debentures are issued at a discount, however, the discount must be shown clearly in the company's balance sheet by the board. In this connection the director should be aware of the principles governing the future treatment of the discount.

Writing Off Discount on Debentures.

The Companies Act, 1929, does not lay down any rules as to the method by which discount or debentures shall be extinguished. The director should consider the particular circumstances of his company's issue and only sanction a method for amortizing the discount which will give full weight to those circumstances. It is impossible to list all possible methods in this present volume, but a reference to one or two common alternatives may prove beneficial.

If the debentures are perpetual then any system of amortization is suitable, the only factor needing consideration being the company's own convenience. If, on the other hand, debentures are redeemable it is usual to adopt such a scheme of writing-off as will ensure the extinction of the debenture discount by the time the debentures have been fully repaid. For example, issues of debentures are sometimes made with the proviso that an equal amount shall be repaid each year during the full term of the issue. In such cases it is clear that the company has the use of the greatest amount of money in the first year, and that thereafter there is an equal annual diminution. The director could, therefore, advise the adoption of appropriate rates of amortization proportionate to the benefit derived by the company from the debentures in each of the years. The discount written off in the earlier years would be heavier than in the later years.

If the debentures have been issued with a stipulation that they shall be repaid all at once at the end of a specified term, the discount may correctly be divided by the number of years in the term and one of the resultant equal instalments written off each year.

Repayment of Debentures at a Premium.

The director may encounter debentures issued at par but repayable at a premium. In these cases the company's liability, during the currency of the debentures, is represented by the par value only. At the redemption date, however, the liability is increased by the amount of the premium. On these grounds the debentures appear in the accounts at par, with a note as to the date of redemption and the premium which will be due when that date arrives. The Redemption Account or Redemption Fund, built up for the repayment of the debentures, should be calculated to provide for the premium as well as for the par value of the debentures, and the board should see that this is done.

Reissue of Redeemed Debentures.

Unless a company's Articles of Association—or its Debenture Trust Deed—specifically forbid, it is possible to reissue redeemed debentures. This right is conferred by Sect. 75 of the Companies Act, 1929, which stipulates that particulars of the debentures which can be . reissued shall be inserted in the company's balance sheet.

The director should note carefully that a reissue of redeemed debentures is regarded as a new issue for the purposes of stamp duty.

Conversion of Debentures.

A company may issue debentures to which there is attached a provision permitting conversion into shares.

This provision must not be framed in such a way as to lead to the issue of shares at a discount. For example, a company may not issue debentures of £100 nominal value at 80 and then permit the conversion of those debentures into shares at the rate of 100 shares of £1 each, fully paid, in respect of each £100 of debenture.

The Capital Account in the Balance Sheet.

In Chapter IV we gave several illustrations of the Balance Sheet together with an explanation that those simple examples could not be treated as representing actual published accounts. The form in which annual accounts should be laid before shareholders is given in a later chapter, but it will be convenient, at this stage, to explain the method of setting out the company's capital account.

EXAMPLE I.

Authorized Capital. Sect. 124 of the Companies Act, 1929, provides that every balance sheet of a company shall contain a summary of the *authorized* share capital and the *issued* share capital.

The A.B. Company, Ltd., has an authorized capital of £500,000 divided into 500,000 shares of £1 each; 250,000 shares have been issued and are fully paid. This capital appears in the balance sheet, on the *liabilities* side, as follows—

	£
Authorized Share Capital—	
500,000 shares of £1 each	500,000
Issued Share Capital—	
250,000 shares of £1 each fully paid . .	250,000

EXAMPLE 2.

Preference Capital. Sect. 46, to which reference was made on page 70, lays down that if a company has issued redeemable preference shares the Balance Sheet must show which part of the capital consists of such shares and the date on or before which those shares are, or are to be liable to be redeemed.

A. The C. D. Company, Ltd., has an authorized and issued capital of £120,000, divided into 20,000 7 per cent Redeemable Preference Shares, redeemable at the option of the company, and 100,000 ordinary shares—

THE C. D. COMPANY, LTD. (LIABILITIES SIDE)

Authorized and Issued Capital—

	£
20,000 7% redeemable preference shares of £1 each (redeemable at the option of the company)	20,000
100,000 ordinary shares of £1 each . .	100,000
	120,000

B. The E. F. Company has an authorized and issued capital of £250,000, divided into 50,000 5 per cent preference shares of £1 each, redeemable on or before 31st December, 1945, and 200,000 ordinary shares, all of £1 each.

THE E. F. COMPANY, LTD. (LIABILITIES SIDE)

Authorized and Issued Capital—

	£
50,000 5% redeemable preference shares of £1 each (redeemable on or before 31st Dec., 1945)	50,000
200,000 ordinary shares of £1 each . .	200,000
	250,000

EXAMPLE 3.

Shares Bearing Interest out of Capital. Under Sect. 54 a company may, with the consent of the Board of Trade, pay interest at a rate fixed by Order in Council on shares issued for the purpose of constructing works, buildings, etc., which cannot be made profitable for a considerable period. This is the only exception to the rule that interest or dividends on share capital cannot be paid except out of profits. It must cease at a date not later than the end of the half-year next after the half-year in which the construction work is completed. The accounts of the company must show the capital on which, and the rate at which, interest has been paid during the period to which the accounts relate.

The Eastern Construction Co., Ltd., has an authorized capital of £500,000, of which £250,000 is issued. Interest at 4 per cent has been authorized for the year 1940 during the building of the ferry which the company intends to operate.

THE EASTERN CONSTRUCTION CO., LTD.
(LIABILITIES SIDE)

Authorized Capital—

	£
500,000 shares of £1 each	500,000

Issued Capital—

	£
250,000 shares of £1 each fully paid (interest at 4% p.a. has been paid during the year to date, on this capital, in accordance with Board of Trade Sanction, dated . . . .) . . .	250,000

EXAMPLE 4.

Shares Issued at a Premium. If shares are issued at a premium the capital is shown at the nominal amount only. The premium is credited to Premium on Shares Account and appears as a separate item on the Balance Sheet. It is a capital profit and is available, if desired, for writing down capital assets.

The Success Co., Ltd., has an authorized capital of £500,000. It increases its issued capital from £250,000 to £500,000 by allotting 250,000 shares at 30s. per share.

THE SUCCESS CO., LTD. (LIABILITIES SIDE)

	£
Authorized and Issued Capital—	
500,000 shares of £1 each fully paid . .	500,000
Premium on Shares Account	125,000

EXAMPLE 5.

Issue at a Discount. The rules governing the issue of shares at a discount are set out on page 69.

The L. M. Co., Ltd., issues 50,000 ordinary shares

of £1 each at a discount of 20 per cent, the shares being of a class already issued. More than one year has elapsed since the company became entitled to commence business. The capital now consists of 100,000 5 per cent preference shares and 100,000 ordinary shares.

THE L. M. CO., LTD.
(Extract from Balance Sheet)

LIABILITIES	£	ASSETS	£
Authorized and Issued Capital—		General assets .	
100,000 5% preference shares . . .	100,000	Discount on Shares Account[1] .	10,000
100,000 ordinary shares . . .	100,000		
	200,000		

EXAMPLE 6.

Expenses of Issue. Under Sect. 124 the expenses of issue of shares or debentures must be set out in the balance sheet separately until written off. Similarly, under Sect. 44, any commission paid on the issue of shares or debentures must be shown on the assets side.

The O. P. Company has an authorized capital of £500,000 of which £200,000 has been issued. It now issues 100,000 shares at an expense of £4,000 and pays a commission of 5 per cent to an issuing house.

THE O. P. CO., LTD.
(Extract from Balance Sheet)

LIABILITIES	£	ASSETS	£
Authorized Capital—		General assets .	
500,000 shares of £1 each . . .	500,000		
Issued Capital—		Expenses of issue of shares made on	4,000
300,000 shares of £1 each fully paid .	300,000	Commission on shares .	5,000

[1] This fictitious asset will be written down out of profits in the manner already described.

EXAMPLE 7.

Debentures. The rules governing the treatment of debentures in the balance sheet are very similar to those relating to shares. One special point, however, must be noted; as mentioned on a previous page, debentures may be reissued under the provisions of Sect. 75, but the balance sheet must include a note of the amount of any debentures which have been redeemed and can be reissued.

The M. N. Company has an authorized and issued capital of £500,000. It has also an authorized debenture issue (5 per cent first mortgage) of £250,000, of which £125,000 have been redeemed and are now available for reissue.

THE M. N. CO., LTD. (LIABILITIES SIDE)

Authorized and Issued Capital—	£
500,000 Shares of £1 each fully paid . .	500,000
5% First Mortgage Debentures (in addition £125,000 of 1st Mortgage Debentures have been redeemed but are available for re-issue)	125,000

In connection with debentures and other charges which give the holders rights over certain assets, the director should note that the charge must be indicated. Sect. 124 (3) provides that—

" Where any liability of the company is secured *otherwise than by operation of law* on any assets of the company the balance sheet shall include a statement that that liability is so secured, but *it shall not be necessary* to specify in the balance sheet the assets on which the liability is secured."

If the charge is one which automatically attaches by operation of law the fact need not be published; such charges would be the normal commercial liens which often arise and debts such as those incurred under the Private Streets Improvement regulations. The deposit of investments with the bankers to secure an overdraft is the type of charge which must be disclosed. It is sufficient, however, to state " Overdraft at Bankers, Secured "; no reference to the specific asset charged is required.

From time to time a company may be forced to deposit debentures with bankers without issuing them formally. When this occurs the balance sheet should include a note to the effect that debentures for such and such a sum have been deposited with the company's bankers by way of collateral security.

CHAPTER VIII

THE CONTROL OF WORKING CAPITAL

IT is imperative that the directors should keep a proper control of the working capital of the company at all times. The control must be exercised in such a manner that it covers not only the actual conservation or disbursement of the finances of the company but also the policies directing those acts.

A large proportion of the concerns recently liquidated might have weathered the storm had a proper margin of working capital been maintained during periods of prosperity. The cause of their failure was often due to lack of working capital rather than to trading losses, even though these two are ordinarily corollaries. A reasonable margin of working capital can be maintained only by a strict control of finance, not only during times of adversity, but also during times of good fortune.

The annual balance sheet and accounts are practically valueless from the point of view of keeping a grip on finance, and it is essential that a statement of working capital be prepared at least every month. It is the duty of every director to see that such a statement is circulated to the board with unfailing regularity.

Fixed and Working Capital.

There is no fixed or standard form of capital control statement. Each company may adopt a form adapted to its own particular requirements. We shall set out, in a few moments, one or two popular forms, but we must first consider a very important matter of principle upon which all such statements are based. Without a knowledge of this principle it is impossible to make full use of the form which the secretary will lay before the board.

All capital control statements are designed to distinguish between the capital which has been locked up in fixed assets, such as plant, machinery, buildings, etc., and working or liquid capital, such as cash, debtors, stock, bills, etc. The former type of capital does not change its form and is therefore not available for use as trading capital; the latter type of capital is constantly changing its form in the process of earning revenue. It is clear, therefore, that we must classify the assets of every company before we can ascertain whether or not there is any over-trading with a consequent shortage of working capital.

Classification of Assets.

The four main classes of assets are the following—

(a) FIXED ASSETS. These are assets of a permanent nature, such as buildings, plant and machinery, etc., which are retained in the business for the purpose of earning revenue.

(b) FLOATING ASSETS. Floating assets are those which constantly change their form in the process of earning revenue, e.g. cash which becomes raw materials, then stock-in-trade, then book debts or bills receivable, then cash again, and so on.

(c) INTANGIBLE ASSETS. Intangible assets have no intrinsic value in themselves, but are of value to the company as a going concern, e.g. goodwill, trade marks,

(d) FICTITIOUS ASSETS, e.g. preliminary expenses, etc.

Classification of Liabilities.

Of slightly less importance in the compilation of capital control statements is the classification of liabilities. Liabilities fall under the two main headings of Fixed Liabilities and Floating or Current Liabilities. The fixed liabilities consist of those which cannot be called in at all or which can only be called in at long notice, e.g. share capital, debentures, mortgages, fixed term loans, etc. The floating liabilities are those which are current and payable at short notice, e.g. creditors' balances, short loans, bank overdrafts, etc.

Composition of Control Statements.

Having grasped the distinction between the types of assets and liabilities, the director will be able to appreciate the general principle upon which all control statements are built up. The fixed assets are balanced against the fixed liabilities and the floating assets against the current or working liabilities. If there is an excess of fixed assets over fixed liabilities it is clear that working capital has been diverted from its proper course. Slight excesses are, of course, of little consequence, but if too much has been locked up in assets which cannot be realized readily the company may find itself in a very difficult position.

Floating assets are compared with the current liabilities. If there is an excess of assets, then the position is satisfactory, except that future commitments and contingent liabilities must be borne in mind. If the liabilities exceed the assets, immediate action on the part of the board is necessary.

Examples of Statements.

We give below a preliminary simple example of a Capital Control Statement. It relates to the A.B. Company, Ltd., which has an issued capital of £100,000. It will be observed that the statement is prepared in columnar form so that the fluctuations from month to month may be watched.

7— (1641)

EXAMPLE "A."

CAPITAL CONTROL STATEMENT

THE A.B. COMPANY, LTD.

	JANUARY		FEBRUARY		MARCH	
	£	£	£	£	£	£
Fixed Capital—						
Freehold land, buildings, etc. . . .		35,000		35,000		35,000
Machinery . . .		25,940		26,110		28,500
Fittings, fixtures, and furniture . .		2,350		2,780		2,794
Wagons, horses, etc. .		4,320		4,300		4,219
		£67,610		£68,190		£70,513
Floating Capital—						
Cash at bank and in hand	13,100		12,519		14,720	
Debtors . . .	27,830		28,290		26,436	
Stocks of raw material.	4,887		5,180		4,590	
Finished stocks . .	16,310		16,318		16,469	
		62,127		62,307		62,215
Less Sundry creditors .	7,102		5,397		6,258	
Bills payable .	445		900		500	
		7,547		6,297		6,758
		£54,580		£56,010		£55,457
Summary—						
Issued capital . .		120,000		120,000		120,000
Accumulated profit .		2,190		4,200		5,970
Represented by—						
Fixed assets . .	67,610		68,190		70,513	
Net floating assets .	54,580		56,010		55,457	
	£122,190	£122,190	£124,200	£124,200	£125,970	£125,970

It is clear from the foregoing that the company is keeping well within its capital position. Such a state of affairs is referred to as being "Liquid." In the next example we will consider the Control Statement of a company in an "illiquid" or "frozen" position.

The director will see from this statement that whilst the position is just clear in March and April, the surplus of working capital cannot be regarded as sufficient to carry any additional trade. In spite of this, new leasehold premises and machinery have been purchased in May with the result that there is a shortage of £23,300 in the liquid assets. The fact that the company is making regular monthly profits has little

EXAMPLE "B."

CAPITAL CONTROL STATEMENT
THE B.C. COMPANY, LTD.

	MARCH		APRIL		MAY	
	£	£	£	£	£	£
Fixed Capital—						
Freehold land		60,000		60,000		60,000
Buildings		25,000		25,000		25,000
Leasehold premises		—		—		20,000
Machinery		35,000		37,500		46,800
		£120,000		£122,500		£151,800
Floating Capital—						
Debtors	12,300		13,970		15,270	
Stock-in-trade	22,250		25,690		27,800	
Bills receivable	2,100		3,700		2,900	
		36,650		43,360		45,970
Less Creditors	29,500		32,750		42,620	
Bank overdraft	3,050		6,910		26,650	
		32,550		39,660		69,270
		£4,100		£3,700		£23,300
Summary—						
Issued capital		80,000		80,000		80,000
First mortgage debentures		40,000		40,000		40,000
Accumulated profit		4,100		6,200		8,500
		124,100		126,200		128,500
Fixed assets	120,000		122,500		151,800	
Fixed capital excess (*or deficiency*) carried down	4,100		3,700		23,300	
	£124,100	£124,100	£126,200	£126,200	£128,500	£128,500
Fixed capital excess (*or deficiency*) brought down		4,100		3,700		23,300
Net floating assets	4,100		3,700		23,300	
	£4,100	£4,100	£3,700	£3,700	—	—

bearing on the position. Immediate steps must be taken to remedy the situation by finding some permanent form of finance to replace the bank overdraft.

Alternative Forms.

As mentioned earlier, there are many alternative forms of Capital Statements which may be adopted. As long as they reveal clearly the proportion of net fixed assets to net floating capital, the details are immaterial. Some companies make use of a summarized statement only, drawn up somewhat on the lines given on page 89.

Working Capital Statements.

Occasionally boards of directors employ a monthly statement recording only the movements of the net working capital. This type of statement is not quite so satisfactory, as it is difficult to follow the effect of capital commitments in the way of plant, machinery, buildings, etc. The form appears somewhat as under—

	JANUARY		FEBRUARY		MARCH	
	£	£	£	£	£	£
Assets—						
1. Stock in trade.		4,900		5,600		3,700
2. Investments .		1,100		1,100		500
3. Book debts .		7,950		8,320		9,480
4. Cash .		3,670		4,280		3,960
5. Bills receivable		2,100		2,650		1,290
6. Other liquid assets .		1,000		1,000		1,000
		20,720		22,950		19,930
Liabilities—						
1. Creditors .	11,420		13,620		9,980	
2. Bills payable .	3,840		3,970		3,800	
3. Loan .	4,100	19,360	4,100	21,690	4,100	17,880
		£1,360		£1,260		£2,050

This statement does not include a note as to the monthly profit, and it cannot be assumed that such profit is represented by the fluctuations in the net monthly balance. The monthly accumulated profit might be £1,360, £3,240, and £5,640. If such were the case, then it needs a calculation to show that among the creditors at March there are commitments of £3,590 in respect of fixed assets, entered into in the two preceding months. On account of the liability to error to which this form of statement lends itself, its adoption is not recommended.

Monthly Profit and Loss Accounts.

It is always advisable that approximate monthly

193–	Issued Capital	Debentures	Profit	Total Fixed Capital	Fixed Assets	Balance	Floating Assets	Current Liabilities	Net Working Capital
	£	£	£	£	£	£	£	£	£
January	300,000	100,000	—	400,000	323,528	76,472	122,670	46,198	76,472
February	300,000	100,000	2,109	402,109	324,670	77,439	121,690	44,151	77,439
March	300,000	100,000	4,675	404,675	338,790	65,885	118,752	52,867	65,885
April	300,000	100,000	7,320	407,320	359,880	47,440	115,616	68,176	47,440
May	300,000	100,000	8,210	408,210	375,900	32,310	101,600	69,290	32,310
June	300,000	100,000	9,760	409,760	435,600	25,840	98,700	124,540	25,840
July	350,000	100,000	10,320	460,320	436,780	23,540	148,629	125,089	23,540
August	350,000	100,000	8,650	458,650	436,780	21,870	144,720	122,850	21,870
September	350,000	100,000	4,302	454,302	436,780	17,522	138,660	121,138	17,522
October	350,000	100,000	1,001	451,001	436,780	14,221	132,100	117,879	14,221
November	350,000	100,000	- 500	449,500	436,780	12,720	119,600	106,880	12,720
December	350,000	100,000	- 3,500	446,500	436,780	9,720	88,642	78,922	9,720

NOTES.
1. New factory was in course of erection January/June, accounting for decrease of working capital from £76,472, to a deficiency of £25,840.
2. 50,000 new shares issued in July, rectifying deficiency and leaving working capital at £23,540.
3. Losses, August/December, result in decrease of working capital from £23,540 to £9,720.

profit and loss accounts should accompany and support the return of working capital. It is sometimes
advanced that, owing to the difficulties of arriving at
the value of stock-in-trade, it is impossible to produce
reliable accounts. The director may take it, however,
that in these days of efficient Stock and Stores Records
there is no company which cannot overcome the
difficulty. It is true that such accounts may not be
wholly correct, but they can be presented with sufficient accuracy to permit the proper control of working
capital.

Gauging Capital Requirements.

So far we have only considered the preparation of
control statements. We have not examined the duty
of the director in determining the margin of free liquid
capital which should be maintained to support a given
quantity of trade.

Initial Working Capital.

Many businesses have failed, during recent years, on
account of the failure of the promoters adequately to
provide for initial working capital. The calculation is
made by the company's technical staff, but the director
should be aware of the general lines on which it is
based. The estimated income and expenditure on
revenue account is scheduled for the number of
months in which the incomings will be less than the
outgoings. The shortages are then added together for
the several periods. To the result is added a margin to
cover any expected increase in turnover which may
follow such matters as the appointment of additional
travellers, the engagement of foreign representatives,
or the opening of branch showrooms.

In arriving at the final figure it is customary to
divide the working capital into two portions—the basic

and the variable. The basic portion is that which should be found in the business at all times, irrespective of periods of depression or boom months. It should be regarded as the minimum below which the liquid resources should not be allowed to fall. The variable portion is that which must be available in times of seasonal activity or emergency. In times of temporary slackness it is the amount which may be invested in first-class and readily realizable securities.

Sources of Capital.

Needless to say, the whole or the bulk of the basic working capital should be provided—at the outset—by the shareholders or the debenture holders. Once the business is established, one or two other sources will reveal themselves. For example, the accumulations of profit will offer a source of basic working capital; again, the trade creditors, once they have complete confidence in the management, may grant larger credit on bulk purchases or offer liberal terms for the purchase of raw material. In addition, the systematic discounting of the bills given by the company's best customers may constitute part of the minimum working capital upon which the company can safely work. All these sources, however, must be used warily, and in particular, care should be taken not to let too great a proportion of the working capital be furnished in the form of an overdraft from the company's bankers.

Seasonal or Emergency Capital.

Seasonal or emergency working capital must not be confused with the capital which is raised frantically in a crisis arising from continued trading losses. Such capital is not seasonal capital, but loans raised to meet serious inroads which have been made into the basic or minimum working capital.

Seasonal or emergency working capital is the excess temporary finance required to carry the company through a period of increased demand for its products. It is called into use after the variable working capital has been "flung into the line," including the portion which may have been invested in gilt-edged stocks or put out as "call money." It may be raised from the company's bankers, or from extended credit from suppliers, or by means of loans from associated companies. Occasionally it may be provided by the directors on open loan from themselves and—less desirably—by pressing for bills from debtors for discounting purposes. As soon as an emergency or seasonal demand assumes the aspect of a permanent increase in turnover it is impossible to meet it by pressing the company's debtors or by asking for still longer terms from the creditors. The time has arrived for the raising of additional fixed finance from the shareholders or from the public. The arrival of this time is indicated very clearly by the Capital Control Statements which we have discussed in this chapter.

CHAPTER IX

In addition to the capital control statement the director will receive periodical returns, financial and otherwise, from various departments of the business. The object of these returns is, of course, to enable the director to acquaint himself with the vital points in the company's progress from time to time and to render himself familiar with any matter of policy which may arise at board meetings.

Danger of Elaboration.

Unless these returns are prepared with discrimination there is a danger of the directors becoming flooded with masses of figures which they have neither the time nor the disposition to consider. It is a good plan, therefore, for the board of directors to indicate to the secretary the information desired and the periods at which it will be required.

If this procedure is adopted the directors will know exactly what to expect. The matter may be, and often is, left to the secretary; it is not unknown, however, for a secretary to prepare returns on vital matters demanding instant attention only to find that the members of the board do not understand or appreciate their importance. For this reason it is always advisable for directors to work out logically a list of the returns they require and to discuss the list with the secretary or with other members of the board.

Presentation of Statistics.

The presentation of figures in a readily assimilable form has received much consideration during the past few years and the various professional bodies are to be congratulated on their efforts to encourage their members to acquire a practical knowledge of the science of statistics. Many types of statistical data can better be expressed in graphs or curves than in mere columns of figures. Directors should not allow themselves to become immersed in masses of figures ; they should require the secretary to present facts in just that form they understand most readily. The secretary will be found quite willing to simplify a statement which he himself understands thoroughly on account of his daily contact with the figures, but which is perhaps obscure to the board.

Useless Returns.

At this point reference may be made to the unprofitable habit of calling for special returns—involving a great deal of work—the use of which to any director is problematical. Some directors seem blessed with bright ideas and call for involved statistics which can serve no useful purpose whatever. Often the train of thought leading to the demand is a good one, but the resulting request is a wrong one. The time of the secretary and his subordinates should be regarded as valuable, and requests for extraordinary information should be made only after consultation with the secretary. He will readily understand the idea at the back of the inquirer's mind and will doubtless produce the required information by shorter methods than those suggesting themselves to the director himself. A secretary may often waste a great deal of time, for instance, preparing statistics from wages sheets and time cards in order to convey information to a director which might readily have been given from the wages book or private ledger, had he known the line of inquiry running through the director's mind.

Essential Returns.

The returns which are considered essential for most classes of business are set out hereunder. It is recommended that they be prepared for the directors *monthly* and that they should be available within a few days of the end of the month. Delay in presenting them reduces their value in proportion to the period of the delay.

1. Return of Total Sales or Business Done.

The figures of this return will usually be best expressed in sterling, but in some businesses a unit of weight or quantity is found more satisfactory. The return should show the comparison with the preceding month and also with the corresponding month of the previous year.

The object of these comparisons is to indicate whether the variation is due to an abnormal factor or to a normal one, such as a seasonal variation.

An unusual drop in the sales figure will warrant close investigation into the cause. In order to identify the largest variations it is very desirable in those businesses possessing more than one sales department, or selling several classes of goods, that the return should be analysed to show the separate sales of the departments or types of product.

The inquiry into the causes of an unusual reduction in sales will proceed upon the following lines—

(*a*) *Is the reduction due to increased competition caused by*—

(1) Reduction in competitors' prices, or

(2) Improvement in quality of competitors' commodities, or

(3) Greater efficiency of competitors' sales organization ?

(b) *Is the reduction due to a fall in the general demand caused by—*

(1) Efficient substitutes at lower prices, or

(2) Changes in public taste or fashion, or

(3) Reduced purchasing power due to trade depression ?

It is not within the scope of this book to deal in detail with the remedies which must be applied when the cause or causes have been ascertained. The necessity for finding out the true causes cannot be urged too strongly, and directors should not be satisfied with mere excuses from their officials but should take all possible steps themselves to ascertain the root of the trouble.

Accumulation of Stocks.

If a reduction in sales is likely to continue for some time, immediate consideration must be given to the question of keeping stocks within reasonable limits and preventing the locking up of working capital in stocks which can be realized only at a loss. In a merchanting business such steps will be taken to cancel goods on order from suppliers as may be considered expedient, according to the peculiar circumstances of the case. In a manufacturing concern the limiting of the production may prove necessary. In the latter case it must be borne in mind that any appreciable reduction in output will increase the cost of the articles produced, on account of the fact that the standing charges such as rent, rates, management salaries, etc., will be apportioned over a smaller output. There is the further possibility of losing skilled workmen who may not be available when it is desired to resume increased production.

If the reduction in sales is due to the lower prices

of competitors it may be found necessary to increase production substantially in order to lower costs.

These factors must be carefully considered and a definite decision reached. It is dangerous and demoralizing to continue without a definite policy in the face of such conditions.

UNACCOUNTABLE INCREASE IN SALES. An unaccountable increase in the sales figures does not necessarily indicate an improved trading position. It may be that selling prices are too low and that either no profit or an insufficient margin of profit is being made. There is the further possibility of stocks becoming exhausted to the detriment of standing orders or the goodwill of regular customers. Again, the financial position of the company may not be strong enough to stand the strain of carrying a considerable increase in book debts requiring, say, 3 to 4 months' credit while the payments for wages and supplies have to be made promptly or within one month.

Unexpected increases in sales may point to overtrading and cannot always be taken as indications of prosperity.

2. Return of Production or Output.

Production or output of a business has a direct bearing on the cost price of each unit. Where selling prices are fixed, any substantial variation in the cost prices affects the profit directly. It is therefore important that periodical returns of production should be laid before the board. Some businesses lend themselves to weekly returns, others to monthly, and others to quarterly returns. Each business must select the most suitable period, but just as in the case of trading accounts, so with production returns— they must be prepared as frequently as possible, regularly and promptly.

The production return is designed to show either the quantities produced or the sterling value at cost or selling prices of each unit. A specimen return is shown on the next page.

In businesses carrying out large contracts over lengthy periods it is possible that no production report will be available. In such cases the amount expended during the month on wages and materials will be a satisfactory guide to the volume of business done and a statement embodying this information should be called for.

3. Return of Outstanding Orders.

In most classes of business it is not practicable to execute all orders received immediately on receipt. Businesses which are accustomed to carry a large number of unexecuted orders are therefore obliged to gauge their progress from the amount of orders on hand at any time.

Directors can obtain valuable information from this return which, in many respects, is of greater value than the ordinary sales return. It often anticipates drastic variations in the sales returns by several months and enables changes of policy to be effected before any serious loss has been sustained through falling off in sales. Again, it enables manufacturing and financial arrangements to be made for a largely increased output without disorganizing the general arrangements of the business.

The period and form of this return will vary with the peculiarities of the business, but, generally speaking, it is desirable that it should be prepared at least once a month and that it should show quantities of goods on order, classified under types of commodities. Comparison should be made with the quantity of orders unexecuted at a corresponding date in the

PRODUCTION RETURN

Month ending...............19....

Branch or Department.

(a)

	QUANTITIES (in appropriate Units), and/or VALUES.											
	LAST YEAR.						THIS YEAR.					
	Month.			Year to date.			Month.			Year to date.		
	Class "A."	Class "B."	Class "C."	Class "A."	Class "B."	Class "C."	Class "A."	Class "B."	Class "C."	Class "A."	Class "B."	Class "C."
Opening Stock												
Production for month												
TOTAL												
Invoiced during month												
Outside Customers												
Associated Companies												
TOTAL												
Closing Stock												

preceding year and also with the preceding two or three months of the same year.

4. Return of Working Capital.

This return has been fully dealt with in the previous chapter, but reference must be made to it in connection with book debts and stocks.

It is a strange but established fact that these two assets always tend to increase unnecessarily unless there exist satisfactory arrangements for keeping them constantly under review.

No company can afford to have money locked up in book debts and stocks unnecessarily. Neither of these assets produces revenue; both cost money to preserve, and one of them requires warehousing—an expensive item, even when the warehousing is provided in the company's own premises.

Stocks rarely improve in value with warehousing, and book debts certainly do not appreciate if allowed to remain outstanding. It may be stated with certainty that with the exception of such stocks as maturing spirits, both stock and book debts, if held for long periods, depreciate more rapidly than any other asset—fixed or circulating—owned by the company.

These two assets must be kept constantly under review. If the relation which each bears to the amount of the preceding month's sales shows a gradual consistent increase each month, then this constitutes a danger signal which cannot be ignored. It is imperative that investigation should be made immediately into the production, sales and accounting organization and for the company's policy in these matters to be brought under review. The secretary and the sales manager are the two officers to whom the directors must turn for information in this matter.

5. Monthly Profit and Loss Accounts.

Reference has already been made to this form of periodical return in connection with the object of a company's accounting system. The remarks were restricted, however, to pointing out the importance of periodical trading and profit and loss accounts. The monthly profit and loss accounts prepared for the information of the board need not necessarily be compiled with that meticulous care necessary in the case of the annual accounts. The object of the monthly account is to give the directors an opportunity of ascertaining weak points in the company's affairs before serious damage is done, and to enable them to take steps to prevent their continuance.

In certain classes of businesses only approximate monthly accounts can be prepared. Provided the margin of possible error is not excessive compared with the trading results shown in the final accounts, then the monthly accounts are of great use. The ideal is, of course, to obtain monthly accounts with the greatest possible degree of accuracy consistent with the expense and time of the staff available. The value of these accounts lies chiefly in their comparison with the figures of the preceding months. The form in which they are presented should enable comparisons to be made with as much facility as possible. Any substantial increase in an item of expense, or reduction in an item of receipt, should be the subject of immediate inquiry.

CHAPTER X

THE FINANCE AND ACCOUNTS OF SUBSIDIARIES

IT is now possible to deal with an important matter of finance with which the director must be familiar, namely, the financing of subsidiaries. The extension of joint stock company enterprise from that of single companies to combines of parent and subsidiary companies has produced many new problems in company finance. The Companies Act of 1929 recognizes this fact in no uncertain manner, and several of its clauses deal specifically and exclusively with the accounts of parent and subsidiary companies. The finance of subsidiaries has to be considered by the parent company from many aspects, particularly to ensure that capital is not locked up in certain of the subsidiaries unnecessarily at the expense of others which might make use of it more profitably.

The main methods of financing subsidiary companies are these—

(*a*) By taking up issued share capital.

(*b*) By advancing money on secured debentures or loans.

(*c*) By open loan.

(*d*) By supply of goods on credit.

The matters affecting these methods which require careful weighing one against the other are set forth hereunder—

Issued Share Capital.

As a general rule it is advisable that the issued share capital of a subsidiary company should be kept at the minimum level considered sufficient to induce suppliers to give the company the necessary amount of credit. This ensures that the stamp duties will not be prohibitive. Secondly, a small issued capital does not act to the detriment of the parent company from a dividend or taxation standpoint. Rather does it assist the parent company in these respects in a manner to be explained later. A small issued capital has an added advantage that in the event of the liquidation of a subsidiary the parent company's cash advances rank for repayment with the other creditors' claims and are not deferred as is the parent company's claim for return of share capital.

Secured Debentures or Loans.

The advantage of this method of financing a subsidiary is that the parent company can become a secured creditor for sums advanced (other than share capital) and ranks before the ordinary creditors up to the value of the security.

The objections to this method are that such charges must be registered with the Registrar of Joint Stock Companies. The information becomes public knowledge and may affect the subsidiary's credit. An *ad valorem* stamp duty is also payable on the amount secured. The parent company's position from dividend and taxation standpoints is not assisted by this method of financing. The only advantage of this method, therefore, is that the parent company apparently obtains priority in repayment of its advances as against the ordinary trade creditors. The word " apparently " is used because in practice it is generally found that if a parent company permits one of its subsidiaries to go into liquidation without paying the trade creditors in full, the credit of the parent company is so seriously affected that it withstands the shock to its own goodwill with great difficulty.

Open Loans.

The advantages of this method of financing as compared with the share capital or secured loan methods may be stated as follows—

(1) No stamp duties are payable.

(2) The credit of the subsidiary is not damaged, because the creditors' rights are not affected, except to the extent that the parent company ranks *with* the trade creditors for repayment of its advances instead of *after*, as in the case of share capital.

(3) The position of the parent company as shareholder, from a dividend standpoint, is assisted. If the subsidiary sustains such heavy losses in one or more periods that several years would be required in which to wipe off the debit balance, the parent company can, if it so desires, remit part or all of any open loans outstanding. The remission of these loans can then be applied by the subsidiary towards the extinction of the debit balance on profit and loss account. The extinction of the debit balance will permit the subsidiary to declare dividends to the parent company as soon as profits are made. By this means the accounts of the parent company will present an accurate view of each year's trading of the whole group. That is to say, the parent company will charge to revenue, in each year in which the subsidiary makes a loss, a sum equal to the amount of the loss, and will credit this sum to the subsidiary's loan account. The subsidiary will credit profit and loss account and extinguish the amount of the year's loss, debiting the parent company's advance account. In the years in which the subsidiary makes profits, a dividend will be declared to the parent company to the extent of the year's profit.

Apart from profits or remission of debts and advances as outlined above, the only other alternative method of extinguishing a debit balance on profit and loss account is by a reduction of the issued share capital. The objections to this method are that application to Court is necessary, considerable publicity regarding the reduction is inevitable with consequent damage to credit, and legal and other expenses must necessarily be incurred. It will be appreciated, therefore, that the extinction of profit and loss debit balances by means of remission of advances has considerable advantages.

(4) The parent company's taxation position is assisted. The Inland Revenue has not so far admitted that a subsidiary company is for income tax purposes owned by the same persons as those owning the parent company. For all practical purposes the shareholders of the parent company are the owners of the subsidiary company, but this practical view is not accepted by the Inland Revenue. When a parent company makes profits and a subsidiary makes losses, the parent company pays income tax on its own profits but obtains no taxation relief in respect of its subsidiary's losses. When a parent company makes trading losses but the subsidiary makes profits a similar position arises, except that if the subsidiary company declares dividends to the parent company the latter can claim a refund of the tax deducted by the subsidiary on payment of the dividend, up to the amount of tax on the trading loss. It is important, therefore, from a taxation standpoint, that subsidiaries should declare the largest possible dividends whenever a substantial loss is sustained by the parent company.

It has already been indicated that the method of financing subsidiaries by means of open loans which can be waived when circumstances necessitate enables subsidiaries to declare dividends at the earliest possible moment. In this respect, therefore, the open loan method of financing may considerably assist the parent company from a taxation standpoint. It must be mentioned, however, that when advances are remitted by a parent company the loss thus sustained by the latter is not allowed as a bad debt in the income tax computation of the parent company.

Supply of Goods on Credit.

When a parent company supplies a subsidiary with goods, the subsidiary can be financed by allowing it to pay for the goods after as long a period of credit as is found to be necessary. The advantages of this method are—

(1) No stamp duties are payable.

(2) The credit of the subsidiary is not damaged.

(3) The position of the parent company as shareholder from a dividend standpoint is assisted.

(4) The parent company's taxation is assisted.

The details of the advantages are similar in this case to those under the open loan method, with this addition, viz., that in the event of the liquidation of the subsidiary any amount not recovered by the parent company will be allowed as a bad debt in the parent company's income tax computation. There is also every probability that in the event of it being found necessary to remit debts owing by the subsidiary without actual liquidation of the latter, the amounts remitted will be allowed as bad or doubtful debts in the income tax computation of the parent company.

In order that the trading results of subsidiaries may appear in proper perspective it is essential that interest should be charged to subsidiaries at current rates on the amounts advanced by the parent companies. Some parent companies charge interest at current rates on the issued share capital of the subsidiary, and credit any dividends to the interest account. Such a procedure gives the parent company a correct view of the result of its investments in subsidiary companies and is to be commended. It must be remembered, however, that credit should not be taken in a parent company's profit and loss account for interest charged to a subsidiary unless the subsidiary company's profit and loss account shows a profit after charging the interest.

Legal Meaning of Subsidiary.

The legal definition of "subsidiary" is somewhat wider than is generally understood. Section 127 of the Companies Act runs as follows:

127.—*Where the assets of a company consist in whole or in part of shares in another company* whether held directly or through a nominee and whether that other company is a company within the meaning of this Act or not—

(a) the amount of the shares so held is at the time when the accounts of the holding company are made up *more than fifty per cent* of the issued share capital of that other company or such as to entitle the company to more than *fifty per cent of the voting power* in that other company; or

(b) *the company has power* (not being power vested in it by virtue only of the provisions of a debenture trust deed or by virtue of shares issued to it for the purpose in pursuance of those provisions) *directly or indirectly to appoint the majority of the directors* of that other company,

that other company shall be deemed to be a subsidiary company within the meaning of this Act, and the expression " subsidiary company " in this Act means a company in the case of which the conditions of this section are satisfied.

(2) Where a company the ordinary business of which includes the lending of money holds shares in another company as security only, no account shall for the purpose of determining under this section whether that other company is a subsidiary company be taken of the shares so held.

It will be seen from this that a company becomes a subsidiary if a majority of its shares or a preponderance of its voting powers is held by another company or if another company holds the power to appoint a majority of the directors.

The Parent Company.

The parent company owning subsidiary companies, within the meaning of Sect. 127 quoted above, is called upon to set out very full details in its balance sheet. It must show, as a separate asset, the shares in or the amounts owing from a subsidiary and, similarly, it must distinguish between debts due to its subsidiaries and those payable to ordinary creditors. It is provided, however, that these assets and liabilities connected with subsidiary companies need only be given in aggregate amounts. The text of the section dealing with this point includes the following—

Sect. 125. Where any of the assets of a company consist of shares in, or amounts owing (whether on account of a loan or otherwise) *from* a subsidiary company or subsidiary companies, the aggregate amount of those assets, distinguishing shares and indebtedness, shall be set out in the balance sheet of the first-mentioned company separately from all its other assets, and where a company is indebted, whether on account of a loan or otherwise, *to* a subsidiary company or subsidiary companies, the aggregate amount of that indebtedness shall be set out in the balance sheet of that company separately from all its other liabilities.

Losses of Subsidiary Companies.

In order to overcome the abuses under which heavy losses of a group of companies were concealed in the accounts of subsidiary companies, the Companies Act of 1929 requires disclosure of the method adopted in dealing with the losses of subsidiaries. It is now necessary to annex to the balance sheet of the parent company a statement setting out how such losses have been dealt with, and in particular how far provision has been made to meet the losses either in the subsidiary or in the parent or in both. The actual amount of the profits or losses need not be given ; neither need the statement show the exact amount of profit or loss which has been dealt with in any particular manner.

The statement must show how the losses of subsidiaries have been taken into account in arriving at the profit or loss shown by the parent company. The section dealing with this matter is Sect. 126, and runs as follows—

Sect. 126.—(1) Where a company holds shares . . . in a subsidiary company . . . there shall be annexed to the balance sheet of the holding company a statement . . . stating how the profits and losses of the subsidiary company . . . have, so far as they concern the holding company, been dealt with, in/or for the purposes of, the accounts of the holding company, and in particular, how, and to what extent—

(a) provision has been made for the losses of a subsidiary company, either in the accounts of that company or of the holding company, or of both; and

(b) losses of a subsidiary company have been taken into account by the directors of the holding company in arriving at the profits and losses of the holding company as disclosed in its accounts.

The attention of the director is drawn to the fact that it is not, as is sometimes supposed, the duty of the auditor to make up the necessary statement. It is the duty of the company, and the statement should not appear above the auditors' report to the shareholders, but below it.

Auditors' Report on Subsidiary Companies.

A further important sub-clause of Sect. 126 deals with the auditors' report on the accounts of subsidiary companies. It is laid down that if the auditors have given a qualified certificate, then the details of the qualification must be disclosed in the statement annexed to the accounts of the parent company. This, again, is a duty falling upon the directors, and the text is accordingly given below—

(2) *If in the case of a subsidiary company the auditors' report* on the balance sheet of the company *does not state without qualification that the auditors have obtained all the information and explanations they have required* and that the balance sheet is properly drawn up so as to exhibit a true and correct view of the state of the company's affairs according to the best of their information and the explanations given to them and as shown by the books of the company, *the statement* which is to be annexed as aforesaid to the balance sheet of the holding company *shall contain particulars of the manner in which the report is qualified.*

(3) For the purposes of this section, the profits or losses of a subsidiary company mean the profits or losses shown in any accounts of the subsidiary company made up to a date within the period to which the accounts of the holding company relate, or, if there are no such accounts of the subsidiary company available at the time when the accounts of the holding company are made up, the profits or losses shown in the last previous accounts of the subsidiary company which became available within that period.

(4) If for any reason the directors of the holding company are unable to obtain such information as is necessary for the preparation of the statement aforesaid, the directors who sign the balance sheet shall so report in writing and their report shall be annexed to the balance sheet in lieu of the statement.

The Parent Company's Accounts.

The practical effect of the sections quoted above upon the *parent company's* balance sheet will be dealt with at greater length in a subsequent chapter.

PART III
The Director and Control of Production

CHAPTER XI

ECONOMIC PRODUCTION

IT is often said with some truth that the success or failure of a company can depend upon the control of its production to a greater extent than upon any other factor. Certain it is that the companies fortunate enough to receive a continuous and steady flow of orders are rare ; the remainder are faced, periodically, with a problem which is no less critical than that involved in the control of cash. Periods during which the factories of the company suffer from lack of orders may be covered in two ways—the closing of the factories, or at least certain of the shops, and the continuation of the factories on stock orders. The execution of the policy to be followed may usually be left in the hands of the managing director, subject to the sanction of the board before either alternative is adopted. The decision to continue on stock production or to close a works is one of importance and should invariably be supervised by the directors.

Comparison of Cost.

Whenever it is found necessary to turn to stock production for any length of time the directors will be provided with an estimate of the stock to be produced, its value and the cost of its production. They will also receive a statement of the expense which will be entailed in closing the factory, and in re-opening at a later date. The latter is extremely important, for in certain businesses it happens that loss on stock production will be less than the cost of the re-lighting of furnaces, the re-starting of machines, and the cost of maintenance during the silent period.

Class of Stock Produced.

If it is decided that the factory shall be employed on stock production, a schedule of the class of goods to be produced will usually be prepared by the sales manager, in consultation with the works executive or the managing director. These schedules from the sales manager and the works manager must be examined by the board. It is always unwise to allow the sales manager to dictate a production programme to a works manager or to allow a works manager to produce according to his own inclination. The sales manager usually knows little or nothing about the methods of production, the shortcomings of workpeople, or the peculiarities of plant ; and his programme will naturally be to produce the goods most easily saleable. The works manager quite naturally, on the other hand, will choose a programme of goods most easily produced.

The directors must consider the scheme of production from every aspect and particularly from the point of view of capital available. They alone have the wider knowledge on such matters as capital-control, which enter into these problems to a far greater extent than into those affecting the departmental managers. The directors will not only take into account the cost of production of the stock and the possibilities of its adaptation to fill orders when they arrive, but they must consider the cost of financing this asset over a period. The cost may include warehousing, insurance, handling, re-packing, and charges for interest on bank loans. The capital control statement will furnish a great deal of the information required, particularly showing the influx of cash which may be expected and the amount required to meet the wages and materials charges.

Only after an exhaustive examination of the cash position and an inquiry into the effect upon this at the end of one, two, or three months, should a decision be recorded adopting one or other alternative. If it is decided to proceed with stock production, then the decision should be recorded and the matter allowed to take its course. Although it is advisable for the directors to approve the schedules governing the production for stock, they should not endeavour to dictate details of procedure either to the sales manager or the works executives. The sales manager may be relied upon to improve the position by turning stock into debtors, and the works manager should be left to produce the goods as efficiently and economically as he can. The rule of non-interference does not preclude the tendering of advice, which will usually be accepted and followed. Unfortunately, however, there is a tendency to interfere with works management, especially in times of stress, when it is necessary to produce goods for stock to keep the works going.

Shortage of Orders.

The occasional necessity of making for stock on account of temporary shortage of orders will usually be overcome without causing the time of the board to be occupied in discussions of policy. All concerns naturally pass through these periods and emerge from them quite successfully with a small stock produced after consultation between the sales manager and works manager; the stock itself finds a ready market soon after the temporary lull has passed. There are many advantages in filling in gaps between sufficient volume of orders with stock production. In the first place it is necessary to retain the confidence of skilled employees in the permanency of their work. False economy often leads to the dismissal of experienced workmen during temporary slack periods, the difficulty of replacement at a later and busier period proving no slight obstacle to the company's welfare. Again, the production of stock leads to speed in the execution of customers' orders as soon as they arrive. In this way goodwill is fostered and a reputation for efficiency is engendered. Lastly, the maintenance of production at its maximum preserves the allocation of standing charges over each unit. To refrain from making the fullest output on account of shortage of orders causes the spreading of the overhead charges over a smaller number of units and may lead to production of the goods for order at a cost higher than the price obtained for them.

Production in Economic Quantities.

It is an established principle of scientific management that it is cheaper to produce a large quantity of one article at one time than to manufacture several smaller quantities at different times. It will often pay to make a larger quantity of goods than is required for the fulfilment of immediate orders, and to place the balance in stock. This principle, which is due to the increased accuracy and efficiency attained by the worker during a long spell at one class of article, should be borne in mind when considering production programmes.

Danger of Over-Production.

Production of stock lines indiscriminately must be discouraged. The sales manager is always in a position to provide tables showing the average monthly sales of standard articles in quantities and the average amounts and quantities held in stock. It is possible to fix a maximum and minimum stock from this information and to direct that the limits be adhered to. The stock-keeper will inform the works manager whenever a stock line has been depleted below the minimum, and the manager will take steps to include that line in his next programme of output. The details of such a method as this will not usually concern the director but it is advisable that he should be acquainted with the procedure followed in his own company. Generally speaking, the minimum stock of a standard line should represent the average demands of the customers over a period corresponding to the period of manufacture of that article.

The Director and Production.

It will be seen from the foregoing that the director can only maintain a general control over the production of his company. Once he has sanctioned any scheme he must allow the departmental managers to carry out their own duties. There is, however, nothing to prevent him from following the effect of production programmes upon the financial statements and reports presented to him, and this should always be done. The decision of the director upon production is nevertheless the deciding factor, and nothing should be done to lessen the control which lies in his hands over excessive production, economic production, or closing the factory, should the latter policy be dictated by the information afforded him from time to time. In the first place, he must guard against sanctioning the locking up of working capital in stock under such circumstances that difficulty will be experienced in meeting running charges and the demands of creditors. He must give full consideration to the representations of the sales manager as to seasonal demands or seasonal periods of slack trade. The effect of excessive handling and storing upon the stock must be weighed, and last but not least, the estimates of costs under alternative programmes must be carefully understood.

CHAPTER XII

THE COSTS OF PRODUCTION

COSTS of production are prepared by means of a Costing System. This is a method of accounting ancillary to, and explaining, the main results of the company's book-keeping. Whereas the accounting system provides the directors and other executives with information concerning the loss or profit of the whole concern over a period, a costing system reveals the cost of production per unit or department. It is not necessary for the director to delve into the details of Costing, but he will be well advised to grasp the principles underlying the matter in order that his knowledge may assist him in the consideration of production control.

The aim of a costing system is to ascertain the cost of production of each unit of the company's manufacture. The term " unit " is used to indicate that measure of output or service upon which a cost may most easily be placed. Thus a " ton of coal " may be the unit for a colliery company, a " department " may be the unit of a multiple or retail stores, " a ton mile " in the case of a railway company, " a printing job " in the case of a printer, and so on. The periodical financial accounts reveal the total cost of the whole of the company's manufacture over a period, the losses sustained in the manufacture and disposal of one type of article being masked by the profit arising from the manufacture and sale of others. The aim of costing is to analyse the items of expenditure, to split up the manufacture into units, and to allocate the cost to each unit concerned. In this way it is ascertained whether any of the company's products are manufactured at a loss or at uneconomical profit, such

117

sources of drain upon the company's capital then being eliminated from the programme of production; alternatively the system of manufacture is overhauled with a view to turning the loss into a profit.

Costing Personnel.

The practice of costing is now fast becoming a science. No little credit for the benefit it confers upon industry is due to the admirable work of the Institute of Cost and Works Accountants. This Institute has for its aim the training and examination of costing personnel, research into scientific methods of costing, and the instilling of interest and enthusiasm in the minds of business executives who may not have fully realized the benefits to be obtained from the science.

It is not always necessary that separate staffs should be engaged for the ascertainment of costs. Indeed, it is always advisable to introduce a system with as little elaboration as possible until the needs of the business are correctly gauged. As elaboration proceeds, however, larger concerns institute a separate costing staff under the charge of a cost accountant. The cost accountant should be given real responsibility, but as it is necessary that his records should agree with those kept by the main accounts office, it is advisable that he should be subject to the authority of the secretary. The work he performs is not only intended to provide information on costs to the sales manager and particulars of production programme costs to the board, but is also designed to assist the works manager in the economical running of his department. For this reason the costing office should be housed in or near the works. Under certain circumstances the costing office should be placed under the control of the works manager, so that there should

be close *liaison* between the cost accountant and the
works manager. The reason for this co-ordination is
that the cost accountant cannot produce any costs
without the fullest information from the works staff
on such matters as time spent on jobs, methods of
working, weights of fuel used, and so on. Unless there
is co-ordination, the result will be either friction or
incorrect costs.

The Objects of Costing.

It is sometimes said that the financial accounts deal
with the expenses of a company in terms of sterling,
and that the cost accounts deal rather in weights
and measures of time. Whereas the financial accounts
show the value of material consumed over a period,
the costs accounts are designed to account for the
weight of the material used, thus revealing excessive
loss, wastage or pilfering. Again, the financial accounts
show the total wages paid, but the cost accounts,
while accounting for the total wages paid and agreeing
the amount with the financial accounts, go farther
and show how much time has been expended by the
workers on each unit and what the cost of that time
has been. Lastly the financial accounts give the
total overhead or oncost charges of the whole company.
The cost accounts split up or allocate the overhead
charges over each unit or department. It will be seen
therefore that costing is designed to show the wages,
material, and overhead charges per unit or department,
and the loss or profit arising on each, the summarized
results agreeing with the composite figure shown or
to be shown in the financial accounts. The expression
" to be shown " is an important one, for it covers one
of the principal advantages to be derived from the
installation of an efficient costing system.

The financial accounts, as explained in previous

chapters, are only made up periodically. In some businesses it is possible to produce approximate profit and loss accounts each month, but in many manufacturing businesses it is impossible to compile accurate accounts at shorter intervals than six months. Costing accounts, on the other hand, are running continuously. No sooner is a job completed than its cost is known, and information is therefore available immediately concerning either a general loss or a loss on any particular contract or job.

Constituents of Cost.

The three main constituents of costs were mentioned above under the terms " wages," " material," and " oncost." In costing nomenclature it is usual to term wages and material by the single term " prime cost." Overhead or running charges, such as salaries, office expenses, selling expenses, and so on, are termed " oncost." The director is likely to meet with these terms on many occasions and he should therefore understand what they are intended to convey. It is sometimes customary to divide oncost into two classes—" works oncost " and " office oncost." Works oncost consists of that portion of the overhead charges attributable to the factory, e.g. works lighting and heating, foremen's and supervisors' salaries, and the proportion of rates, water rent, and similar outgoings chargeable to the factory, based upon floor space, meter readings, or similar methods of allocation.

The other terms which the director is likely to meet are those which indicate the method of costing in use. " Terminal costing " is that applied to the costing of businesses in which the contract or job is terminal or definable, e.g. contracting businesses.

It is possible to charge each particular contract with the exact wages and materials consumed, and after allocating oncost and crediting the contract price, the exact profit or loss is known.

"Single costing" is adopted in companies producing but one standard article. The cost per single unit is obtainable by dividing the output into the total cost.

"Multiple costing" is applied to businesses engaged in the manufacture of more than one type of article. It is designed to reveal whether each class of product is produced at a loss or a profit, indicating whether the prices charged are too low or too high.

"Departmental costing" is adopted by such concerns as retail shops engaged in more than one class of trade. The cost—and therefore the profit or loss—of each department is given.

"Operating costs" are used by undertakings engaged in the provision of services, e.g. lighting companies, railways, tramway companies, aviation concerns, and gas companies, and the cost per train mile, per therm, or per traffic mile is thereby derived.

The Benefits of Costing.

The benefits to be derived from the installation of costing may be summarized as follows—

Cost accounts—

(1) Indicate whether the selling price of a particular commodity or unit of service results in a profit or loss.

(2) Indicate the price which must be charged for a commodity to show a profit.

(3) Reveal any substantial variation in cost of production within the shortest possible time, enabling steps to be taken to curtail heavy loss or to take advantage of increased trade.

(4) Provide information as to the effect on cost of any variation in output.

(5) Indicate the economic output which must be maintained to produce the maximum profit.

(6) Enable concentration to be exerted by the sales department in pushing the disposal of profitable lines, and eliminating the sale of unprofitable items whenever the cost of the latter cannot be reduced to an economic figure.

(7) Provide information concerning the separate running cost of different types of machines, comparison of the cost of different workmanship, and the varying cost of such items of plant as furnaces, kilns, etc.

(8) Furnish data upon which quotations may be based.

(9) Reveal loss of time, wastage of material, defalcations of cash and similar loss of the company's assets. They account for, and confirm, the expenditure in weight and value of every charge appearing in the financial accounts.

(10) Point out the occasions upon which it is more profitable to let out work on sub-contract than to take into the factory any work previously placed with sub-contractors.

It will be realized from the foregoing that there is no better aid to the director in any efforts he makes towards economy or efficiency in his company than costing. By its aid he is enabled to review separately the three classes of expenditure charged in his company's accounts, at the same time studying the effect of projected economy upon production as well as expense. The items over which the director should exercise control are—

(a) Raw materials.

(b) Wages.

(c) Oncost generally.

With regard to raw materials, it is advisable that the execution of contracts for supply of fuel, oil, steel, and any chemicals subject to convention should be carried out by the board. Power to make such contracts is occasionally granted to subordinate officials but there is every reason why contracts which commit the expenditure of considerable portions of the working capital, and which contain clauses mulcting the company in damages in the event of agreed amounts not being taken up, should invariably be laid before the directors for sanction. The proposed contracts will be supported by a memorandum from the buyer and only in exceptional cases should his advice be disregarded. Exceptional cases arise whenever the capital-control statement indicates that the laying-in of extra stocks cannot be financed without difficulty. The company will benefit from the moral effect caused by an instruction that all forward commitments relating to raw materials and fuel shall be approved by the directors before execution. The control of stocks will depend upon the efficiency of the works manager and upon the system of stores recording, the latter duty falling within the province of the cost accountant. Although it is advisable for the director to interest himself in the material purchases of his company as much as possible, he should never over-ride the recommendations of the buyer to the extent of ordering the purchasing of different brands of goods. The practice of influencing the purchasing of raw materials from other companies in which a director happens to be interested can cause great dissatisfaction among works executives. They should be credited with knowing the particular class of raw material best suited to their work, and it stands to reason that any materials foisted upon them for the private benefit of a director will seldom be judged suitable by them. In certain cases it may be desirable for the works to purchase their supplies from particular companies, especially when the supplying company happens to be a subsidiary company. There are ways by which the works executives may be induced to order those goods in preference to others without the necessity of giving direct orders to that effect.

Wages.

The control of the board over wages should be general, but at the same time sufficiently wide to enable them to deal with matters of policy connected with the worker, labour disputes, increases of rates, and betterment of conditions connected with wages. It is impossible to understand questions affecting wages without spending some time in consultation with the works manager, and for this purpose the directors should arrange for frequent conferences between the board and those who directly control the worker and fix his pay. Wages, of course, are subject to many factors other than the whims and dictates of directors, and it is not suggested that conferences of the nature referred to should be held for the purpose of fixing rates of pay. They should be held for the purpose of enabling the director to gain a correct idea of the conditions prevailing in the factory, of the wages earned, and of the hours worked. He will then be in a position to take part in the settlement of disputes which may arise from time to time. Too often do directors ignore this matter beyond asking the secretary the average rates paid, or the highest rates paid, or the number of hands employed, or confining their attention to the item of wages expressed only in sterling figures in the costing or production reports laid before them. These spasmodic requests should never permit a director to imagine that he is controlling this item of his company's expenditure.

Oncost.

The company's oncost will be brought before the

directors in many forms, but usually in an oncost sheet
prepared by the costing department. This class of
expenditure is more readily grasped by the director
than the other constituents ; it is fairly constant
from month to month, and fluctuations can readily
be explained by the secretary or cost accountant in
whose department the expense is summarized. The
oncost sheet sets out the salaries paid, the charges
for rates, water, lighting, cleaning, office expenses,
stationery, travelling expenses and advertising. The
director should compare the sheets from month
to month and satisfy himself that the effect of
oncost fluctuations has been fully realized in the
consideration of all production programmes.

There is one other matter into which the director
should inquire whenever he reviews the revenue expenditure outlined above, and that is the outlay of the
company in capital expenditure. The question arises
on many occasions, but particularly when changes
in methods of production are under consideration.
Slight changes in production programmes are often
sufficient to call for capital outlay. A rule should always exist that capital expenditure be authorized by
the board. Capital expenditure does not necessarily
imply the purchase of new plant or the erection of
new buildings by outside builders and contractors. It
covers the employment of the company's workmen and
the use of the company's material in the building of
new machinery, the installation of new furnaces, the
erection of additional producers, or the laying of new
mains. Any proposal to divert revenue expenditure
to capital purposes should be brought before the
directors immediately, and their sanction should be
obtained before the work is commenced. This rule
should be extended to the employment of the company's workmen, its materials or its technical staff in

experimental work. Although it is undesirable to curtail experimental work considered necessary by the company's experts, its pursuit should receive the authority of the board in every case, after consideration of the financial aspect.

CHAPTER XIII

In the brief reference to sales organization in Chapter II, it was explained that this side of a company's activity is committed to a separate department under the charge of a Sales Manager. This division is one of the three main groups into which the whole administration is split up, the other two being production management and financial management. The officer in charge of the financial management is not regarded as the sole financial manager, for the real control of his department is subject to the detailed consideration of the board. The position is similar regarding the head of the production department. The Sales Manager, however, is rather more independent of control. It is therefore necessary for the director to ensure that the lessened control he himself possesses is rendered as effective as possible. The sales manager should be a man of specialized experience and he should also possess an all-round knowledge of the administration and organization of joint-stock companies and the principles underlying their finance. The latter qualification will enable him to preserve a *liaison* with the finance management, without which successful salesmanship is practically impossible.

Relative Importance of the Sales Manager.

The importance of the sales manager usually varies with the nature of the sales policy which his company is able to adopt. The adoption of a policy is not always a matter of choice, for the fixing of selling prices—which is the chief factor in the policy—depends upon whether the company is able to quote according

to costs and estimates, or whether it can impose monopoly prices, or whether it must follow trade practice.
These three divisions represent the main methods upon
which selling prices may be based. The importance
of the sales manager will be relatively less when his
company's prices depend upon the work of a costing
office than when he is left to follow trade practice, and
by his own initiative prove himself a sales manager in
actual fact.

The Director and the Sales Manager.

Except when the sales department disposes of the
company's products upon terms dictated by other
departments, e.g. by commercial estimators or a costing department, the profit or loss on the company's
accounts may depend entirely upon the efficiency of
the sales manager. An inefficient sales manager who is
allowed to fix selling prices without supervision may
easily dispose of the whole of the margin between cost
and a fair selling price. In his anxiety to force up his
sales he may cast aside the co-operation of other
departments and forego any production profit which
may have been made. It is quite possible, however,
for the director to control the sales without trespassing
upon the sales department's province, and the following
methods should be considered—

Production Profit.

In Chapter VI illustrations of a manufacturing and
a trading account were given. The manufacturing
account was based upon a business in which selling
prices were fixed by trade practice. It was therefore
possible to transfer the production to Trading Account
at market or wholesale prices, the balance on the
account representing the production profit made by
the works. Now if the transfer to the trading account

is regarded as a sale of the production to the sales manager at wholesale prices a ready means of gauging the efficiency of that official is provided. The *production* profit in that example amounted to £19,675, indicating that the efficiency of the production management resulted in the manufacture of the goods at a cost of £19,675 less than would have to be paid for the products in the wholesale market. The gross profit shown in the trading account, amounting to £40,410, represents the trading profit earned by the efforts of the sales manager. This is the first method by which a certain control may be maintained by the director over the sales department. It is not advanced that either amount of profit indicates maximum efficiency; other indications must be examined before that conclusion is adopted. It is clear, however, that whenever the first balance (on production account) shows a profit on wholesale prices, and the second balance (on the sales manager's account) shows a loss, the board must act at once. An investigation into the methods of the sales manager is imperative.

Disposal of Production.

Turning next to the capital control statement given in Chapter VIII, we observe that monthly increases or decreases of stock are ascertainable by comparing the entries under this heading month by month. This point is of considerable value to the director in his control over the sales. In order to obtain a clear view of the work of the sales department over a period, it is necessary to examine, simultaneously, the return of sales, the return of production, and the capital control statement. A decrease in the sales and an increase in the stock must be explained by the sales manager very fully. A decrease in the sales without an apparent effect upon other items will lead the director to compare the schedule of outstanding orders with the schedule prepared for the previous month. It may be found that the works manager is not co-operating efficiently with the sales manager.

It is the duty of the director to investigate the matter and to pursue inquiries in both directions. The capital control statement itself may show that a remarkable increase in the sales has led to a too heavy increase in the sundry debtors. The directors, and not the sales manager, are responsible for the control of working capital, and such an occurrence as this, which may conceivably hamper the company's finance, must be attended to by the board. It is one of the cases in which the directors must preserve strict supervision over the sales department, examining the terms of credit it is allowing to customers, and deciding whether those terms can be continued.

The lines of inquiry based upon the periodical returns as set out above cannot be regarded as exhaustive. Enough has been written, however, to indicate that by making full use of the periodical returns outlined in a previous chapter the director may maintain a close watch on the sales policy of the company, however much it may be committed to one man.

Sales Statistics.

Reference was made in a previous chapter to the fact that the sales department keeps no books of account. The daily, weekly, or monthly total of sales invoiced is compiled in the accounts office and may be laid before the board by the secretary, or it may be passed on to the sales manager for incorporation in his own report. Totals of sales invoiced are not, however, always sufficiently indicative of the results of the sales department. It may happen, for instance, that very good results achieved by the sales manager in a particular month may not be seen until some time later when the goods have been manufactured or the orders received from abroad. For this reason it is desirable that the sales manager should prepare sales statistics suitable for the particular business, and that he should submit them to the directors.

The compilation of the statistics will not involve much clerical labour, but it will be found that many sales managers are averse from keeping such records on the ground that their travellers are required for selling goods and not for writing up records. This excuse is a plausible one, but the inclusion of sufficient data by the travellers in their reports cannot possibly over-burden them to the extent of causing the neglect of the primary object of their employment. In any case the traveller must make reports, and it will be found that where insufficient co-operation is maintained between the works manager and the sales department the traveller will always find time to set out customers' complaints in his reports, in this way providing an excuse for his own poor results.

If the director arranges for the furnishing of statistics based upon orders, he will be in possession of fairly complete information regarding the sales department of his concern. It will be necessary to read together the following returns—

From the Secretary	*From the Sales Manager*
(a) Value of goods invoiced, daily, monthly, or at other regular intervals	(a) Quantities or approximate value of orders under headings of different commodities
(b) Value of goods returned by customers	(b) Report on nature of complaints leading to return of goods by customers
(c) Classification of goods invoiced	(c) Values of orders from different travellers or different territories
(d) Amount of sales for which customers have not paid (in Control Statement)	(d) Quantities or values of goods ordered but not yet produced

Inquiries based upon these returns will provide the director with information concerning the last remaining point upon which he should satisfy himself. This last point is whether co-operation, to which passing reference has been made, is fully maintained.

Co-operation with the Accounts Officer.

The usual result of lack of co-operation with the accounts officer is that the sales department grants credit to all and sundry customers, no matter what their past record may have been. The natural outcome is a debit in the company's accounts for abnormal bad debts, and for this loss the finance officer is usually left to make what explanations he can. The director should see that the finance officer is consulted before large orders are accepted from customers who may eventually fail to meet their obligations. It should not be possible for travellers to take definite orders without restriction of some kind. In many companies the travellers are encouraged to obtain orders at all costs, or at least they are not restricted in the matter of the terms they grant. Wherever this occurs it will be found that additional allowances, extra discounts, and long credit are promised freely by the traveller, and that on many occasions he fails to notify the accounts department fully or fails to give the finance officer an opportunity of approving the concession. This lack of co-ordination inevitably leads to complaints from good customers as soon as the accounts department presses for payment on the usual terms, ignorant of the magnanimous conditions granted by the traveller or his manager. This state of affairs is, unfortunately, of frequent occurrence. It is due, in no small measure, to the growing custom of investing the sales manager and his subordinates with an unfettered authority and regarding their work as paramount in the whole organization. That sales management is indeed a field for specialization is not denied. The improvement of the status of the sales manager cannot fail to have a beneficial effect on the company. At the same time it is to be regretted that selling the company's products should be regarded as the only factor upon which the success of a concern depends. An eminent business man recently remarked that " if the process of elaboration of sales departments continues on this side of the Atlantic with the same disregard of cost as is indulged in upon the other side, the majority of concerns will be selling goods for the manufacture of which they have no means." This reference, incidentally, is sometimes applicable to other departments in a company's organization.

In order to foster the co-operation which is so necessary between the accounts office and the sales department, the sales manager should not be given supreme authority to sell goods indiscriminately. His work certainly consists in the disposal of the company's production, but it should not be possible for him to convert a tangible asset into one of more or less problematical value. Whenever the remuneration of a sales manager, traveller, or agent consists in part of a commission on sales, the director should ensure that the commission is payable only on cash received, or that the commission account is charged with bad debts and excess discounts.

Fixing Prices.

The compiling of catalogues, and the preparation of price lists, is carried out by the sales manager, but it is advisable that the directors should supervise the work. The case of contract companies in which prices are based on costs and quoted by the estimator need not be considered. The board will naturally have an opportunity of approving or rejecting contracts of any magnitude. In the case of monopoly commodities or goods sold at trade-practice prices, however, the directors will receive two lists—one containing the suggested base selling prices, and the other setting out the cost.

It is not possible to give a list of the full considerations governing the fixing of prices in either case within this volume. As a general rule it may be stated that the process of discovering the economic price giving the highest return on a monopoly (not necessarily the highest price) can be carried out with success only by following the costs. It is the duty of the sales manager to advise the board upon economic selling prices in such businesses, and the directors may arrive at their decision from that information, considered in conjunction with the costs laid before them.

It may be mentioned at this point that even where the commodity sold is a patent or is controlled by a trust, the economic price will usually be a reflection of the trade-practice price obtainable for substitutes, or for the goods of competitors outside the convention. With regard to trade-practice prices, the director will be well advised to make full use of the schedule of costs. Unfortunately, he cannot be advised to insist on a rigid cost basis for selling prices, for trade practice in almost every type of business in England continues to reveal glaring fallacies when compared with analysed cost. The selling price must continue to follow the trade until the adoption of standard rates revealed by standard trade costing becomes universal. This does not mean that the cost schedules cannot be used. On the contrary, it may be found that departure from trade practice by substituting lower prices justified by the costing can be carried out immediately. Again, the director may find that many suggested selling prices, if adopted, would result in a heavy loss to the company. In such cases it is obvious that the production of the lines concerned must be eliminated or an inquiry must be made into the method of manufacture. The use of the two schedules and the part to be played by the director is thus clearly seen. The sales manager is quite justified in following trade practice; it is the director's duty to examine the prices, and to link the sales department's policy with that demanded by the statistics of manufacture.

Co-operation with the Works.

The director should pay particular attention to the portions of the sales manager's report which deal with complaints from customers, and with the quantities of goods ordered but not produced. These sections of the report may often enable the director to arrange better co-ordination between the sales department and the factory. When proper arrangements do not exist, it may be found that allowances for goods alleged to be faulty are granted too freely by the sales officials. This procedure does not lead to harmony in administration. As a general principle, the production executives should be given an opportunity of inspecting the goods returned before any allowance is made and before an apology, containing recriminations against the works, is sent out by the sales department. In the majority of cases it may be arranged that allowances for faulty work shall be made only on the joint sanction of the works manager and the head of the sales department.

Outstanding Orders.

With regard to the orders outstanding, the director should ascertain whether the delay is due to an abnormal rush of orders, shortage of stock, or to a breakdown in the factory. Satisfactory explanations will usually be forthcoming, but the cause may be found to lie in a failure of the sales department to realize the limitations of production. Orders may have been taken indiscriminately for goods of a pattern not usually · produced, with a general assurance to the customer that the peculiarity in type can be overcome. There is a good deal to be said for promotion of a company's goodwill by refusing to disappoint a customer ; at the same time it is not advisable for the sales department to follow the practice without keeping well in touch with the department responsible for executing the orders. By co-operation it will be found that the practice can be rendered beneficial to the company, for the production manager will be able to advise the sales manager to what extent, and in which direction, he can cope with the results of that policy. Without co-operation, it is possible for the practice to become a real hindrance to profitable production.

Another factor which frequently leads to the accumulation of orders is the practice of promising delivery of particular orders at stated dates without previous consultation with the works manager. As a general principle, it should be laid down that work commenced and running through a factory should continue running until it reaches the finished stores. To send in production orders for execution before completion of goods in course of manufacture, and without first conferring with the works manager, naturally leads to an all-round delay, increased cost, and to imperfect workmanship. The works manager will, however, often be able to promise early delivery of many orders which will not delay output in other parts of his shops. By such methods as those outlined above the director should be able to satisfy himself that co-ordination is maintained. Information indicating lack of co-operation may be gathered from the returns presented for his consideration.

PART IV
The Director and the Annual Accounts

CHAPTER XIV

THE PREPARATION OF THE ANNUAL ACCOUNTS

At the close of the company's financial year the director is called upon to prepare an account of his directorship for presentation to the proprietors covering the year since he last reported to them. It is again emphasized that the accounts are the accounts of the Board. The fallacy still persists, in some quarters, that the annual Balance Sheet is that of the auditors. Where this belief is held it may be taken for granted that the Board is inefficient and that the members have not a proper conception of directorship. The preparation of the draft accounts is carried out by the Board through its officers—either the secretary or accountant—and they are laid before the Board for discussion. Alterations and adjustments are then made and the accounts are afterwards handed to the auditors for examination. In all probability the auditors will have carried out certain of the detail checking work in order that the presentation of the final accounts may not be delayed. In many cases also the auditors may attend at the deliberations of the directors, assisting the Board in the capacity of accountants, and advising the directors upon the form of the accounts. Even though they do so the accounts remain the accounts of the Board and the report at the foot continues to be the only part of the accounts belonging to the auditors.

The Formation of Committees.

Occasionally the preparation of annual accounts is delegated to small committees composed of three or four members of the Board. It may happen that this practice, at times, is found advantageous. Unfortunately, however, it is not one which can be fully commended. It may be considered a welcome relief by directors whose attendance at accounts meetings would in no way assist the deliberations; but it will not safeguard the incompetent director. No director can possibly afford to neglect the principles upon which his accounts are prepared. The accounts sent out to the shareholders are as much his accounts as they are those of any other member of the Board. No director should retain a seat on the Board of a company unless he understands the information sent out to the shareholders in his name. That many directors still do not realize the importance and meaning of their own accounts is common knowledge. And this anomaly is due, in no little degree, to the system of leaving the preparation of accounts to committees.

Where the number of directors on a Board is not unwieldy, the committee system should be avoided whenever the annual accounts are under discussion. If there are too many directors to permit of sufficient progress being made in the preparation of accounts, the committee system should only be adopted with the proviso that full reports and all draft documents be circulated to each non-committee member, accompanied by the recommendations of the accounts committee. These provisional documents must be examined and sifted thoroughly, and power should alway be reserved to any director to attend an accounts committee should he so desire, so that any particular suggested procedure may be thrashed out in his presence.

How the Accounts are Prepared.

In order that subsequent remarks may be perfectly

clear we will consider, for a few moments, the preliminary steps in the preparation of accounts. The first is the preparation of a Trial Balance. This consists of nothing more than a list of all the balances appearing in the company's Ledger. As the director is now well aware, the Ledger is the only essential book of account, but on account of the magnitude of the business the Ledger may have been split into a considerable number of parts. For instance, the Ledger accounts of customers may—and in all probability will—have been bound in separate books called Sales Ledgers. The accounts of the suppliers, on the other hand, will be contained in Bought or Purchase Ledgers. The bank account, generally the most unwieldy of the personal accounts in the Ledger, will be bound up separately and called a Cash Book. The expense and revenue items will be contained in a Nominal Ledger, and so on.

As soon as the financial year of the company comes to an end the books are " closed off " and the balances are carried down. This means that no further entries are made, the two sides of each account are added up, ruled off, and the net balances carried down to the new year. An exception to this general statement is that the Bought Ledger is usually left open for a few days so that invoices in respect of goods delivered in the day or so before the end of the year may be included.

THE TRIAL BALANCE. The Trial Balance is drawn up by the secretary or the accountant. The balances on the Private Ledger usually appear first, followed by Nominal Ledger balances, then the balances on the Sales and Purchases Ledgers, and, lastly, the bank balance or balance on the Cash Book.

Stock-in-Trade.

Whilst the clerical staff are engaged in ruling off the books and laying the material for the Trial Balance before the secretary, the technical staff are employed in listing and valuing the stock-in-trade. This work naturally varies in magnitude in different businesses. In a merchanting business there may be little or no stock to be valued; in a retail business the departmental valuations of stock displayed for sale at retail prices may be considerable; and in a manufacturing business the separate treatment of raw material, work in progress, and finished goods calls for the exercise of great care and intelligent supervision.

As explained in an earlier chapter, the stock-in-trade must be taken into account before the profit or loss on a year's trading can be arrived at. It must appear as a credit in the Trading or Profit and Loss Account, and constitutes a " gain," which offsets the " loss " or expense represented by the stock-in-trade held at the commencement of the trading period.

Stock-in-trade is valued at cost or at market price, whichever is the lower. The effect of this practice is that no unrealized profit is taken into credit in the company's account. If the stock were valued at selling price the profits would be inflated by an amount which might never be realized. This situation could easily arise if an unexpected slump set in immediately following the close of the company's financial year.

Reserves and Apportionments.

The next step in the preparation of the accounts is the calculation of Reserves and Apportionments. The meaning of these terms will be clear if it is remembered that debits to expense accounts do not necessarily represent the full charge under each heading appropriate to the company's financial year. Thus the rates demand entered in "Rates Account" may relate to a six months' period in advance. On the other hand, the debits appearing under " Insurance Account " may not represent the full year's outlay, on account of the non-receipt of a demand note for the renewal premium. It is necessary, therefore, to calculate reserves for charges not yet entered in the books and to apportion the charges paid in advance. These adjustments have the effect of debiting the accounts with the appropriate charge under each heading—and no more. In order to complete the double entry the reserves are entered in the Balance Sheet among the liabilities, thus off-setting the additional debits made in the Profit and Loss Account. The apportionments, on the other hand, are carried forward as assets, i.e. debits, the corresponding credits consisting of diminutions of the Expense Accounts paid in advance.

Bad Debts and Depreciation.

The secretary, or accountant, next calculates the Bad Debt Reserve and the Depreciation Charges. Whilst the director need not examine the minute details of these charges and reserves, he should call for a summary at the next accounts meeting. The clarity, or otherwise, with which the summary is presented depends entirely on whether the company has a capable secretary or not. If he is efficient, the schedule of bad debts to be written off *with the sanction of the Board* will show full details of the principal debts and the grounds on which they are believed to be bad. Adequate references to liquidations, receiverships, or other causes which prevent the recovery of debts, will be available.

The calculations of the reserves against *possible* bad debts should be presented to the director very clearly. A list of the over-due accounts, giving the dates on which the goods were supplied, should be available; and if the reserve suggested by the secretary is calculated as a percentage of the whole of the debtors, the

THE SUCCESS CO., LTD.

Preliminary Trial Balance, 31st December, 1935

	£	£
1. Land and buildings, at cost . .	145,000	
2. Plant and machinery as at 1st January, 1935 (Depreciation rate 10%). .	263,888	
3. Fixtures (Depreciation rate 10%) .	39,444	
4. Goodwill, patents, and trade marks .	12,200	
5. Issued 5% Preference Share Capital Account (Authorized £250,000) .		50,000
6. Issued 6% Redeemable Preference Share Capital Account (Authorized £500,000)		50,000
7. Issued Ordinary Share Capital Account (Authorized £500,000) . . .		400,000
8. Trade debtors per schedule of Sales Ledger Balances	113,495	
9. Investments in Quoted Securities at book value	93,725	
10. Reserve Account		100,000
11. Investments in Subsidiary Companies (A B, C D, and E F) . . .	45,000	
12. Debentures in the A B Subsidiary Co., Ltd.	12,000	
13. Current Account with the E F Subsidiary Co., Ltd.	13,400	12,400
14. Rates Account (including £105 paid in advance)	905	
15. Stock-in-Trade, 1st January, 1935 .	150,490	
16. Cash at bankers	44,010	
17. Preliminary expenses . . .	9,200	
18. Trade creditors per Bought Ledger Balances		25,200
19. The X Y Co., Ltd. Secured by deposit of investments		10,500
20. Rent Account—Sidings—including £250 paid in advance	900	
21. Mr. Walton, cash creditor, temporary deposit		1,500
22. Loan to Mr. Benson, director, as at 1st January, 1933, repaid 1935 . .	1,000	1,000
23. Loan to Mr. Jameson, director, as at 1st January, 1935	2,500	
24. Loan to Mr. Smithers, director, made during year and repaid . . .	3,500	3,500
25. Purchases, *less* returns . . .	459,780	
26. Sales, *less* returns		748,900
27. Wages	98,779	
28. Salaries (£1,200 paid in advance) .	44,330	
Carried forward	£1,553,546	£1,403,000

grounds on which any given percentage is chosen should be set out fully.

The depreciation which it is proposed to write off should be presented to the director in much the same form as the bad debt calculation. The exact rates and amounts applicable to each type of asset should appear in the secretary's summary. In this way the director is enabled to offer his own comments on the adequacy or otherwise of each proposed charge. He is also able to join effectively in the discussion which will take place

PRELIMINARY TRIAL BALANCE—(contd.)

	£	£
Brought forward . .	1,553,546	1,403,000
29. Lighting, heating, and power (£220 due but not entered)	4,840	
30. Advertising (Reserve of £700 necessary)	2,200	
31. Office expenses	1,900	
32. Travellers' salaries (£1,000 reserve necessary)	7,800	
33. Directors' fees	5,000	
34. Reserve for bad debts . .		10,000
35. Dividends from investments .		8,400
36. Stationery, telephone, etc. (Telephone reserve £45)	1,980	
37. Preference dividend, 5% shares . .	2,500	
38. Preference dividend, 6% shares . .	3,000	
39. Dividends from subsidiary companies.		8,980
40. Capital Redemption Reserve Fund .		50,000
41. Sundry trade expenses . . .	5,434	
42. Carriage inwards	22,980	
43. Income Tax reserve		50,000
44. Carriage outwards	19,020	
45. Profit and Loss Appropriation Account, as at 1st January, 1935 . .		99,820
	£1,630,200	£1,630,200

NOTES:

1. Stock in trade at 31st December, 1935, £102,380.

2. Reserve for bad debts, £13,200.

3. Market value of securities, £95,850.

4. The Redeemable Preference Shares are redeemable at option of company on or before 31st December, 1945.

THE SUCCESS COMPANY, LTD.
SECOND TRIAL BALANCE, 31ST DECEMBER, 1935

No.	Particulars	Balance Sheet Items		Profit and Loss Account Items	
		Dr. £	Cr. £	Dr. £	Cr. £
1.	Land and buildings	145,000			
2.	Plant and machinery, *less* Depreciation at 10% per annum	263,888	26,388	26,388	
3.	Fixtures, *less* Depreciation at 10% per annum	39,444	3,944	3,944	
4.	Goodwill, patents, and trade-marks	12,200			
5.	Issued 5% Preference Share Capital Account (Authorized £250,000)		50,000		
6.	Issued 6% Redeemable Share Capital Account (Authorized £100,000) redeemable on or before 31st December, 1945		50,000		
7.	Issued Ordinary Share Capital Account (Authorized £500,000)		400,000		
8.	Trade debtors per schedule of Sales Ledger Balances	113,495			
9.	Investments in Quoted Securities at book value (market value £95,850)	93,725			
10.	Reserve Account		100,000		
11.	Investments in subsidiary companies (A B, C D, E F)	45,000			
12.	Debentures in the A B Subsidiary Co., Ltd.	12,000			
13.	Current Accounts with the E F Subsidiary Co., Ltd.	13,400	12,400		
14.	Rates Account (including £105 paid in advance)	105		800	
15.	Stock in trade at beginning and end of year	102,380		150,490	102,380
16.	Cash at bankers	44,010			
17.	Preliminary expenses	9,200			
18.	Trade creditors per Bought Ledger Balances		25,200		
19.	The X Y Co., Ltd.—Secured by deposit of securities		10,500		
20.	Rent Account—Sidings—Including £250 paid in advance	250		650	
21.	Mr. Walton, cash creditor, temporary deposit		1,500		
22.	Loan to Mr. Benson, director, as at January, 1933, repaid 1935 (need not be disclosed)				
23.	Loan to Mr. Jameson, director, as at 1st January, 1935	2,500			
24.	Loan to Mr. Smithers, director, made during year and repaid (must be disclosed)	3,500	3,500		
25.	Purchases, *less* returns			459,780	
26.	Sales, *less* returns				748,900
27.	Wages			98,779	
28.	Salaries (£1,200 paid in advance)	1,200		43,130	
29.	Lighting, heating, and power (£220 due but not entered)		220	5,060	
30.	Advertising (Reserve of £700 necessary)		700	2,900	
31.	Office expenses		1,000	1,900	
32.	Travellers' salaries			8,800	
33.	Directors' fees			5,000	
34.	Reserve for bad debts		23,200	13,200	
35.	Dividends from investments				8,400
36.	Stationery, telephone, etc. (Telephone Reserve £45)		45	2,025	
37.	Preference Dividend—5% shares			2,500	
38.	Preference Dividend—6% shares			3,000	
39.	Dividends from subsidiary companies				8,980
40.	Capital Redemption Reserve Fund		50,000		
41.	Sundry trade expenses			5,434	
42.	Carriage inwards			22,980	
43.	Income Tax Reserve		80,000	30,000	
44.	Carriage outwards			19,020	
45.	Profit and Loss Appropriation Account, as at 1st January, 1935				99,820
	Balances	62,700	62,700	62,700	

on suggestions that the depreciation rates be varied from time to time.

The Draft Accounts.

When the secretary is in possession of the stock figures, the bad debt schedules, lists of reserves, and the depreciation calculations, he gives effect to the adjustments in his second Trial Balance. This second draft then includes the final figures ready for inclusion in the Draft Accounts. The two steps must be understood by the director, and we give below a detailed illustration of the process. We take, first of all, the preliminary Trial Balance of the Success Company, Ltd., and then prepare the second draft, incorporating the reserves, apportionments, etc. Lastly, we draw up the Balance Sheet for the consideration of the Board at their first accounts meeting.

The Trial Balance, as shown on page 142, sets out the balances taken roughly from the company's books of account. Beyond a few notes as to reserves and apportionments, the secretary has made no attempt to adjust the balances for inclusion in the draft accounts. In his second draft he makes the appropriate allowances, deductions, and additions, and he also prepares his Trial Balance in such a way as to distinguish the Balance Sheet items from the Profit and Loss Account entries. As explained fully in a previous chapter, *all* debits are either assets or losses, and all credits are either liabilities or gains. Following this invariable and immutable rule the analysis of the balances is carried out easily, as indicated in the second Trial Balance illustrated on page 144.

THE DRAFT ACCOUNTS. The draft accounts of the Success Company, Ltd., prepared from the Trial Balance given on page 142, are now laid before the director in the following form.

THE SUCCESS COMPANY, LTD.

Balance Sheet as at 31st December, 1935

Liabilities	£	£	Assets	£	£
Authorized Capital :			Land and buildings, at cost . .		145,000
250,000 5% Preference Shares of £1 each .		250,000	Plant and machinery *less* depreciation .	263,888	
100,000 6% Redeemable Preference Shares of £1 each .		100,000	*Deduct :* depreciation at 10% per annum	26,388	
500,000 Ordinary Shares of £1 each .		500,000			237,500
		£850,000	Fixtures *less* depreciation .	39,444	
			Deduct : depreciation at 10% per annum	3,944	
Issued Share Capital :					35,500
50,000 5% Preference Shares .	50,000		Debtors and apportionments . .	115,050	
50,000 6% Redeemable Preference Shares (Redeemable on or before 31st Dec., 1945) .	50,000		*Less* Reserve for bad debts .	23,200	
400,000 Ordinary Shares . .	400,000				91,850
		500,000	Investments in subsidiary companies—		
Creditors and accrued expenses . .	27,165		Shares at cost	45,000	
Loan Account (secured)	10,500		Debentures at cost.	12,000	
Amount due to subsidiary company .	12,400		Current Accounts .	13,400	
Reserve Account .	100,000				70,400
Reserve for taxation .	80,000		Loans to Directors, as at 1st Jan., 1935 .	2,500	
Loan Account, unsecured	1,500		*Add* loan made during year . .	3,500	
Capital Redemption Reserve Fund	50,000			6,000	
Profit & Loss Appropriation Account .	62,700		*Less* loan repaid .	3,500	
					2,500
			Investments at book value (Market value £95,850)		93,725
			Stock in trade, at cost or market value, whichever is the lower .		102,380
			Cash at bankers		44,010
			Preliminary expenses		9,200
			Goodwill, patents, and trade marks . .		12,200
		£844,265			£844,265

TRADING AND PROFIT AND LOSS ACCOUNT

For the Year Ended 31st December, 1935

Dr.   Cr.

	£		£
To Stock in trade, 1st Jan., 1935 . .	150,490	By Sales, *less* returns . .	748,900
,, Purchases, *less* returns .	459,780	,, Stock in trade, 31st Dec., 1935 . . .	102,380
,, Carriage inwards . .	22,980		
,, Wages . .	98,779		
,, Gross Profit carried down .	119,251		
	£851,280		£851,280

Trading and Profit and Loss Account (*contd.*)—
Dr.   Cr.

	£		£
To Salaries	43,130	By Gross Profit brought down.	119,251
,, Lighting, heating, and power	5,060	,, Dividends from investments	8,400
,, Advertising . . .	2,900	,, Dividends from subsidiary	
,, Office expenses . .	1,900	companies . . .	8,890
,, Travellers' salaries . .	8,800	,, Net loss for year carried to	
,, Directors' fees . . .	5,000	Appropriation Account .	1,620
,, Rates . . .	800		
,, Rent of siding . . .	650		
,, Stationery, telephone, etc..	2,025		
,, Sundry trade expenses .	5,434		
,, Carriage outwards . .	19,020		
,, Reserve for bad debts .	13,200		
,, Depreciation . . .	30,332		
	£138,251		£138,251

APPROPRIATION ACCOUNT
Dr.   Cr.

	£		£
To Dividend on 5% Preference		By Balance, 1st Jan., 1935 .	99,820
Shares, paid Feb., 1935 .	2,500		
,, Dividend on 6% Preference			
Shares, paid Feb., 1935 .	3,000		
,, Reserve for Income Tax .	30,000		
Net loss for year transferred			
from Profit and Loss A/c	1,620		
,, Balance carried to Balance			
Sheet	62,700		
	£99,820		£99,820

In our illustration of the accounts of the Success Company, Ltd., we have creditors and one secured liability; we include the accrued expenses with the creditors and we disclose the general nature of the liability by describing it as " Creditors and Accrued Expenses." The secured loan from the X Y Company, Ltd., is shown as " Loan Account (Secured) £10,500."

The amount due to the E. F. Subsidiary Company, Ltd., could, quite correctly, be deducted from the amount owing by that company; it is shown separately as a liability, however, in order to draw attention again to Section 125, which was set out in full on page 108. On referring to the text of that section it will be seen that the company must disclose the aggregate amount of any indebtedness to a subsidiary or subsidiary

companies.   It need not specify the particular company
or companies to which the debts are due.

Treatment of Liabilities.

It will be convenient to consider the liabilities first.
The director must examine each item in turn and see
that the provisions of the Companies Act are complied
with.   We have dealt with the method of setting out
the Capital Account in the Balance Sheet, and we
therefore turn to the Trade and Secured Creditors.

Section 124 provides that the Balance Sheet must
contain the company's liabilities together with such
particulars as are necessary to disclose their general
nature; secured liabilities must be so described, although
it is not necessary to specify the assets which have been
charged.

The other items on the liabilities side of the Balance
Sheet are reserves of varying nature.   Some reserves,
such as that for taxation, represent actual provisions
against liabilities.   Other reserves consist of allocations
of profit and are somewhat similar in nature to the
liability to the shareholders; that is to say, they represent profits belonging to the members which they agree
to leave in the business as additional temporary capital.
Again, there are reserves designed to conserve funds
for the replacement of assets or the repayment of fixed
liabilities.   In view of these distinctions we leave their
consideration over until we examine the rules governing
the allocation and distribution of profits.

Treatment of Assets.

The principal regulations governing the treatment
of assets in the published accounts are contained in
Sec. 124 of the Companies Act, 1929.   It is laid down
that every Balance Sheet must contain such particulars
as are necessary to distinguish between the *fixed* and

the *floating* assets. In addition, it must be shown how the value of the *fixed* assets have been arrived at. It is for this reason that we describe the land and buildings, in the illustration, as " at cost " and the plant as being " less depreciation at 10 per cent."

There are also these important rules in Sec. 124 for the director's attention—

1. The preliminary expenses must be shown separately until written off. (See illustration on page 146.)

2. Any expenses incurred in connection with issues of shares or debentures must be stated. (See illustration on page 80.)

3. The amount of goodwill and of any patents and trade marks must be given separately. If the goodwill is already merged with other assets in the books, then steps must be taken to ascertain its amount by reference to contracts or other documents under which it was acquired.

Investments in Subsidiaries.

The legal requirements as to the disclosure of interests in subsidiaries were set out at length in Chapter X. The directors must give particulars of—

(*a*) Shares in subsidiaries.

(*b*) Loans to subsidiaries.

It is advisable to distinguish between ordinary indebtedness and advances on current account, but it is unnecessary to do more than give aggregate figures under each heading. The extent of the necessary disclosure is illustrated in the draft accounts of the Success Company, Ltd.

The director must then comply with Sec. 126 (p. 109) and see that a statement is annexed to the Balance Sheet setting out—

1. How the profits and losses of subsidiaries have been dealt with in the accounts of the parent company.

2. Whether, in particular, provision has been made for the losses of subsidiaries, either in their own accounts or in the accounts of the parent company, or both.

3. How far the losses of subsidiaries have been taken into account in arriving at the profits or losses of the parent company.

4. A reference to any qualifications made in the reports of the auditors of the subsidiary companies to the members.

There is no set form in which the foregoing information must be given, and the following illustrations indicate the general method of complying with the Act—

(a) Assuming that the subsidiaries have made profits, with one exception, and that dividends have been received from all save that one, the statement would read somewhat as under—

Statement made in compliance with Sec. 126 of the Companies Act, 1929: The profits of the subsidiary companies, to the extent of dividends declared, have been included in the company's accounts ; provision has been made to cover a loss sustained by one subsidiary company in the accounts of that company.

(b) Assuming that the subsidiaries have made losses but that they have been covered by reserves, partly in their own accounts and partly in the accounts of the holding company—

Losses sustained by subsidiary companies have been provided for partly in the accounts of the companies concerned and partly in the accounts of this company.

(c) Assuming that a subsidiary company has made a profit and declared a dividend, and that the auditors have made a reservation in their report—

The profits of a subsidiary company, to the extent of dividend declared, have been taken into account in arriving at the profits of the company ; in their report to the members of the subsidiary company the auditors state that " no provision has been made for depreciation."

Loans to Directors.

A salutary provision of the Companies Act, 1929, is that which insists on the disclosure of loans to directors and officers. The Balance Sheet must set out the following—

(*a*) The amount of such loans made during the period to which the accounts relate, whether repaid or not.

(*b*) The amount of loans made during the period by other parties and guaranteed by the company.

(*c*) The amount of loans made during previous periods and outstanding at the date of the Balance Sheet under review.

All these items may be shown in aggregate amounts on the lines indicated in the illustration on page 146. There are two exceptions to the rule : firstly, the company need not disclose loans made *in the ordinary course* of its business if that business includes, as part of its usual and ordinary activities, the lending of money ; secondly, a loan to an employee not exceeding £2,000 need not be shown if the directors certify that such loan is made in accordance with a practice adopted by the company governing loans to its employees.

Employees and Shares.

It is illegal, in the ordinary way, for a company to purchase its own shares or to lend money for that purpose. If, however, a scheme is adopted for aiding salaried directors and employees to purchase shares through trustees, then advances may be made for that purpose. This exception is designed to foster the promotion of co-partnership and similar schemes for giving the employee an actual participation in the company for which he works. Sec. 45 provides that, although these loans may be made, they must be disclosed separately in the Balance Sheet.

Directors' Remuneration.

The final point to be considered by the director in connection with the draft accounts is the publication of the amount of the Board's remuneration. It is now obligatory (under Sec. 128) to show, in the accounts laid before the company in general meeting—

> The total of the amount paid to the directors as remuneration for their services, inclusive of all fees, percentages, or other emoluments paid to or receivable by them, by or from the company or by or from any subsidiary company.

In the draft Profit and Loss Account given on page 147 the directors' remuneration is correctly disclosed as " Directors' Fees £5,000 "; but it is only remuneration in the nature of fees which need be shown. The remuneration paid to the managing director and to other directors in respect of salaried posts they may hold in the company can be included in the general salaries account, an account which rarely appears as a separate item in the abbreviated published Profit and Loss Account. This exemption is contained in Sec. 128—

> The provisions shall *not* apply in relation to a managing director, and in the case of any other director who holds any salaried employment or office in the company there shall not be required to be included in the said total amount any sums paid to him except sums paid by way of directors' fees.

The Final Accounts.

Whilst the directors have been examining and passing the draft accounts we have illustrated, the auditors have been completing the audit. In all probability they have submitted a report to the directors on the draft, containing their recommendations. These are considered carefully by the Board and any necessary amendments are carried out, after which the directors' own report is prepared and the accounts are sent for printing.

As mentioned elsewhere, a Profit and Loss Account must be laid before the members once in every calendar year. This account must be made up to a date not earlier than nine months prior to the date of the meeting, although an exception is made in the case of companies trading abroad; these companies may present an account made up to a date not earlier than twelve months before the meeting. Unfortunately, the Act does not insist on the circulation of the Profit and Loss Account to the members. The Balance Sheet must be sent out to all members at least seven days before the meeting, but the Profit and Loss Account need only " be laid before the meeting." Advantage has been taken of this technicality on many occasions, but the director is advised to insist on the circulation of the Profit and Loss Account with the Balance Sheet.

The amount of information given in published Profit and Loss Accounts varies considerably, but there is a hoary tradition that the account shall be condensed to the utmost extent. As time goes on it is inevitable that this tradition will die down, but it is so ingrained in directorates at the moment that one cannot do more than exhort the director not to resist the demand which is becoming more and more insistent for the disclosure of informative details of trading results to the proprietors.

The reason given for the elimination of the Trading Account and condensation of the Profit and Loss Account is the well-worn phrase about giving information to competitors. The suppression of accounts certainly prevents competitors from gaining information; that fact cannot be denied. What information they could gain from the usual revenue account is a question to which it is difficult to find a reasonable answer. In fact, it will be found that only one excuse can be given—that the rate of gross profit could be ascertained by any competitor. Assuming for a moment that the Trading Account could not be cast in such a way as to conceal the rate of gross profit, it may be mentioned that satisfactory means exist of ascertaining gross profit percentages in trade practice prices adopted by competitors; and sales managers of competing concerns have no need to resort to calculations based upon figures which may contain items quite foreign to the particular trade concerned.

The Directors' Report

Under Sec. 123 of the Companies Act, the directors must attach to every Balance Sheet their report on the state of the company's affairs. They must notify the shareholders, in this report, of the following matters—

1. The amount, if any, which they recommend should be paid by way of dividend.

2. The amount, if any, which they propose to carry to the reserve fund, general reserve, or reserve account *shown specifically* on the Balance Sheet.

The words " shown specifically " are significant; they mean that if directors determine to transfer profit to a secret reserve, which, of course, is not set out separately on the Balance Sheet, the fact need not be disclosed in their report. We deal with this matter in greater detail in the next chapter when considering the allocation and distribution of profit.

Summary of Rules.

We conclude the chapter on the director's duty regarding the accounts with the following table of the statutory rules. The items are arranged in the normal order of the Balance Sheet, the liabilities being given first and then the assets. This summary can be utilized whenever draft Balance Sheets are laid before the Board for discussion—

Section.   *Liabilities*

124. The Balance Sheet must give a summary of authorized and the issued capital.

46. If any part of the capital consist of Redeemable Preference Shares the Balance Sheet must specify the part and give the date on or before which the shares are to be redeemed.

54. Capital upon which interest is payable with the consent of the Board of Trade during constructional work must be set out in the accounts.

75. If a company has power to re-issue redeemed debentures, the fact must be disclosed in the Balance Sheet.

124. The general nature of the ordinary debts of the company must be distinguishable in the Balance Sheet and if a liability is secured, otherwise than by operation of law, the fact must be stated.

125. Debts due to subsidiary companies must be given separately.

123. The Balance Sheet must set out the General Reserves or Reserve Accounts and Funds, but not the secret reserves.

46. The Capital Redemption Reserve Fund arising out of the redemption of Preference Shares must be shown in the Balance Sheet.

Assets

124. Every Balance Sheet must distinguish the Fixed Assets and state how the values of such assets have been arrived at.

124. The Floating Assets must be distinguishable from the Fixed Assets; Goodwill and Patents to be separated.

125. Shares in, or indebtedness by, subsidiary companies must be segregated from the other assets.

128. There must be disclosure of loans to directors and officers of the company.

45. If the company has power to advance money to employees for the purchase of the company's shares, then any resulting loans must be set out in the Balance Sheet.

124. Preliminary expenses must be given as a separate asset until written off; also expenses of issues.

124. The Balance Sheet must contain, as an asset, the expenses of the issue of any share capital or debentures.

44. Commission paid on shares or debentures and discount on debentures must be disclosed as a separate item until written off.

NOTES, FOOTNOTES, REPORT

128. There must be a note as to any guarantees given by the company in respect of loans to directors or officers.

126. A statement must be annexed stating how the profits or losses of subsidiaries have been dealt with.

128. The remuneration of the directors must be disclosed.

123. A Profit and Loss Account must be laid before the meeting.

130. The Balance Sheet and the Directors' Report must be circulated at least seven days before the meeting of the members.

CHAPTER XV

THE allocation of the company's profit is made in the
Appropriation Account. This is the account in which
appropriations of profit—as distinct from charges
against profits—are made. It contains debits in respect
of the dividends declared at the preceding annual
general meeting and any interim dividends subsequently paid.

Although the dividends are formally passed by the
members, the decision as to their amount rests with
the directors. A serious responsibility therefore rests
upon the Board when deciding upon the dividends to
be recommended in their report to the shareholders. In
the preceding chapter we saw that the directors' report
must set out the amounts of the recommended dividends and the amounts of any transfers to reserves
shown specifically in the Balance Sheet. It follows
from this that the secret reserves receive treatment
first, because it is only the balance which is disclosed
to the members. Under the circumstances we discuss
the secret appropriations before dealing with the rules
governing the published appropriations.

Secret Reserves.

A secret reserve may be created by excessive writings-
off, by the depreciation of fixed assets at too high
rates, by transfers to contingencies accounts, and even
by the elimination of assets from the Balance Sheet.
Obviously these transactions constitute a formidable
power in the director's hands, and he must use that

power very warily. Some years ago the now defunct Rubber Shareholders' Association put forward the following—

We submit the following postulates, which are, in our opinion, fundamental—

1. The object of all book-keeping should be the providing of a true and complete statement of affairs at any given date.

2. The owners of a business are entitled to the information provided by correct book-keeping.

3. In the case of a joint-stock company the owners are the shareholders.

These postulates constitute a very direct challenge to the whole principle of secret reserves; and there is a very large and influential section of public opinion which endorses the challenge emphatically. On the other hand, the fact remains that the Companies Act itself acknowledges, by implication, the continuance of the practice. In addition, it cannot be gainsaid that there is a great deal in favour of undisclosed reserves from the point of view of commercial prosperity. On many occasions they have been the means of warding off much unnecessary anxiety; they have assisted in the equalization of dividends and in the support of such undertakings as banks, in which public confidence forms a large part of the goodwill.

It is impossible to lay down any hard and fast rules for the guidance of the director in this matter. He must weigh the whole of the circumstances of the particular case which confronts him and keep constantly before him the dangers surrounding the problem. He must remember that cellar reserves tend to destroy confidence in the Board's accounts as soon as the members learn, by implication or direct information, that they exist. Suspicion can be aroused very easily that a steady increase in net profit is not necessarily a real variation from year to year but the effect of utilizing secret reserves put aside in earlier periods.

A good deal depends upon the extent to which undisclosed reserves are used. Within limits, they may be drawn upon to decrease or increase the published profits, but the director should hesitate a long time before agreeing to convert an actual loss into a profit by this means.

Disclosed Reserves.

The disclosed reserves fall into several classifications, but they are all divisible into " Specific " and " General Reserves." A Specific Reserve is one set aside out of profits to meet specific expenditure which will be incurred at some future date, e.g. the renewal of leases, the payment of dilapidations, the redemption of mortgages, etc. A General Reserve is a reserve built up in order to conserve cash in the business. The director will realize that a large credit balance on Appropriation Account cannot always be paid away in dividends. The cash balance may be low and the declaration of a dividend may hamper the normal trading operations. In such circumstances it is customary to retain the capital in the business by transferring the credit balance, or part of it, to a General Reserve.

If cash representing a reserve is invested outside the business it is usual to refer to the reserve as a " Fund." In this connection the director should note that specific reserves should normally be transformed into Reserve Funds. Unless cash to the amount of the specific reserves is invested in gilt-edged or trustee securities there is considerable danger that when the liability falls to be met the resources of the company may be locked up in trading or fixed assets. If this state of affairs arises, the business may be hampered severely by the sudden and compulsory realization of stocks or even of fixed property.

The transfer of profits to a Reserve Fund should be

accompanied by the investment of cash in outside investments at the time of the appropriation. The effect of this policy is that, when the time arrives for the payment of a liability or the replacement of a fixed asset, the investments may be sold and the company placed in funds without delay.

The Nature of Funds.

There is a difference in the treatment of funds built up for the meeting of liabilities and those intended for the replacement of assets. In the first place it is unusual to turn a reserve against a liability into a fund unless the amount is of some magnitude. Appropriations of profit to meet the company's liability to taxation, for instance, are rarely funded. The reserve in such a case, though specific, can be shown as " Reserve for Taxation " in the manner illustrated in the preceding chapter. A reserve to replace an asset, on the other hand, is funded in practically every case.

Funds to Meet Liabilities.

The commonest type of fund under this heading is that built up for the redemption of debentures, mortgages, and similar items of a quasi-fixed capital nature. Profit is transferred every year from the credit side of the Profit and Loss Appropriation Account to the credit of the Redemption Fund. On the assets side of the Balance Sheet the cash at bankers is diminished and a new item appears—" Redemption Fund Investments." If the director studies the published Balance Sheets of other companies he will find an account on each side in respect of all funds of this nature with the exception of the " Capital Redemption Reserve Fund," to which we shall refer in a moment. In some cases the value of the investments representing the fund or funds will not agree exactly with the funds on the liabilities side.

This is only because it is not always convenient to purchase the exact amount of investments in any given year; over the term of the fund, however, they will tend to be equal.

When the time arrives for the repayment of the liability, e.g. the redemption of debentures, the investments are sold, thus providing the necessary cash. The debentures are called in and paid off, and consequently disappear from the Balance Sheet; but whilst the elimination of the debentures from the liabilities side is balanced by the disbursement of cash on the assets side, the company is left with the " Debenture Redemption Account " still standing as a reserve. A little reflection serves to show that this account is a General Reserve and that its title should be changed accordingly. Whereas a proportion of the assets was formerly represented by the debentures, that proportion has now been " acquired " by the shareholders out of the profits set aside to the fund. This is a very important matter, and will be clear if the following simple example is studied—

STAGE I. The Orion Company, Ltd., has an issued capital of £125,000 and a Debenture Issue of a like amount. Its assets may be described, for purposes of illustration only, as: Fixed Assets £150,000, and Liquid Assets £100,000.

THE ORION COMPANY, LTD.

Liabilities	£	Assets	£
Share Capital . .	125,000	Fixed Assets . .	150,000
Debentures . .	125,000	Liquid Assets . .	100,000
	£250,000		£250,000

STAGE 2. The company makes total profits over a period of ten years of £300,000, of which it distributes £120,000 and sets aside £125,000 to Debenture Redemption Fund by means of ten annual instalments of £12,500. The fund is invested in gilt-edged securities. At the end of ten years the company proposes to repay its debentures, and its Balance Sheet, just prior to the operation, appears as follows:

THE ORION COMPANY, LTD.

Liabilities	£	Assets	£
Share Capital . .	125,000	Fixed Assets . .	150,000
Debentures . .	125,000	Liquid Assets . .	155,000
Debenture Redemption		Debenture Redemption	
Reserve Fund .	125,000	Reserve Fund In-	
Profit & Loss Account	55,000	vestments . .	125,000
	£430,000		£430,000

Note.—The balance on Profit and Loss Account is arrived at by deducting the dividend paid (£120,000) and the profit set aside to the fund (£125,000) from the total profits of £300,000.

STAGE 3. The company realizes the fund investments and increases its liquid assets from £155,000 to £280,000. It then repays the debentures, which disappear from the Balance Sheet, and the liquid assets revert to the amount shown in Stage 2, i.e. £155,000. The fund on the liabilities side is re-named Capital Reserve *Account*.

THE ORION COMPANY, LTD.

Liabilities	£	Assets	£
Share Capital . .	125,000	Fixed Assets . .	150,000
Capital Reserve Acct.	125,000	Liquid Assets . .	155,000
Profit & Loss Account	55,000		
	£305,000		£305,000

Note.—Particular attention is drawn to the fact that the Capital Reserve is now an " Account " and not a Fund. It is no longer represented by outside investments.

Capital Redemption Reserve Fund.

As it is now possible to redeem preference share capital, it is obligatory on a company to set aside profits for the purpose, unless the redemption is effected out of the proceeds of a fresh issue. The redemption out of a new issue is a simple operation and needs no illustration. All that happens is that the company receives cash from the applicants for the new shares and then utilizes the money in the extinction of the old shares from the Balance Sheet. The new shares take the place of the old shares in the accounts, and no alteration in the Balance Sheet is necessary.

When the redemption is made out of profits the company sets aside an appropriation, either in annual amounts or in one allocation, to a reserve called " Capital Redemption Reserve Fund." The full procedure is set out in Sec. 46 of the Companies Act and the title of the reserve is specified in Sub-sec. (1) (c). Contrary to usual commercial practice, however, there is no obligation to invest the fund in outside securities. It is perhaps unfortunate that the Act specifies the use of the word " Fund," and the director must regard it as an exception to the rule we have been considering. In the illustration of the accounts of the Success Company, Ltd., given in the previous chapter, the Authorized Redeemable Preference Capital amounted to £100,000 and the Issued Capital to £50,000. The Balance Sheet contained, in addition, a Capital Redemption Reserve Fund of £50,000. This indicates that 100,000 redeemable preference shares had been issued at one time and that 50,000 had been redeemed.

We give below a further example of the procedure, in order to make the matter perfectly clear—

STAGE I. The Orestes Company, Ltd., has an authorized and issued capital of £500,000, of which half is represented by Ordinary Shares and half by 5% Redeemable Preference Shares. The latter are redeemable at the end of ten years.

THE ORESTES COMPANY, LTD.

Liabilities	£	Assets	£
Authorized Capital .	500,000	Fixed and Floating Assets . . .	500,000
Issued Capital—			
250,000 5% Redeemable Preference Shares (redeemable on —) .	250,000		
250,000 Ordinary Shares . .	250,000		
	£500,000		£500,000

STAGE 2. At the end of ten years the company has a credit balance on Profit and Loss Account of £275,000 and proposes to utilize £250,000 in the redemption of the preference capital.

THE ORESTES COMPANY, LTD.

Liabilities	£	Assets	£
Authorized Capital .	500,000	Fixed and Floating Assets . . .	775,000
Issued Capital, as before	500,000		
Profit & Loss Account	275,000		
	£775,000		£775,000

STAGE 3. Cash to the amount of £250,000 is paid out to the holders of the Preference Shares, which are eliminated from the issued capital, and at the same time a transfer is made to Capital Redemption Reserve Fund of £250,000.

THE ORESTES COMPANY, LTD.

Liabilities	£	Assets	£
Authorized Capital .	500,000	Fixed and Floating Assets . . .	525,000
Issued Capital—			
250,000 Ordinary Shares . .	250,000		
Capital Redemption Reserve Fund .	250,000		
Profit & Loss Account	25,000		
	£525,000		£525,000

It should be noted that the Authorized Capital remains at the original figure; it is not affected by the redemption of any portion of the redeemable shares.

Under Sec. 46 it is possible to redeem preference shares at a premium, and possibly also at a discount, but the director need not delve too deeply into these complications. They are subject to certain technical details of procedure which will be dealt with by the company's officials.

Funds to Replace Assets.

The setting-up of funds for the replacement of assets is not very different from that adopted for the repayment of liabilities. An annual charge is made in the company's accounts and credited to the appropriate reserve fund. The type of asset to which it is normally applied is exemplified by leasehold properties which fall in at the end of the lease. In such a case the fund is termed " Leasehold Redemption Reserve Fund." The investment of cash in outside securities is carried out in exactly the same manner as before. When the lease falls in, however, the balance on the asset account, i.e. Leasehold Property Account, is written off against the fund. The investments representing the funds are then utilized in the purchase of a new lease.

It will be seen from this that whilst a fund for the replacement of an asset is built up in exactly the same manner as a fund for the repayment of a liability, there is difference in treatment when the date arrives for utilizing the investments. Whereas in the latter case the company is left with a general reserve, in the former case the fund disappears; it is expunged by transferring to it the book value of the asset, which is now of no value. The following example should be examined and compared with the treatment of the other types of fund we have studied above—

EXAMPLE

The Orama Company, Ltd., builds up a fund for the redemption of its leasehold property valued at £25,000. The lease is for ten years and the company sets aside a fund of £2,500 for the purpose.

STAGE I.

THE ORAMA COMPANY, LTD.

	£		£
Capital . . .	125,000	General Fixed and	
Leasehold Redemption		Floating Assets .	125,000
Fund . . .	25,000	Redemption Fund In-	
Creditors . . .	10,000	vestments . .	25,000
Profit & Loss Account	15,000	Leasehold property .	25,000
	£175,000		£175,000

STAGE 2. The lease falls in and the investments are sold.

THE ORAMA COMPANY, LTD.

	£			£
Capital . . .	125,000	General Fixed and		
Creditors . . .	10,000	Floating Assets .		125,000
Profit & Loss Account	15,000	Cash at bankers .		25,000
	£150,000			£150,000

STAGE 3. A new lease is purchased for £15,000.

THE ORAMA COMPANY, LTD.

	£			£
Capital . . .	125,000	General Fixed and		
Creditors . . .	10,000	Floating Assets .		125,000
Profit & Loss Account	15,000	Leasehold premises .		15,000
		Cash at bankers .		10,000
	£150,000			£150,000

CHAPTER XVI

OCCASIONAL references have been made throughout the preceding pages to the meetings of directors. We now deal in greater detail with the conduct of such meetings and also of the more formal meetings of the shareholders.

Directors' Meetings.

The meetings of directors are termed Board Meetings. There is no settled code of procedure governing them. It is only necessary for the directors to act as a board and not as individuals, and it is legal and possible for a board meeting to take place under quite informal circumstances; but they must meet. It has been laid down that directors cannot think without meeting. This was the decision in a case in 1889,[1] the judge holding that in order to act the directors must get together and that it is not sufficient to procure the separate written authority of a number of directors to any matter, however unimportant. This opinion might not be upheld to-day, but it would be well if directors regarded it as a rule to be observed irrespective of the law on the point. Unfortunately, many Articles of Association contain a provision that a resolution committed to writing and sent round to every member of the board for signature shall have the same force as a resolution passed at a meeting duly convened. There are many dangers attending this provision and if it is adopted in his company the

[1] *Portuguese Consolidated Copper Mines*, 1889.

director is advised to see that such resolutions are brought forward for confirmation at the next subsequent meeting. As a matter of interest, it may be mentioned that Articles of Association including this clause as to written resolutions are not acceptable to the committee of the Stock Exchange when they are considering applications for quotation.

Informal Directors' Meetings.

It was mentioned above that the meetings of directors may be held under informal circumstances. It is important to observe, however, that casual meetings of directors, even at the office of the company, cannot be called board meetings against the wish or intention of any member or members meeting casually in this way. If the Articles stipulate that notice of board meetings must be given, then informal meetings cannot be treated as board meetings unless proper notice has been given.

Proceedings at Directors' Meetings.

The agenda for the meetings of directors is usually prepared by the secretary in consultation with the chairman. The directors are not bound to take the business in the order of the agenda; they may deal with the matters arising in any order they please.[1] This point is one which may easily be of importance should actions arise in which the acts of the directors in the conduct of the company are questioned. The director should therefore note his right in this matter.

The quorum for a directors' meeting is usually fixed in the Articles. If it is not fixed then it consists of a majority of the board present and willing to act.

[1] *Re Cawley*, 1889.

Reference has been made to cases in which the Articles forbid directors to vote upon matters in which they are interested in a capacity other than that of director. This point must be borne in mind in connection with a quorum at board meetings ; whenever a director is present at a meeting at which contracts for his own benefit are under consideration he cannot be counted in the quorum.[1] This rule will not prevent the director from voting as an ordinary shareholder at general meetings when such contracts are laid before the proprietors for acceptance.

Directors' Minutes.

Every company is bound to keep a minute book of its proceedings at general meetings and at the meetings of its directors or managers. Sec. 120 of the Companies Act, 1929, runs as follows—

120.—(1) Every company *shall cause minutes* of all proceedings *of general meetings, and,* where there are directors or managers, *of all proceedings at meetings of its directors* or of its managers to be entered in books kept for that purpose.

(2) Any such minute if purporting to be signed by the chairman of the meeting at which the proceedings were had, or by the chairman of the next succeeding meeting, shall be evidence of the proceedings.

(3) Where minutes have been made in accordance with the provisions of this section of the proceedings of any general meeting of the company or meeting of directors or managers, then, until the contrary is proved, the meeting shall be deemed to have been duly held and convened, and all proceedings had thereat to have been duly had, and all appointments of directors, managers, or liquidators shall be deemed to be valid.

The minute book is *prima facie* evidence of the transactions of the meetings and should be open to the inspection of all the directors, the secretary, and the auditors of the company. Attempts have been made upon occasions to prevent the auditors from inspecting the minute book on the ground that it is not a book of account. This is quite wrong and should not be entertained seriously by any director. The directors' minute

[1] *Greymouth Point Elizabeth Railway and Coal Co.,* 1904.

book is *not* open to the inspection of the shareholders. The minute book of general meetings, on the other hand, must be open for inspection by shareholders for at least two hours per day.

Classes of Meetings.

The meetings of directors do not fall into any defined classes but there are three distinct classes of meeting of shareholders, namely, the statutory meeting, the ordinary general meeting, and the extraordinary general meeting.

The Statutory Meeting.

The statutory meeting is the first important meeting the director is called upon to attend.   It is a meeting of all the shareholders called together not less than one month and not more than three months from the time the company is entitled to commence business. Its object is to acquaint the shareholders with the exact position of the company, and though it is usually of a formal nature it is obligatory to forward a report to the members at least seven days before the meeting. This report is certified by not less than two directors and sets out the number of shares allotted, the amount of cash received, and certain details concerning preliminary expenditure and contracts into which the company is entering.   One result of this meeting is to acquaint the shareholders whether sufficient cash has been received to enable the company to pursue the objects set forth in the Memorandum.   The meeting is at liberty to discuss any matter relating to the formation of the company, the prospects of the company and any matter arising out of the statutory report.

At one time it was doubtful whether the whole of the section in the Companies Acts relating to this matter applied to private companies. Now, however, under Sec. 113 of the Companies Act, 1929, it is perfectly clear that it applies solely to public companies.

Extraordinary Meetings.

Extraordinary general meetings are meetings of the shareholders other than the statutory meeting or the ordinary general meeting. They are held for the purpose of dealing with extraordinary matters outside the usual business of the company, and they may be called by the directors in accordance with the Articles or on requisition of the members or they may be called by the shareholders themselves if the directors fail to convene.

The power of requisition is one which the director must not overlook. It is one of the few rights left to shareholders by which they may exercise control over a board. The text of the section governing the matter is as follows—

114.—(1) *The directors of a company*, notwithstanding anything in its articles, *shall, on the requisition of members* of the company *holding* at the date of the deposit of the requisition *not less than one-tenth of such of the paid-up capital* of the company as at the date of the deposit carries the right of voting at general meetings of the company, or, in the case of a company not having a share capital, members of the company representing not less than one-tenth of the total voting rights of all the members having at the said date a right to vote at general meetings of the company, *forthwith proceed duly to convene an extraordinary general meeting of the company.*

(2) *The requisition must state the objects of the meeting*, and must be signed by the requisitionists and deposited at the registered office of the company, and may consist of several documents in like form, each signed by one or more requisitionists.

(3) *If the directors do not* within twenty-one days from the date of the deposit of the requisition *proceed duly to convene a meeting, the requisitionists*, or any of them representing more than one-half of the total voting rights of all of them, *may themselves convene a meeting*, but any meeting so convened shall not be held after the expiration of three months from the said date.

(4) A meeting convened under this section by the requisitionists shall be convened in the same manner, as nearly as possible, as that in which meetings are to be convened by directors.

(5) Any reasonable expenses incurred by the requisitionists by reason of the failure of the directors duly to convene a meeting shall

be repaid to the requisitionists by the company, and any sum so repaid shall be retained by the company out of any sums due or to become due from the company by way of fees or other remuneration in respect of their services to such of the directors as were in default.

(6) For the purposes of this section, the directors shall, in the case of a meeting at which a resolution is to be proposed as a special resolution, be deemed not to have duly convened the meeting if they do not give such notice thereof as is required by section one hundred and seventeen of this Act.

Ordinary General Meetings.

It is with the ordinary general meeting that the director is most concerned, and the detail surrounding the procedure to be observed will be set out at greater length. The ordinary general meeting must be held once in every calendar year and not more than fifteen months after the last preceding ordinary general meeting. Failure to hold this meeting renders every officer liable to a fine not exceeding fifty pounds. The Articles provide the method by which the ordinary general meeting is to be convened, and it is usual for them to stipulate that the meeting shall deal with such matters as the re-election of directors, auditors, and so on.

The first step is to hold a board meeting, at which directions are given for the calling of the ordinary general meeting. This directors' meeting will be the one at which the accounts are passed for publication, as explained in a previous chapter. The secretary then takes steps to print the accounts and to dispatch copies to the members on the register. The insertion of the time and place of the meeting is usually left, by the Articles, to the discretion of the board. It is not uncommon, however, for the Articles to stipulate that a certain amount of notice shall be given—generally seven days.

The details surrounding the summoning of an ordinary general meeting are not fixed and identical for all companies. The particular Articles of each company must be followed and there will therefore be no harm in advising the director to cast aside the very general idea that the annual general meeting is hedged by numerous legal requirements and that it consists of little else but the fulfilment of demands laid down by the Companies Act.

This point is introduced in order to stress a matter which often escapes the director when preparing to attend his first general meeting. The success of joint stock enterprise is undoubtedly enhanced whenever boards of directors regard the occasions upon which they meet the shareholders as opportunities for acquainting them fully and even informally of every possible item of interest to which the proprietors are entitled. Too often is the general meeting invested with a solemnity and with a legal significance which prevents the director from presenting a frank and open front to the inquiries of those whose interests he is appointed to safeguard.

Compliance with the Articles.

To return to the formalities connected with the calling of the general meeting, it is sufficient if the directors consult the Articles. The law will not interfere with the internal management of a company, and, in the matter of fixing the date and place of a general meeting, or the manner in which notice is given, the board need only refrain from selecting times and places with the object of preventing shareholders from exercising their voting powers. This item connected with general meetings has been dealt with at some length in order to insist upon the importance of observing the maxim that every assistance should be given to the shareholder to meet the directors upon the very occasional opportunities presented to him. In recent years there have been many cases in which places and dates

of meetings have been chosen with the obvious intention of defeating fair criticism.

CONTENTS OF THE NOTICE. The Articles often stipulate that specified matters shall be dealt with at general
meetings. Somewhat similar rules govern the compiling
of the notices. Here again the director should see that
any express rules in the Articles as to the contents of
the notice are observed. If, in addition to this, he
adopts the method of ensuring that the notice of a
meeting—ordinary or extraordinary—gives the recipient sufficient information to permit him to judge
whether he should make a special point of attending,
the director will have done his duty. The notice should
show clearly whether the agenda consists of none but
routine business or whether matters of importance will
come up for discussion. If a notice does not give
sufficient detail of " general business " to show that
certain of the business is of great importance then
the meeting may be invalid and any resolutions pur-
ported to have been passed may subsequently be
declared void (*Normandy & Co.* v. *Ind, Coope & Co.*,
1908).

THE CHAIRMAN. The chairman of the annual
general meeting is usually the chairman of the board
of directors, but not necessarily so. It must not be
imagined that chairmanship of a board carries with it
a right to the chair of the shareholders' meeting. The
Articles generally provide that the chairman of the
board shall take the chair at the general meeting, and
in that case he takes charge of the meeting as a matter
of course. If the Articles are silent then the Act
allows the election by the members of any person to
preside over their own meeting. It is perhaps regrettable that the Articles of Association of companies
generally set out detailed provisions on the matter
of chairman of the general meeting. It is only in

those companies which permit the shareholders to choose a chairman that the one upon whom their choice falls controls the meeting with a true conception of his position. The chairman is always the representative of the shareholders at a general meeting ; he collects his authority from the *members* and not from the board ; the members, and not merely the board of directors, have given him the power to control those present at the meeting.

Unless the Articles lay down rules for the conduct of the meeting the director must, on his own responsibility, preserve order, see that the proceedings are carried out in a proper manner and ensure that the true feeling of the members is ascertained in connection with each point laid before them.

READING THE NOTICE. It is customary to commence the meeting by calling upon the secretary to read the notice convening the meeting. This practice is not required by statute, but it is useful—as also is the less usual practice of reading out the previous minutes—as a means of permitting the directors, and particularly the chairman, to settle down before commencing their speeches. The next matter is the reading of the auditor's report. In this case it is necessary that the remarks of the auditor shall be actually read out to the meeting in order to comply with the Act. Under Sec. 134 of the Companies Act, 1929, the auditor has a right to attend any general meeting of the company at which accounts examined by him are to be considered. He is also given a statutory right to make any statements or explanations he desires regarding the accounts.

The reading of the actual accounts is usually omitted because each shareholder has a copy. The formalities concluded, the chairman makes his speech, explaining the affairs of the company and providing as much additional information as he can. He concludes his speech by formally moving the adoption of the accounts. Another director seconds and the meeting is thrown open to discussion, the shareholders being invited to ask questions upon, or to criticise, the report, accounts, and speech. Whenever the temper of the meeting runs high the chairman must keep a firm hand and be insistent upon any rulings he makes. He should refuse all dilatory resolutions and amendments firmly and, without appearing to be antagonistic, repress unruly spirits, urging them to air their grievances in a reasoned manner.

Appointment of Committee.

Whilst the chairman should be firm, he should never baulk reasoned critical speeches by shareholders. The unfair repression of shareholders gives rise to several of the major troubles with which joint-stock enterprise is faced to-day. It leads to the everlasting cry for the appointment of a committee of inspection, coupled with all manner of amendments to the motion to pass the accounts. When this common trouble arises it is well for the director to explain, in an impartial manner, that a committee of inspection can be appointed only by a special resolution. It should also be made clear that it is doubtful whether an informal committee, as distinct from a properly constituted committee of inspection, can be appointed except by a motion upon which all the shareholders have had a chance of voting. This method is preferable to the more usual one of calling upon the solicitor to state baldly that the proposal is out of order. This treatment inevitably adds fuel to the fire.

In spite of the law on the subject, it is sometimes unwise for a board to resist an honest attempt to investigate the affairs of the company. If all is in order, then the fact that a committee carries out an inquiry can only enhance the prestige of the board when the committee's report is presented to the members.

If cases arise in which policy indicates the wisdom of accepting a committee, the chairman should first give the explanation referred to above. The meeting should be told that a demand for a committee except on a special resolution is of no avail, but that the directors welcome an *informal* delegation chosen from among the members. The delegation should be promised every assistance by the board. It is a most inadvisable proceeding for any chairman or director to endeavour to ward off inquiry by threatening to resign if an appeal for a committee is persisted in. This practice is rife and is in some degree responsible for the feeling of injustice with which many shareholders depart from annual general meetings.

Personal Apologies.

There is perhaps no more unfortunate aspect of annual general meetings than the growing tendency to occupy the time and attention of the proprietors with the personal explanations and apologies of individual directors. The habit appears to be widespread during the periods of depression immediately following a boom in trade. These periods inevitably reveal cases of shortsighted policy. They demonstrate that although the direction of a company may be entrusted to all and sundry persons during times of brisk trade, the temporary profit is liable to disappear as soon as the period in which it was impossible to make losses has passed away. Such times emphasize the distinction between direction and speculation. As far as the director is concerned there is no necessity whatever for him to make excuses to the shareholders for his own lack of judgment. He is but the officer and

servant of a separate legal *persona*—the company—
and the members must expect to suffer for errors of
judgment or inefficiency of those they appoint.   If the
director feels that the responsibility is his, then he can
take no better course than that of resigning, thus
safeguarding the company from further possible losses
on account of his own admitted shortcomings.   If
his fault consists of inefficiency then personal apologies
are quite unnecessary ; if he has been guilty of acts
in the nature of misfeasance, as distinct from innocent
incompetence, then the shareholders will require an
explanation from him under different circumstances
from those obtaining at a general meeting, and possibly
before a court.

Vendors and Dividends.

Another custom which has little to recommend it,
but which appears to have gained some degree of
popularity, is that of offering to make good a dividend
when the results of a company's trading prove otherwise than was predicted in a prospectus.   This custom
is sometimes followed by the vendor-directors of a
business and is designed to counter the inevitable
disappointment of those who placed their trust in
optimistic forecasts of handsome dividends.   The
habit is an unnecessary one.   The vendors are under
no obligation to make gratuitous offerings to companies
and if they do so they are apt to be misunderstood.
In any case they are doing much to undermine the
principle of independent constitution which is at the
base of all joint-stock finance.   When prospectus forecasts are not realized the public have only themselves
to blame if they have permitted the vendors to take the
whole of their consideration in cash, instead of insisting
that they should retain a share interest in the company's
fortune.

Meetings and the Press.

The director should remember that his object is not to counter the inquiry of the shareholders with skill. The board must not be secretive or antagonistic. Frankness is the best policy. Needless reserve or the unnecessary baulking of questions will only cause the members and the Press to sift the matter to the bottom. The Press, in particular, will leave no stone unturned—and rightly, too—to provide information on points concerning which there is any appearance of anxiety to resist criticism.

In this connection the new director should realize the power and authority which is now vested in those controlling the financial columns of our daily newspapers. The days when the city editor confined his attention to the money article, and nothing else, are long past. He is the guardian of the public conscience in so far as it concerns the investment of the public's money. Whether he has insinuated himself into this position is beside the point; the fact is that the director of every public company is subject to the well-informed and reasoned criticism of men who profess openly to stand between the public and those who control their money. And the efficient director cannot help agreeing that this status to which the city editor has forced himself is all for the good.

It is to the financial press that the unearthing of many of the 1928–29 scandals is due. Its power led to the pressure on companies to hold general meetings, to the improvement in the presentation of prospectuses, and—in some measure—to the adoption of more stringent Stock Exchange regulations. Many chairmen still resent the self-constituted authority of the financial editor, but this attitude is indefensible. City Press criticism, whatever may be said of the views appearing in the other pages of our national newspapers, is absolutely fair and impartial. Those companies whose affairs are conducted with rectitude have all to gain and nothing to lose, from the reasoned comments of men whose very detachment enables them to appreciate the views and interests both of the directorate and the general body of shareholders in the public companies of this country.

THE SPEECH. An examination of the reports of chairmen's speeches reveals the strange fact that many of them commence with a mass of uninteresting information concerning the accounts, which might well be left unsaid. The new director might advantageously consider these speeches, placing himself in the position of the inquiring shareholder, and endeavour to find out the reason why the greater part of these orations are delivered at all. It is safe to say that in a large number of cases he will fail. By noting down carefully the type of information which does not enlighten him he will be able to avoid superfluity when preparing his own speeches later. He will find that the addresses consist, to a great extent, of comparison of figures appearing in the balance sheet with the corresponding amounts of the previous year. He is first informed that the sundry creditors amount to " £101,362 4s. 9d. as against £110,696 5s. 2d. last year, a reduction of £9,334 0s. 5d. on the year." There may possibly be some motive underlying this information, but when it is remembered that the balance sheet just happens to show the position at a certain date, it is difficult to appreciate the reason for expatiating on "reductions of sundry creditors." It is quite possible that twelve hours before the closing of the accounts the sundry creditors were many thousands of pounds in excess of the amount appearing in the last balance sheet, and that the reduction upon which stress is laid merely resulted from the fact that the company's monthly pay-day occurred one day before the end of the year. Cash at bank is reported as " now standing at £65,220 as against £22,000 last year, an increase of £43,220." This useful information is also designed to enlighten the shareholder who draws some conclusion or other which may not be identical with that he would form if he noted, for instance, that a loan had just been made to the company and that the cash received was offset by a charge on the company's property. It should not be necessary to bore shareholders with these and similar " explanations." If the directors are of opinion that the shareholders should be in possession of the knowledge required to appreciate variations in figures of assets or liabilities, then the disclosure could be made in the printed report. There is some ground for suspecting that information is given in speeches which materially affects the printed accounts. If the speeches are not afterwards published in order that the shareholders may study the exact effect at their leisure, then the explanations cannot be fully appreciated.

FORM OF SPEECH. Assuming that the accounts have been set out in sufficient detail to enable the shareholder to understand the form in which his property exists, then the speech should be framed to give—

(a) An outline of the company's activities during the past year.

(b) An account of improvements effected in the company's management and manufactures.

(c) A report on changes carried out in main policy.

(d) A statement of the company's trade, orders in hand, and prospects for the ensuing year.

(e) Recommendations as to dividends and other appropriations of profit, supported by the foregoing portions of the speech.

Ample opportunity should be given to shareholders to ask questions upon matters arising out of the accounts or the speech. Answers to these questions should be given at the meeting itself, and any appearance of endeavouring to omit answering should be avoided. Occasionally, answers are not given at the meeting itself, the inquiring shareholder being requested to present himself at the company's office at a later date for the information he seeks. This artifice is a weak one and never engenders confidence. It must be remembered that a competitor may, by becoming a shareholder, place himself in a position to acquire any information not given openly at a meeting. Suspicion can be disarmed only by frankness.

The director concludes his replies to the inquiries of the shareholders by "putting the question." The report and accounts are then either adopted or they are rejected. The chairman should be firm in the event of rejection and should rule out any amendments not strictly relevant to the original motion. If the meeting will not adopt the accounts it will usually be found sufficient to agree to an informal investigation by a committee, and an adjournment.

If the report and accounts are adopted, one of the directors moves the payment of any dividend recommended. Occasionally shareholders endeavour to procure the payment of a higher dividend than that recommended. If such an attempt is made the Articles should be consulted. Most Articles provide that no higher dividend than that recommended may be declared, but that the shareholders may declare a lower one.

If the Articles are silent then Table " A " makes a provision similar to that just outlined and the directors may rightly resist attempts to pass a higher dividend.

Election of Officers.

The election of auditors should be left entirely to the shareholders, but the directors must remind the meeting that none but the retiring auditors may be elected unless previous notice has been given. The report generally informs the members which of the directors retire and whether those directors are willing to be re-elected. The actual election of the directors should also be left to the meeting. If any of the formal proposals of the directors as to these routine matters are questioned, the board must be careful to preserve the harmony of the meeting.

Misuse of Proxies.

Reference has been made, in several places in this book, to the abuse of proxies. Although these instruments now play so large a part in joint-stock company administration, there are no provisions for their use in the Companies Act of 1929, except in a very incidental fashion in Sec. 116 and Table " A." Moreover, there is no common law right to vote by proxy. It is all the more strange, therefore, that proxies have been allowed to intrude so far into the affairs of joint-stock finance.

If they were always used properly then little or no objection could be raised to the adoption of what are, after all, very convenient instruments. Unfortunately, they are so far misused that their present position in company finance is entirely unwarranted. The fact is that the nature and uses of a proxy are imperfectly understood by the general body of shareholders. They accompany a very considerable proportion of the annual accounts sent to shareholders. Their general appearance, and the peremptoriness of the requests that they shall be signed and returned without delay, undoubtedly lead many members to give proxies

without realizing that they may be assisting in the
maladministration of their affairs. If any proof of this
statement were needed it is to be found in the case of a
company in which the auditor's certificate stated that
the Balance Sheet did *not* set out the true state of
affairs. Incredible as it may seem, numerous rural
investors signed and sent in proxies which with un-
paralleled audacity the directors had issued with the
accounts.

We leave the matter with a quotation from a speech
by Mr. Henry Morgan—

It is hardly surprising that shareholders display apathy with
regard to the administration of their companies. In those cases
where shareholders have attempted to make themselves felt their
task has been difficult, arduous, and thankless. Attendances at
general meetings and general proxies, *which in practice are almost
invariably useless except to the directors*, are of little value to shareholders, all of whom cannot possibly attend annual meetings. An
effective remedy would be to provide that a copy of every resolution
to be proposed at a company meeting should be sent to every
shareholder, with such explanations as may be necessary, and
a voting paper on which he can vote either for or against such
resolution.

CHAPTER XVII

DIRECTORS AND TAXATION

THE provisions of the various enactments relating to the taxation of companies are too numerous and complicated for directors to acquire more than a general knowledge of principles.

Some directors who have had professional careers may possibly be well versed in these matters. Generally speaking, the actual settlement of taxation affairs is left in the hands of the company's professional advisers unless the secretary or accountant has made a special study of the matter, in which case he may be authorized to deal with it. It is desirable, nevertheless, that the director should have a general knowledge of the main principles of taxation, because his decisions upon many of the financial problems which come before the board will have a material effect upon the taxation liability of the company.

This fact was emphasized in Chapter X, in connection with the financing of subsidiaries. It was there shown that lack of knowledge of the general principles of taxation may lead the company into making inter-company financial arrangements which may increase the income tax assessment of the group. Moreover, there are special circumstances under which a company may be entitled to reliefs or reductions in the amount of income tax normally payable, and it is desirable that directors should be aware of these circumstances so that, when such occasions arise, they may ensure that the appropriate relief is not overlooked.

The remarks which follow are intended to give the director that general knowledge which will enable him to take a certain amount of interest in this aspect of company finance.

The Normal Basis of Assessment.

The financial year of a company may run from any date, but the fiscal or taxation year runs from the 6th April in one year to the 5th April of the next, and the company pays tax on a hypothetical profit which it is deemed to make during the fiscal period. Until 1926–27 the profits of a company in respect of each fiscal year were taken to be the average of the profits of the three preceding financial years. From 1927–28 onwards, this method was discarded and the normal basis of assessment is now the profit made by the company during the *preceding* financial year.

EXAMPLE.

Profits for Financial Year Ended 31st December		Assessed for Tax in Fiscal Year 6th April to 5th April
	£	
1930 . . .	4,000	1931–32
1931 . . .	5,000	1932–33
1932 . . .	6,000	1933–34

It will be seen from this simple illustration that profits upon which a company may be paying tax over the course of the fiscal year may have no relation to the actual profits of that period. In the year 1932–33 given above, the company seems to be making profits at the rate of £6,000 per annum, but it is paying tax in that year on £5,000. In actual practice the disparity may be even more marked; a company may pass suddenly from a year of no profit to a year of exceptional prosperity, but this fact will not alter the rule that the profits of one year will not be taxed until the following year. The assessment during the year of high profits will be nil, as it is based on the results of the previous year, viz. no profit. In the subsequent year a further loss may be sustained, but, normally, this will not relieve the company from paying tax on the high profits of the preceding year.

Relief in Respect of Losses.

If a company sustains a heavy loss in one year followed by several years of profits it would obviously be penalized unless relief were available. Provision is therefore made under Sec. 33 of the Finance Act, 1926, for carrying forward losses and setting them off against subsequent profits over a period of six years, thus—

			Assessment	Carry Forward
	£		£	£
1930 Loss	− 50,000	.	1931–32 Nil	− 50,000
1931 Profit	+ 10,000	.	1932–33 Nil	− 40,000
1932 Profit	+ 10,000	.	1933–34 Nil	− 30,000
1933 Profit	+ 12,000	.	1934–35 Nil	− 18,000
1934 Profit	+ 6,000	.	1935–36 Nil	− 12,000
1935 Profit	+ 6,000	.	1936–37 Nil	Nil
1936 Profit	+ 8,000	.	1937–38 8,000	—

It should be noted that the right to carry forward losses extends for a period of six years *immediately following* the year in which the loss is made. In the above example, therefore, the right to carry forward expires in 1936–37, and no relief can be obtained in respect of the balance of the loss of £6,000.

This rule is subject to adjustment if a claim for refund of tax is made under Sec. 34, with which we deal below.

SEC. 34. CLAIMS. Sec. 34 of the Income Tax Act, 1918, provides that if a company makes a loss in any year it may claim to set off that loss against the assessment upon the business for that year. If the loss exceeds the assessment, the balance may be utilized in obtaining a refund of tax paid on any other items of income, e.g. income from investments. It is provided, however, that if a loss is utilized in this way it cannot be taken into account again; that is to say, the company is debarred from carrying the loss forward for six years as explained in the preceding paragraph.

EXAMPLE.

		£			Assessment	£	Carry Forward £
1930	Profit	10,000	.	.	1931–32	10,000 reduced to Nil under Sec. 34	—
1931	Loss	12,000	.	.	1932–33	Nil	2,000
1932	Profit	10,000	.	.	1933–34	8,000	Nil

It is sometimes difficult for a company to determine whether to make a claim for relief under Sec. 34 or whether to allow the loss to go forward under the six years' clause. Generally speaking, if there is a tendency for the rate of tax to fall it is better to obtain the relief at once. If there is a likelihood of the rate being increased, then it usually pays to carry the loss forward.

In all cases consideration must be given to the question whether sufficient profits are likely to be made during the following years to absorb the loss.

ALLOWANCES. A company is a " person " but not an " individual " for taxation purposes, and on this account it does not receive any of the allowances to which an individual is entitled. A private taxpayer is granted various personal allowances and, in addition, is charged at only four-ninths of the standard rate of tax on the first £250 of his income. A company, on the other hand, pays at the full standard rate on the whole of its assessable profits.

DEDUCTION OF TAX FROM DIVIDENDS. The company is allowed to deduct tax from dividends paid to shareholders at the full standard rate; it thus recovers from its members tax on that portion of its profit which is distributed to them. In this connection the director should note that under Sec. 33 of the Finance Act, 1924, the tax deducted from shareholders' dividends must be set out clearly and fully on the dividend counterfoil; if the dividends are paid " free of tax " the counterfoil must show the gross and the net amount of the dividends; both the rate and amount of any tax deducted must be given.

Tax at the full standard rate must also be deducted from all debenture or mortgage interest, ground rent, annuities, patent royalties, and other annual payments made by the company; these payments, as will be seen later, are not allowed as deductions from profits in arriving at the assessment on the company.

The effect of deducting tax from dividends is that a company passes on the tax it pays. It usually happens, however, that there is a " lag," and the tax paid rarely coincides with the tax recovered from shareholders at any given moment.

DISCONTINUANCE OF BUSINESS. Although a company is assessed on its profits " one year in arrear," the director will appreciate that so long as the concern goes on it will ultimately be paying tax on the profits made and no more. An exception would arise, however, if a company ceased business and were permitted to escape tax on the profits of its final year. To meet this case it is provided, by Sec. 31 of the Finance Act, 1926, that the assessments are adjustable for the tax year in which a business comes to an end and also for the year immediately preceding. In the case of the final year the company itself and the Inland Revenue authorities have the right to adjust the assessment to the actual apportioned profits; in the case of the preceding year the Inland Revenue alone have the power to adjust. The assessment for the last year is based on the actual profit from 6th April to the date of discontinuance. The assessment on the penultimate year may be raised to the actual profit of that financial year.

EXAMPLE.

	£	Normal Assessment £	Adjusted £
1930 Profit	40,000	.	
1931 Profit	50,000	. 1931–32 40,000	50,000
1932 Profit	60,000	. 1932–33 50,000 ¾ of 60,000 = 45,000	

Business ceases 31st December, 1932.

New Businesses.

To deal with the first fiscal years of a company's trading, for which preceding accounts are naturally not available, special provisions are made. The first year is assessed on a proper proportion of the profits shown by the first accounts of the business. The second year is assessed upon the actual profits of one year from the date on which the business was commenced.

EXAMPLE.

	Actual Profits £	Assessment £
Year to 31st December, 1933	40,000	1932–33 10,000 (i.e. ¼ representing the period 1st January to 5th April, 1933)
Year to 31st December, 1934	60,000	1933–34 40,000

There are complications if the first accounts cover a period of less than twelve months, but this is a technical point which should not worry the director. It may be mentioned, though this also is a technical detail, that on application in writing by the company the assessment for the second and third years may be amended to the actual apportioned profits for the fiscal years. The necessity for making claim to this relief would arise if the profits for the second year showed a heavy falling-off as compared with the first year.

Businesses Abroad.

Businesses wholly carried on and controlled abroad are not liable to tax in the United Kingdom, but income derived from investments in such companies is taxable upon the British recipients; non-residents, of course, are not chargeable. The director must note, however, that if the Board of a company trading abroad holds its meetings in this country and so exercises control from the United Kingdom, the company will be held to be carrying on business here. It will then be chargeable on the whole of its profits despite the fact that its trading operations are not carried on in England.

Taxable Profits.

The amount of profit shown by the company's audited accounts does not necessarily represent the statutory profit of the company as viewed from a taxation standpoint. If, in arriving at its profits, the company has provided reserves for equalization of dividends or other purposes, or has written off ascertained capital losses out of profits, then the profit shown by the accounts will be increased for income tax purposes by these non-allowable items. The statutory profits for income tax purposes may consequently be much greater than the profits shown by the annual accounts. In any case depreciation is not allowed as a charge against profits and must be added back in calculating the tax payable.

Disallowable Items.

There is no need for the director to be acquainted with every item which is disallowed as a charge for taxation purposes. He should, nevertheless, memorize the more important classes of expenditure which, in the eyes of the Inland Revenue, are not charges " wholly and exclusively laid out for the purposes of the trade " of his company. They are as under—

(1) Capital expenditure.

(2) Exhaustion of wasting assets.

(3) Structural alterations, additions, or improvements.

(4) Dilapidations on expiry of leases.

(5) Income tax paid or reserved.

(6) Removal expenses, except in cases where the removal is compulsory.

(7) Charitable subscriptions, except to charities from which the companies derive direct benefit.

(8) Legal expenses connected with capital matters, e.g. acquisition of leaseholds, etc.

(9) Depreciation.

(10) Interest and other annual payments from which tax is deducted at source.

(11) Dividends, reserves, and all appropriations of profit.

On the other hand, if any income which has suffered tax by deduction, or which is subject to taxation under some other schedule, has been credited to Profit and Loss Account, this may be deducted from profits in computing the company's assessment.

WEAR AND TEAR ALLOWANCE. Although depreciation, as such, is disallowed in the company's tax computation, an allowance is made in respect of wear and tear of plant, machinery and mills, factories, and other premises of a similar character. No allowance is granted for *wasting* assets, and, consequently, the depreciation of mines and the amortization of leases is not recognized by the Inland Revenue.

Wear and tear allowances take the form of a percentage deduction calculated on the annual written-down value of the assets concerned. It is deducted from the assessment and not included in the Profit and Loss Account as a trading expense. The settlement of the rates to be allowed is usually a matter for the company and the Inspector of Taxes, although applications may be made to the Commissioners of Inland Revenue to fix rates for particular trades. The Board of Referees have fixed rates of allowance for various types of machinery in a large number of trades, and these rates will be allowed where applicable.

Occasionally a company may have a nil assessment for income tax but a substantial claim for wear and tear. In cases such as this the claim may be carried forward and set off against the assessments of subsequent years until it is completely exhausted.

The Computation.

The director is not called upon to deal with the detailed computations of his company's liability to tax. At the same time it is useful for him to know how the calculation is carried out. For this purpose we give below a simple example of the form the computation takes.

THE X Y COMPANY, LTD.
PROFIT AND LOSS ACCOUNT FOR THE YEAR ENDED 31ST DECEMBER, 1934

	£		£
To Stock at 1st Jan., 1934	321	By Sales . . .	10,649
,, Purchases . .	8,625	,, Discount .	131
,, Discount . .	121	,, Dividends on Invest-	
,, Rates and taxes .	240	ments (Net) . .	25
,, Advertising . .	25	,, Stock at 31st Dec. .	836
,, Salaries . .	800	,, Loss for year carried	
,, Wages . .	680	to Balance Sheet .	284
,, Travelling expenses	48		
,, Freight . .	170		
,, Interest on mortgage	90		
,, Preliminary expenses	240		
,, Structural alterations	195		
,, Repairs . .	150		
,, Depreciation of plant	220		
	£11,925		£11,925

NOTES.

1. Advertising includes £12 charitable subscriptions.
2. Rates and taxes includes £120 Income Tax.
3. The Income Tax value of the plant is £2,500 and the rate of wear and tear agreed is 5 per cent.
4. The dividends received from investments have borne tax already.

COMPUTATION OF LIABILITY TO TAX, YEAR 1935–36

	£	£
Loss per Accounts		284
Items to be added back—		
Taxes	120	
Interest on mortgage	90	
Preliminary expenses	240	
Structural alterations	195	
Depreciation	220	
Charitable subscriptions	12	
		877
		593
Item to be deducted—		
Dividends on investments		25
· Adjusted Profits		568
Less Wear and Tear allowance—		
Plant as at 31st December, 1933, £2,500—		
5 per cent thereon		125
Amount assessable for 1935–36		£443

The director's attention is drawn to the fact that the company may be liable for tax on profits computed according to the Income Tax Acts, although the actual commercial accounts—as in the foregoing example—may show a trading loss.

Supervision of Inter-Subsidiary Trading from Taxation Standpoint.

Considerable attention was given to this matter in a previous chapter under the heading of " Financing Subsidiaries," and there is no necessity to take up further space in explaining it, except to emphasize the importance of giving proper consideration to the taxation aspect of the matter before definitely committing a subsidiary to a particular method of financing.

CHAPTER XVIII

DESPITE de-rating relief the burden of local taxation is still a heavy one. It is therefore important that a company which occupies a factory should take full advantage of every right to claim a reduction in its rating assessments. It is somewhat remarkable that the circumstances under which a works rating assessment can be reduced are not generally known and appreciated, and that the right to claim a reduction is often overlooked. It is the duty of the directors to inquire into this question from time to time so as to ensure that the possibility of reducing the amount payable in rates is kept constantly in view by one or other of the responsible officials of the company.

There are two main points connected with rating assessments with which the director of a manufacturing company should be acquainted—

(1) The general principles upon which assessments are calculated.

(2) The circumstances under which a rating assessment, reasonable at one period, may subsequently become excessive.

Recent Legislation.

During the last few years there has been a considerable volume of legislation with regard to rating but, in the main, the new Acts have been designed to modernize the administration rather than to alter principles. In particular, the Rating and Valuation Act, 1925, is directed chiefly to the simplification of the methods of making and collecting rates and the establishment of uniformity in valuations. It brought about the reduction in the number of rating authorities from 15,300 to approximately 2,000; it resulted also in the abolition of the parish as the separate area for rating and substituted the county borough, the urban and the rural district. A subsequent Act, passed in 1928, made the improvement of the 1925 Act, regarding the valuation of machinery, applicable to the London area. Finally, mention must be made of the derating Acts. These Acts (the Rating and Valuation Apportionment Act, 1928, and the Local Government Act, 1929), provide for the derating of agricultural, industrial, and freight-transport properties.

The Rating and Valuation Act, 1925.

The only point of this Act with which the director need concern himself is that relating to the valuation of machinery. It is laid down that certain plant and machinery is definitely to be excluded from the valuation of properties whilst, on the other hand, the following items are to be treated as though they formed part of the hereditament—

Machinery and plant used chiefly for generating power, heating, cooling, lighting, ventilating, draining, and supplying water.

Machinery or plant used for protecting the properties from fire.

Lifts, railway lines, tramlines.

Gasholders, blast furnaces, tar-distilling plants, coke ovens, water towers, etc.

All loose plant, tools, and manufacturing or process plant, which does not form part of the structure, is to be excluded from the valuation of the building. Needless to say there is a considerable amount of uncertainty in deciding whether particular items form part of the structure, but to meet this position a committee, to which all doubtful cases may be submitted, has been set up.

Fixing Rateable Value.

Rateable value is the net annual value, and this is obtained by deducting from the gross annual value certain statutory allowances which are set out in a scale known as the Second Schedule to the Rating and Valuation Act, 1925. But not all properties are scheduled in the Act, and it is therefore provided that premises not so listed shall be valued at the annual rent which a tenant might reasonably be expected to pay if he undertook to bear not only the tenant's burdens but also the cost of repairs, insurance, and similar maintenance items. The director will find that the property with which he is likely to be concerned falls into this latter class. The Second Schedule sets out the deductions to be made from land and buildings (10 per cent) and land without buildings (5 per cent), but it is laid down that the properties listed in the schedule are not to include " mills, factories, or premises used wholly or mainly for industrial purposes, or hereditaments valued as part of any railway, dock, canal, gas, water, or similar undertaking. In arriving at the value of factories, therefore, it is necessary to fix a hypothetical rent.

Hypothetical Tenants.

The hypothetical rent is the rent which a tenant would pay and not necessarily the rent actually paid. That is to say, the inquiry which is made is directed to the annual rental value which might reasonably be expected, taking one year with another, and where the owner is the occupier, he is to be regarded as though he were a tenant.

Profits and Valuation.

Although rent is the measure of rateable value, and not profits, it will be understood that profits must be regarded as a factor in determining the amount at which business premises could be let. If a company's property is such that it offers special facilities for carrying on a particular business profitably, then those facilities must undoubtedly enter into the hypothetical rent. On the other hand, an inability to make profits in any given property may give grounds for relief.

FACTORIES. In valuing a factory it must be ascertained what rent it would command after considering the purposes for which it can be used. We ignore, for a moment, the derating proposals of the 1928 Act. The equipment of the factory must be taken into account, especially if it has become, or is becoming obsolete; the rapid changes which take place in methods of manufacture may result in a great reduction of the hypothetical rent. So, also, will an uneconomic lay-out or a structural default be grounds for claiming that a lesser rent could be expected for an out-of-date factory as compared with a modern, well-designed plant.

The whole of the factory falls to be considered in the valuation, unless definite portions are thrown out of commission permanently. The temporary disuse of certain of the shops does not give rise to a claim for reduction.

If the factory is freehold, the site and the building are the two chief items in the valuation. Percentages, varying with the local conditions, are applied to the capital value of the land and the present value of the buildings. In fixing the percentages, the factors and special circumstances already discussed are taken into account. In the provinces the percentages used

14—(1641)

for the land vary from 3, 3½, to 4 per cent; for the buildings and the structural plant enumerated in an earlier paragraph the percentages range from 5 to 7 per cent.

EXAMPLE.

ASSESSMENT ON A FACTORY (EXCLUDED FROM THE SECOND SCHEDULE)

	Rate	£
Freehold land—Capital value £50,000 . . .	4%	2,000
Buildings, £100,000	5%	5,000
Boilers, generating plant, lifts, draining, heating and cooling, and water supply, £12,000 . . .	5%	600
General plant and machinery, £50,000 . . .	—	—
		7,600
Deductions under Second Schedule . . .		Nil
Rateable Value		£7,600

NOTE. The structural plant must be included in accordance with Section 24, Rating Act, 1925.

The foregoing example relates to a provincial property, for the Metropolis is governed by the Valuation (Metropolis) Act, 1869, and although certain types of premises are now dealt with as though they came under the Act of 1925, mills and factories continue to be treated under the original Act and are subject to a maximum deduction of 33⅓ per cent from the gross annual value.

The general principles underlying valuations in the London district are not very different, but special tables of deductions were laid down in the Third Schedule of the Valuation (Metropolis) Act, 1869. Under the Rating and Valuation Act, 1928, the inclusion of structural plant was extended to valuations in the London district, and as from 6th April, 1931, the deduction of certain of the allowances specified in the Third Schedule of the 1869 Act is superseded by the provisions of the Second Schedule to the 1928 Act.

Rating Relief Acts.

We turn now to the Acts which provide for the de-rating of industrial properties. The Rating and Valuation (Apportionment) Act of 1928 was the precursor of the de-rating enactments. It prescribed the machinery by which the Valuation Lists were to be revised in readiness for the statutory changes which were contemplated. As far as possible it laid down the distinction to be drawn between the properties to be de-rated and those which were to be charged in full. Broadly speaking, the relief is given to—

(a) Agricultural hereditaments.

(b) Industrial hereditaments.

(c) Freight-transport hereditaments.

The distinguishing of industrial properties entitled to relief is far from settled, but the following types of premises are not exempt—

Dwelling-houses, even if used as a workshop.

Retail shops.

Distributive wholesale businesses.

Storage premises.

Public supply undertakings.

On the other hand, extensive premises used for ship repairs are derateable, and also creameries, bakeries, oil-blending factories, newspaper offices other than the editorial rooms, motor garages, beer-bottling premises, printing works, and wool-sorting rooms.

There is no relief for cold storage companies, estate sawmills, cement merchants, duty-free warehouses, jewellers' workshops, seed-cleaning stores, distillers' warehouses, photographic studios, and warehouses used for carbonizing and bottling beer.

The Local Government Act, 1929 (Part V), is the Act which confers the actual de-rating relief.

In respect of industrial and freight-transport properties which are entitled to relief, it is provided that if they are devoted entirely to industrial purposes, the rateable value is to be reduced *three-fourths*. If they are used partly for a trade which would entitle the owners to relief, then the assessment is apportioned; relief is given to the extent of three-quarters of the assessment on the excepted portion of the premises only.

Agricultural property is given total relief.

How to Appeal against Rates.

Appeals against rates are governed by Sec. 14 of the Act of 1925 and, with regard to London, by Secs. 18–41 of the Valuation Act of 1869. Secs. 26–36 of the Rating Act, 1925, also set out the procedure for appealing against valuations.

Under Sec. 14 an appeal may be made against a rate in accordance with a right which has existed since 1601. In that year an Act was passed permitting appeals to quarter sessions. Great care is necessary here, however, because if relief could have been obtained by objecting to the draft valuation list the right to go to quarter sessions is lost.

Sec. 26 of the 1925 Act permits a company to lodge an objection to a draft valuation list within 25 days of the deposit of the list. The assessment committee meets to hear objections and the company is entitled to be heard. The draft list may then be revised—or confirmed—and if the company is still aggrieved it may proceed under Secs. 31–36. These sections provide that ratepayers who have failed to obtain satisfaction before the assessment committee may appear before the court of quarter sessions, which will either confirm the valuation or give effect to the contention of the appellant company.

A director is not concerned with the routine of appeals, but no harm is done if he satisfies himself that the right to relief is claimed before it is too late. In any case he should see that relief is obtained if a reasonable assessment subsequently becomes excessive.

A Reasonable Assessment May Subsequently Become Excessive.

The circumstances under which a rating assessment which at one time was reasonable may subsequently become excessive can be tabulated as follows—

(1) Where the property was originally assessed on the basis of constructional cost, and the cost of replacement has fallen since the original erection.

(2) Where part of the property has been destroyed by a sudden cause such as fire, explosion or flood, or by a natural cause such as wear and tear, and it is not proposed to re-build.

(3) Where part of the property formerly occupied as a factory is now occupied solely as a store or warehouse or is unoccupied.

(4) Where the property is suitable only for a particular trade or trades, and those trades can be carried on only at a loss, or at a profit insufficient to yield a reasonable return on the capital employed.

(5) Where property which originally had certain special licences, rights or advantages of position ceases to hold these licences, rights or advantages.

If the property is let on long lease at a fixed rent it is necessary to consider whether the value of the property from the point of view of a prospective tenant has varied since the execution of the lease. It should be borne in mind that an assessment committee will not necessarily assess a property on the basis of the rent, if the actual rent appears to be an artificial charge. In any such case the committee will proceed to calculate a hypothetical rent as in the case of property occupied by owners.

Illustrative Cases.

In order to illustrate the general effect of the assessment bases and to indicate the circumstances under which appeals should be lodged, the following examples are given—

(*a*) A factory is devoted to the manufacture of a commodity commonly made in the district. *The factory is suitable for any ordinary trade,* but it has a peculiarity of construction which renders it incomparable with other properties. It is occupied by the owners or by lessees on a long lease. It has no special licences, rights or peculiarities which render abnormal profits possible.

In this case a basis of 4 per cent to 6 per cent on *present* cost of the land, premises and fixed plant as previously indicated will usually be adopted. The occupiers of such property should ascertain the cost of replacing the factory at current building rates. This is particularly important if extravagance was indulged in at the time of the original erection or if the factory was built at the instance of Government departments at high war cost.

(*b*) A factory devoted to a manufacture *entailing a peculiar layout and construction,* e.g. special furnaces, kilns, gasometers, or unusual shaped shops, is situated in a parish in which there is no similar property. It is occupied by the owners or by lessees with a long lease.

The rules applying to such a case are—

(1) If the factory could possibly be used for any ordinary trade, then normally 4 per cent to 6 per cent on present cost will be the basis. If the cost of replacing the construction falls then an appeal should be made for adjustment.

(2) If the peculiar construction of the factory precludes its use for *any other business* then evidence of profits most support any objection to the valuation. It may happen that the valuation was made at a time

when the profits were abnormal. With a return to normal trading times it may be found impossible to make any profit. Whether consistent losses or inadequate profits can be attributed to the situation of the factory or to general depression in that trade is a matter of fact. Consistent losses may sometimes be ascribed to indolence, ineptitude or to carelessness on the part of the factory occupier, but unless definite evidence of this can be produced, the actual profit or loss made is *prima facie* evidence of normal trading results.

Assuming, however, that even a normal manufacturing company failed to make a profit equal to the amount upon which its assessment is based, after deducting interest on working capital, its evidence before the assessment committee for a reduction of its assessment will be substantiated by the production of the balance sheet and profit and loss account. The explanation may possibly be found in the item " Carriage and Cartage." The company will give evidence that the distance from the railway sidings to the factory is such that it eats into the margin of profit and places it at a disadvantage as compared with its more fortunately situated competitors in other districts. Again, its site may be liable to flood and its stock exposed to damage by water. The factory may be situated at a long distance from the source of supplies of raw material. Labour may be scarce in the district or the rates of pay in the parish may be above the normal for that particular trade.

Supported by such evidence the company should be able to obtain a reduced assessment varying according to circumstances from something below the normal rateable value based on constructional cost down to that which would be applied if the factory were but a warehouse.

(c) A factory, similar to the one considered in example (a), is occupied by the owners or by a lessee with a long lease, but the peculiarity of construction *permits the making of abnormal profits*.

In this case the basis will take into consideration the profit which an ordinary tenant (including the present occupiers) might be expected to make in a building not possessing the particular advantage, plus the additional profit due to the peculiarity of construction. This economic " surplus " will only be taken into account if any ordinary tenant could make it, and it is necessary to differentiate between abnormal profit attributable to the advantages of the factory and the abnormal profit attributable to the special ability of the occupiers. The former is taken into account, but the latter is not.

These examples cover the three main classes of property occupied by factory owners or by lessees of factories on long lease. The director should apply them to his own case, and take steps to ensure that a reduction is obtained if his company's property is over-assessed. In every case a periodical review should be made ; preferably on each occasion the notice of the settlement of a rateable valuation list for the parish is posted on the church doors.

Whenever any change occurs in the construction of a factory or in the uses to which it can be put, or whenever a general depression occurs in a particular industry, the director should ask himself whether the change affects his company's assessment. Similarly if a fire or explosion occurs, or if from any other cause part of the factory is thrown into disuse, or if furnaces or shops are closed down or otherwise thrown out of commission, or if an appreciable fall occurs in the cost of factory construction, then steps should be taken to secure a reduction of the rating assessment.

PART V

Miscellaneous Matters

CHAPTER XIX

DIRECTORS AND PROSPECTUSES

THE duty of a director with regard to a prospectus is one of the most important of his duties. We have deferred dealing with the matter until now because this chapter deals with the practical side of a prospectus and not merely the legal details surrounding its issue. The discussion of the practical questions of prospectus issue presupposes a knowledge of accounting principles, and it has been necessary to leave this point in the duty of a director until the accounts of a company had been set out and explained.

The Companies Act, 1929, devotes considerable attention to prospectuses. Many sections are designed exclusively for the protection of the public from the dangers besetting them when they are induced to invest money in companies concerning which they have no information beyond that provided in a prospectus.

No public company can allot shares or debentures, whether originally offering shares to the public or not, until it has filed with the Registrar of Joint Stock Companies a copy of its prospectus or a statement in lieu of prospectus. The prospectus must be signed by every person named in it as a director or prospective director; it must be dated, and every copy issued or published must state that a copy has been duly presented for registration. It is the duty of every director named in a prospectus to see that a copy has been so filed, for neglect carries with it a liability to a fine of five pounds per day from the date of issue until the eventual date of filing. (Sec. 34.)

Contents of the Prospectus.

Part I of the 4th Schedule to the Companies Act, 1929, lays down a long list of detailed information which must be given in prospectuses; directors would be well advised to study this schedule carefully when checking over a draft prospectus handed to them for approval before publication. The principal matters which must be disclosed are set out below—

1. *Except where the prospectus is published as a newspaper advertisement*, the contents of the memorandum, with the names, descriptions, and addresses of the signatories, and the number of shares subscribed for by them respectively.

2. The number of founders or management or deferred shares, if any, and the nature and extent of the interest of the holders in the property and profits of the company.

3. The number of shares, if any, fixed by the articles as the qualification of a director, and any provision in the articles as to the remuneration of the directors.

4. The names, descriptions, and addresses of the directors or proposed directors.

5. Where shares are offered to the public for subscription, particulars as to—

(i) *the minimum amount* which, in the opinion of the directors, must be raised by the issue of those shares in order to provide the sums *required to be provided in respect of each of the following matters*—

(a) *the purchase price of any property purchased* or to be purchased which is to be defrayed in whole or in part out of the proceeds of the issue;

(b) *any preliminary expenses payable* by the company, and any commission so payable to any person in consideration of his agreeing to subscribe for, or of his procuring or agreeing to procure subscriptions for, any shares in the company;

(c) *the repayment of any moneys borrowed* by the company in respect of any of the foregoing matters;

(d) *working capital ;* and

(ii) the amounts to be provided in respect of the matters aforesaid otherwise than out of the proceeds of the issue and the sources out of which those amounts are to be provided.

6. The amount payable on application and allotment on each share, and, in the case of a second or subsequent offer of shares, the amount offered for subscription on each previous allotment made within the two preceding years, the amount actually allotted, and the amount, if any, paid on the shares so allotted.

7. The number and amount of shares and debentures which

within the two preceding years have been issued, or agreed to be issued, as fully or partly paid up otherwise than in cash, and in the latter case the extent to which they are so paid up, and in either case the consideration for which those shares or debentures have been issued or are proposed or intended to be issued.

8. The names and addresses of the vendors of any property purchased or acquired by the company, or proposed so to be purchased or acquired, which is to be paid for wholly or partly out of the proceeds of the issue offered for subscription by the prospectus, or the purchase or acquisition of which has not been completed at the date of issue of the prospectus, and the amount payable in cash, shares, or debentures, to the vendor, and where there is more than one separate vendor, or the company is a sub-purchaser, the amount so payable to each vendor.

9. The amount, if any, paid or payable as purchase money in cash, shares, or debentures, for any such property as aforesaid, specifying the amount, if any, payable for goodwill.

10. The amount, if any, paid within the two preceding years, or payable, as commission (but not including commission to sub-underwriters) for subscribing or agreeing to subscribe, or procuring or agreeing to procure subscriptions, for any shares in, or debentures of, the company, or the rate of any such commission.

11. The amount or estimated amount of preliminary expenses.

12. The payments made to promoters within the two preceding years, and the consideration for such payments.

13. The dates of and parties to every material contract.

14. The names and addresses of the auditors.

15. The nature and interest of every director in property to be acquired and the sums paid to any director to induce him to qualify as a director.

16. Voting powers or rights attaching to different classes of shares.

17. The length of time during which the company, or the company to be acquired, has carried on business.

Minimum Subscription.

Directors should be particularly careful to observe their duty with regard to the minimum subscription. Even if the issue has been underwritten the prospectus must give full information as to the minimum capital with which, in their opinion, the company can carry on. If the minimum subscription is not obtained within 40 days, then the moneys must be returned as provided by Sec. 39. The duty of a director in this matter is now much greater than it was under earlier Companies Acts. Prior to the Act of 1900, directors were able to proceed to allotment even when a very small and insignificant amount of capital had been subscribed. The 1900 Act had for its intention, *inter alia,* the prevention of this practice, but it was difficult to lay down an amount below which allotment should not take place. The Act of 1908 required the directors to state the minimum amount upon which the board would proceed to allotment.

Under the Act of 1929 the restrictions upon directors are much more definite. The conditions are set out fully in Point 5 given above in the details of Part I to the 4th Schedule. To enforce these conditions it is provided that a public company *cannot commence business* until the requirements are complied with (Sec. 39). The text of this section (No. 39) is given below—

39.—(1) *No allotment shall be made* of any share capital of a company offered to the public for subscription, *unless the amount stated in the prospectus as the minimum amount which,* in the opinion of the directors, *must be raised* by the issue of share capital in order *to provide for the matters specified in paragraph 5 of Part I of the Fourth Schedule to this Act has been subscribed,* and the sum payable on application for the amount so stated, has been paid to and received by the company.

For the purposes of this subsection, a sum shall be deemed to have been paid to and received by the company if a cheque for that sum has been received in good faith by the company and the directors of the company have no reason for suspecting that the cheque will not be paid.

(2) The amount so stated in the prospectus shall be reckoned exclusively of any amount payable otherwise than in cash, and is in this Act referred to as the minimum subscription.

(3) The amount payable on application on each share shall not be less than five per cent of the nominal amount of the share.

(4) If the conditions aforesaid have not been complied with on the expiration of forty days after the first issue of the prospectus, all money received from applicants for shares shall be forthwith repaid to them without interest, and, if any such money is not so repaid within forty-eight days after the issue of the prospectus, the directors of the company shall be jointly and severally liable to repay that money with interest at the rate of five per centum per annum from the expiration of the forty-eighth day:

Provided that a director shall not be liable if he proves that the default in the repayment of the money was not due to any misconduct or negligence on his part.

(5) Any condition requiring or binding any applicant for shares to waive compliance with any requirement of this section shall be void.

(6) This section, except subsection (3) thereof, shall not apply to any allotment of shares subsequent to the first allotment of shares offered to the public for subscription.

Vendors.

The names and addresses of the vendors of any property purchased or acquired, or proposed to be acquired by the company, must be given in the prospectus if the property is to be paid for wholly or partly out of the proceeds of the issue. This requirement is a most important one, and must be observed in the spirit as well as in the letter. Not only is it necessary to disclose the names of the actual vendors, but also those of sub-vendors, and the consideration payable to each in cash, shares or debentures. Point 7 of Part I of the 4th Schedule further provides that a prospectus must set out the number of shares or debentures which have been issued otherwise than for cash during the preceding two years and the consideration for which the issue was made. The amount paid or payable as purchase money for property must be given, and it is obligatory to state separately the amount paid or payable for goodwill. (See Point 9 *supra*.) Any payments to a promoter during the two previous years must be disclosed, and reference must be made to all material contracts which have been entered into during the preceding two years, whether with promoters, vendors, or other persons. (Points 12 and 13.)

The Purchase of Property.

It is in connection with the purchase of property from promoters or vendors that the director is bound to exercise particular vigilance. He may be perfectly satisfied with the price paid by the company for the property, but when checking the draft prospectus he should insist upon seeing the originals or certified copies of all the contracts leading up to the sale. The person who completes the last contract for sale with the company is not always the only vendor within the

meaning of the Act.   The word includes any person who
has entered into a contract, either absolute or condi-
tional, for the sale, purchase, or option of purchase, of any
property to be acquired by the company if the purchase
money has not been fully paid at the date of the issue of
the prospectus or if the purchase money is to be paid
wholly or in part from the proceeds of the invitation to
the public, or if the contract depends for its fulfilment
on the result of the issue.   It will be observed then, that
if A agrees to purchase the X works as a going concern,
and pays a deposit on the purchase one month before
the prospectus, the balance to be paid two months
after the public issue, and then agrees to give an option
to B to buy within two months, and B sells his option
to C, who enters into an agreement with the company
to sell the works for cash payable one week after the
issue, all these people are vendors within the meaning
of the Act.   The interest of each, the name and address
of each, and the manner in which they are to be paid
must be disclosed to the public.   The object of the
provision is naturally to ensure that the public is made
aware of the circumstances under which a company
to which it subscribes pays £1,000,000 for a concern
which was sold to a sub-vendor for £500,000 but two
months previously.   Occasionally a company purchases only a lease of a factory instead of buying a
concern outright.   The fact that the lessor does not
receive " purchase money " and does not sell his
property will not excuse the company from disclosing
the name of the lessor or sub-lessees in the same
manner as the names of vendors would be disclosed.

Directors' Interest.

The Companies Act, 1929, is equally emphatic as to
the disclosure of directors' interest.   It is necessary
to give details of the nature and extent of the interest

of any director in the company's promotion or in property to be acquired, with a statement of the sums paid or payable to him in cash, shares, or otherwise to induce him to become a director, or to qualify him as a director, or in payment of services rendered to the company by him or by his firm.

The clause dealing with directors' interest is a wide one and was introduced to strengthen the common law liability, which prevented a director making a secret profit but allowed him to take his profit on disclosure of his interest to independent directors. The Act now provides for disclosure in the prospectus itself.

Occasionally directors lend their names to promoters of companies, who use them to enhance the chances of success of the issue. The section relating to directors' interest covers this matter and requires disclosure, in the prospectus, of the cash, shares or consideration paid to a director to induce him to take a seat on the board. This should act as a deterrent to directors who may be tempted to lend their names to promoters for prospectus purposes or for assisting appeals to the public for capital for concerns in which the use of the promoter's own name alone might prove a hindrance rather than an inducement.

Voting Powers.

If the company is formed with different classes of shares the rights and voting powers attaching to each class of shares must be given.

Reports and Documents.

There are several other minor matters which must be set out in the prospectus, but as they are not of so great importance as those set out above, the reader will not be worried by their iteration. Attention

must be paid, however, to other matters which promoters are anxious to disclose as distinct from those
which must be revealed under threat of penalty.
Strangely enough, the Act is practically silent on all
the matters to which most of the space and large type
in prospectuses is devoted. There is no obligation,
for instance, to set out experts' reports, directors' forecasts of future profits, valuation of property, particulars
of patent rights, testimonials or descriptions of the company's processes. There is no objection to the provision
of any information of the nature of the foregoing, in
spite of the fact that it is not legally necessary to give
it. Directors should be at least as careful in the
scrutiny of gratuitous information as in the verification
of information they are bound to include. It is recognized, of course, that due allowance must be made by
the public for enthusiasm, sanguine hopes, and even
exaggeration on the part of promoters. It is essential,
however, that there should be no misstatements or
concealment of any matters of importance.

Misrepresentation.

If a shareholder is induced to join a company
by misrepresentation he has a right to rescission of
the contract, and he may also have a right to action
for damages against every person who has assisted
in the issue of the prospectus. Sec. 37 provides for
damages against directors or any other persons who
have aided misrepresentation or who have sanctioned
the inclusion of the reports of experts when they themselves had no reasonable ground for believing them
to be true. This section is an important one, for it
re-enacts the Directors' Liability Act of 1890, which
laid down that an applicant for damages need only
show that the statements complained of are untrue,
the onus of proving that there were reasonable grounds

for believing the statements resting upon the directors or other defendants.

The directors must not only examine each paragraph of a proposed prospectus, but must grasp the general import of the document as a whole. It may happen that each point, taken separately, could be justified and yet the whole prospectus remain a misrepresentation. On this point the case of *Aaron's Reef* v. *Twiss* (1896) laid down that the true test is— " taking the whole thing together, was there misrepresentation ? If a number of statements give a false impression, the prospectus is none the less false, although it may be difficult to show that any specific statement is untrue."

Occasionally a prospectus is misleading as a whole on account of the suppression of information which would throw a different aspect upon the statements actually published. In such a case there is undoubtedly misrepresentation, for " those who issue a prospectus holding out to the public the great advantages which will accrue to persons who will take shares in a proposed undertaking and inviting them to take shares on the faith of the representations therein contained, are bound to state everything with strict and scrupulous accuracy, and not only to abstain from stating as fact that which is not so, but to omit no one fact within their knowledge the existence of which might in any degree affect the nature or extent or quality of the privileges and advantages which the prospectus holds out as inducements to take shares " (*Kindersley V.C. New Brunswick and Canada Rail Co.* v. *Muggeridge,* 1859).

Past Results.

Prior to the 1929 Act there were no definite regulations as to the disclosure of past results. Several instances arose, in consequence, of the suppression of information as to past losses. Often this was effected by the publication of average profits only, although the practice was condemned both by the Institute of Chartered Accountants and the Society of Incorporated Accountants.

Now, however, the law on the matter is quite specific. In the case of prospectuses two reports must be published—

(*a*) By the existing auditors " with respect to the profits of the company " during each of the three preceding financial years and with respect to the dividends paid on each class of share during those three years.

(*b*) By accountants, to be named in the prospectus, upon the profits of the business where the proceeds of the issue are to be applied in the purchase of a business.

These requirements are contained in Part II of the 4th Schedule and run as follows—

1. *A report by the auditors of the company* with respect to the profits of the company in respect of each of the *three financial years immediately preceding* the issue of the prospectus, and with respect to the rates of the dividends, if any, paid by the company in respect of each class of shares in the company in respect of each of the said three years, giving particulars of each such class of shares on which such dividends have been paid and particulars of the cases in which no dividends have been paid in respect of any class of shares in respect of any of those years, and, if no accounts have been made up in respect of any part of the period of three years ending on a date three months before the issue of the prospectus, containing a statement of that fact.

2. *If the proceeds, or any part of the proceeds,* of the issue of the shares or debentures *are or is to be applied directly or indirectly in the purchase of any business a report made by accountants who shall be named in the prospectus* upon the profits of the business in respect of each of the three financial years immediately preceding the issue of the prospectus.

In the case of statements in lieu of prospectuses there is still no necessity to disclose the company's own past profits. But if it is intended to acquire another business then it is necessary to show " the amount, as certified by the persons by whom the accounts have been audited, of the net profits of the business." Particular attention is drawn to the fact that it must be the certificate or report of the auditors of the acquired business which must be given. The profits to be shown are the actual net profits without adjustment in respect of taxation or exceptional items. This leads us to the important question of the general use of audited accounts in prospectuses, etc.

Auditors' Certificates.

Although the Companies Act, 1929, lays down definite rules as to the disclosure of past results in prospectuses and statements in lieu, it is still open to directors to supplement the information if they desire. The statutory information discussed above, though useful, may not of itself present a clear view to the intending investor. As we have seen, the company is bound to publish only—

In the case of Statements :

1. Profits of acquired businesses during the previous three years, or less if businesses not so long established.

In the case of Prospectuses—

2. Profits and dividends of the company during the previous three years, or less if businesses not so long established.

3. Profits of acquired businesses during the previous three years, or less if businesses not so long established.

In addition to these statements the directors may instruct the auditors to prepare a report upon the " adjusted profits." By this is meant a report showing the effect of eliminating non-recurring items of income and expenditure from the results of previous years in order to show the normal past profits which an intending investor can bear in mind.

The preparation of the certificate of past profits is left entirely to the discretion of the accountants and they follow the usually accepted principles governing adjustments. They examine each of the items which have been credited to, or charged against, profit and loss account during the period under review, and they add back or deduct any items which are not ordinary trading charges or trading profits. Exceptional profits of a non-trading nature which are not likely to recur are excluded. Where secret reserves have been created by excessive depreciation they adjust the charges to normal amounts. In every case they indicate clearly the nature of the adjustments they have made.

In addition to these alterations, the accountants exclude any charges incurred in the past which will be eliminated as a result of the issue of fresh capital, even though these items are ordinary trade charges properly debited to the profit and loss account. Thus, where the proceeds are to be used to extinguish a bank over-draft, the amounts previously charged for bank interest are added back in arriving at the distributable profits under the new conditions. Again, if certain debentures are to be paid off out of the proceeds of an issue of shares, it is correct in principle to add back the debenture interest which has been charged in the previous accounts. In the case of the conversion of a partnership business into a limited liability company, the accountants add back any salaries of the partners which have appeared in the previous accounts. On the other hand, adjustments are made to allow for the directors' fees, which will be payable instead of salaries to partners. Sometimes the cash received by means of a new issue is applied to the purchase of property previously rented. If this is so, the rent charges of former years are added back to the profits in the certificate.

An Example of Adjustments.

In order to illustrate the method of adjusting profits for prospectus purposes, as detailed above, an example is given on page 218, consisting of the summarized results of a business over a period of years, and an account of the profits as they would appear after adjustment based upon the information given concerning the proceeds of the issue.

The A. B. Company, Limited

An issue of 200,000 Ordinary Shares at par, bringing the Authorized and Issued capital up to £400,000.

The proceeds will be devoted to paying off £100,000 5 % Debentures, a Bank overdraft of £50,000, and the purchase of the premises occupied, for which a rent of £5,000 per annum is at present payable.

The profits in the example given, if adjusted for prospectus purposes would be as follows—

	Year 1	Year 2	Year 3	Year 4	Year 5
	£	£	£	£	£
Profits per Accounts (p. 218)	25,670	34,300	29,870	28,640	32,487
Add back the following charges—					
1. Rent of Premises .	5,000	5,000	5,000	5,000	5,000
2. Legal Expenses (connected with special lawsuit). . . .	—	—	—	—	3,500
3. Expenses re Key Industries Bill . .	—	—	520	1,960	—
4. Bad Debt (special non-recurring) . .	—	—	—	—	16,000
5. Bank Interest on Overdraft . . .	2,500	3,400	3,900	2,780	2,550
6. Interest on Debentures	5,000	5,000	5,000	5,000	5,000
7. Compensation to Managing Director	—	—	5,000	—	—
	£38,170	£47,700	£49,290	£43,380	£64,537

The adjustments have the effect of showing the profits at the amounts which would have been available

PROFIT AND LOSS ACCOUNTS

	YEAR 1 £	YEAR 2 £	YEAR 3 £	YEAR 4 £	YEAR 5 £
To Office and Travellers' Salaries and Expenses	89,640	91,380	93,420	94,110	92,876
" Rent of Premises	5,000	5,000	5,000	5,000	5,000
" Directors' Fees	7,200	8,000	8,000	8,000	9,450
" Rates, Taxes, and Insurance	1,750	1,800	1,940	1,970	2,110
" Audit and Accountancy	850	850	850	900	900
" Legal Expenses	530	620	483	550	3,970
" Expenses re Key Industries Bill	—	—	520	1,960	—
" Bad Debts	7,980	6,980	8,290	9,480	25,720
" Lighting, Heating, and Cleaning	1,420	1,375	1,240	1,850	1,740
" Donations and Subscriptions	575	620	490	385	360
" Bank Charges	132	150	149	128	117
" Bank Interest	2,500	3,400	3,900	2,780	2,550
Depreciation— Plant and Machinery	7,420	8,960	8,840	8,590	9,200
Fixtures	838	921	724	639	678
Office Furniture	320	310	290	280	255
Tools	480	460	430	390	370
" Repairs and Renewals	1,100	990	840	730	850
" Interest on Debentures	5,000	5,000	5,000	5,000	5,000
" Pensions and Annuities	1,000	1,200	1,100	1,300	1,250
" Compensation to late Managing Director	—	—	5,000	—	—
	£133,735	£138,106	£146,506	£144,042	£162,396
TO NET PROFIT	25,670	34,300	29,870	28,640	32,487
	£159,405	£172,406	£176,375	£172,682	£194,883

	YEAR 1 £	YEAR 2 £	YEAR 3 £	YEAR 4 £	YEAR 5 £
By Gross Profit from Trading Accounts	150,490	163,136	157,297	137,969	190,549
" Interest on Overdue Accounts	175	240	59	63	184
" Indemnity from Insurance Company					
" Discounts Received	3,940	4,230	15,300	30,700	—
" Agency Commissions	4,800	4,800	3,720	3,950	4,150
	£159,405	£172,406	£176,376	£172,682	£194,883

for the shareholders but for the exceptional and non-recurring charges. The rent of premises will not be chargeable against the profits in future, and the item is therefore excluded. The special legal expenses (£3,500) and the bad debt (£16,000) were connected with a lawsuit over the quality of certain goods which were alleged to be faulty and were so found by the Court. It is unlikely that so large a sum will be lost under similar circumstances in the future, and there is no obligation to provide for such a contingency. The two sums are therefore added back. Bank interest and debenture interest will disappear when the new capital is subscribed. None of the profit items has been added back, but reference would be made to the fire which occurred in Year 3 and a statement of its effect would be furnished. The indemnity received from the insurance company is regarded as a replacement of the profit which would have been made on the burnt stock.

The profits before and after adjustment are therefore as follows—

	Before Adjustment £	After Adjustment £
Year 1	25,670	38,170
,, 2	34,300	47,700
,, 3	29,870	49,290
,, 4	28,640	43,380
,, 5	32,487	64,537
	£150,967	£243,077

Average per annum	£30,193	£48,615
		Or, approximately, 12% on Capital.

Publication of a Balance Sheet.

There is no statutory obligation to publish the company's balance sheet in the prospectus, but whenever a balance sheet is given the directors should see that it is printed in the form in which it was presented to the shareholders at the last meeting. There is a practice now extant of providing the public with an uncertified statement resembling a balance sheet in certain particulars only. Very often a valuation figure taken from a valuer's report is inserted against the fixed assets and directors' estimates against the floating assets, including investments temporarily held for trading purposes. Whilst the inclusion of a valuer's report and figures in a prospectus is a practice to be commended, it is incorrect to use it in making up a balance sheet which materially differs from that presented to the shareholders. A little reflection will convince the reader that this practice quite naturally arouses suspicion that the balance sheet contains undesirable items, the amount of which is covered by an increase of the valuation of fixed assets over the book values.

Issuing Houses and Offers for Sale.

Most of the issues of new capital are now carried out through the medium of issuing houses and trust companies. Sometimes the issuing house purchases the issue and re-sells at a profit ; in other cases, the issuing house merely acts as an agent, placing the underwriting and carrying out the work for an agreed fee. In the former case the resale to the public is carried out by what is known as an " Offer for Sale." At one time " Offers for Sale " provided a means for avoiding certain of the restrictions governing the issue of prospectuses. In addition the public were deprived of the remedy against the Issuing House which they would have had against the directors under Sec. 84 of the Companies Act, 1908 (corresponding to Sec. 37 of the Companies Act, 1929), for misrepresentation.

Now, however, prospectuses and offers for sale are

placed on the same basis. The details of the offer must be filed in compliance with Sec. 34 (see page 255) and the same responsibilities regarding the issue of a prospectus attach to those issuing an offer for sale. It follows that the director must now be conversant, not only with Sec. 37, but also with the new provision (Sec. 38), particularly if he is a party to the issue of his company's shares by means of an " Offer." The text of both sections is set out below—

THE RULES REGARDING PROSPECTUSES.

SEC. 37.—(1) *Where a prospectus invites persons to subscribe for shares or debentures of a company*—

(a) every person who is a director of the company at the time of the issue of the prospectus; and

(b) every person who has authorized himself to be named and is named in the prospectus as a director or as having agreed to become a director either immediately or after an interval of time; and

(c) every person being a promoter of the company; and

(d) every person who has authorized the issue of the prospectus shall be liable to pay compensation to all persons who subscribe for any shares or debentures on the faith of the prospectus for the loss or damage they may have sustained by reason of any untrue statement therein, or in any report or memorandum appearing on the face thereof, or by reference incorporated therein or issued therewith, unless it is proved—

(i) that having consented to become a director of the company he withdrew his consent before the issue of the prospectus, and that it was issued without his authority or consent; or

(ii) that the prospectus was issued without his knowledge or consent, and that on becoming aware of its issue he forthwith gave reasonable public notice that it was issued without his knowledge or consent; or

(iii) that after the issue of the prospectus and before allotment thereunder, he, on becoming aware of any untrue statement therein, withdrew his consent thereto, and gave reasonable public notice of the withdrawal, and of the reason therefor; or

(iv) that—

(a) as regards every untrue statement not purporting to be made on the authority of an expert, or of a public official document or statement, he had reasonable ground to believe, and did up to the time of the allotment of the shares or debentures, as the case may be, believe, that the statement was true; and

(b) as regards every untrue statement purporting to be a statement by an expert or contained in what purports to be a copy of or extract from a report or valuation of an expert, that it fairly represented the statement or was a correct and fair copy of or extract from the report or valuation; and (*c*) as regards every untrue statement purporting to be a statement made by an official person or contained in what purports to be a copy of or extract from a public official document, it was a correct and fair representation of the statement or copy of or extract from the document:

Provided that a person shall be liable to pay compensation as aforesaid if it is proved that he had no reasonable ground to believe that the person making any such statement, report, or valuation as is mentioned in paragraph (iv) (*b*) of this subsection was competent to make it.

(2) Where the prospectus contains the name of a person as a director of the company, or as having agreed to become a director thereof, and he has not consented to become a director, or has withdrawn his consent before the issue of the prospectus, and has not authorized or consented to the issue thereof, the directors of the company, except any without whose knowledge or consent the prospectus was issued, and any other person who authorized the issue thereof, shall be liable to indemnify the person named as aforesaid against all damages, costs, and expenses to which he may be made liable by reason of his name having been inserted in the prospectus, or in defending himself against any action or legal proceedings brought against him in respect thereof.

(3) Every person who by reason of his being a director, or named as a director or as having agreed to become a director, or of his having authorized the issue of the prospectus, becomes liable to make any payment under this section may recover contribution, as in cases of contract, from any other person who, if sued separately, would have been liable to make the same payment, unless the person who has become so liable was, and that other person was not, guilty of fraudulent misrepresentation.

(4) For the purposes of this section—

The expression " promoter " means a promoter who was a party to the preparation of the prospectus, or of the portion thereof containing the untrue statement, but does not include any person by reason of his acting in a professional capacity for persons engaged in procuring the formation of the company:

The expression " expert " includes engineer, valuer, accountant, and any other person whose profession gives authority to a statement made by him.

The Rules Regarding " Offers for Sale."

Sec. 38.—(1) *Where a company allots or agrees to allot any shares in or debentures of the company with a view to all or any of those shares or debentures being offered for sale to the public,* any document by which the offer for sale to the public is made shall for all purposes be deemed to be a prospectus issued by the company, and all enactments and rules of law as to the contents of prospectuses and to liability in respect of statements in and omissions from prospectuses, or otherwise relating to prospectuses, shall apply and have effect accordingly, as if the shares or debentures had been offered to the public for subscription and as if persons accepting the offer in respect of any shares or debentures were subscribers for those shares or debentures, but without prejudice to the liability, if any, of the persons by whom the offer is made, in respect of mis-statements contained in the document or otherwise in respect thereof.

(2) For the purposes of this Act, it shall, unless the contrary is proved, be evidence that an allotment of, or an agreement to allot, shares or debentures was made with a view to the shares or debentures being offered for sale to the public, if it is shown—

(a) that an offer of the shares or debentures or of any of them for sale to the public was made within six months after the allotment or agreement to allot; or

(b) that at the date when the offer was made the whole consideration to be received by the company in respect of the shares or debentures had not been so received.

(3) Section thirty-four of this Act as applied by this section shall have effect as though the persons making the offer were persons named in a prospectus as directors of a company, and section thirty-five of this Act as applied by this section shall have effect as if it required a prospectus to state in addition to the matters required by that section to be stated in a prospectus—

(a) the net amount of the consideration received or to be received by the company in respect of the shares or debentures to which the offer relates; and

(b) the place and time at which the contract under which the said shares or debentures have been or are to be allotted may be inspected.

(4) Where a person making an offer to which this section relates is a company or a firm, it shall be sufficient if the document aforesaid is *signed on behalf of the company or firm by two directors of the company or not less than half of the partners*, as the case may be, and any such director or partner may sign by his agent authorized in writing.

Share-Hawking.

At one time there existed a fairly widespread system of hawking shares and debentures from house to house. The securities were generally very speculative and frequently worthless. The Companies Act, 1929, put an end to the practice and laid down this rule (Sec. 356)—

It shall not be lawful for any person to go from house to house offering shares for subscription or purchase to the public or any member of the public.

The same section renders it illegal to make an offer in writing to the public of shares or securities unless the offer is accompanied by a signed statement containing specified information. Among other matters this specified information must include full particulars regarding the directorate, even though the person making the offer may have no connection with the company. On this account, therefore, directors should be aware of the regulations so that they may exercise a general surveillance over any widespread traffic in their shares. Their duty is not a direct one, as it is in the case of prospectuses, but where statements are published giving past profits, dividends, details of capitalization, and so on, it is obviously desirable that directors should keep an eye on the information sent out by those who have large blocks of shares to sell to the public.

CHAPTER XX

WHEREAS the investigation into a company's accounts by independent auditors is a statutory obligation, the institution of an internal system of audit is quite voluntary. The installation of such a check upon the company's funds is one of the duties of the directors, and must never be overlooked.

The usual annual visits of independent auditors, though leading to the detection of fraud which has been perpetrated since their last audit, will not act as a deterrent except when the time of the visit approaches. Defalcations may possibly commence immediately after the conclusion of the audit and continue for a space of twelve months before the auditors' next investigation. The duty of conserving the company's funds rests upon the directors, and it is therefore imperative that they should satisfy themselves personally that a perpetual check is maintained within the company's own organization.

An internal audit need not necessarily be elaborate. It may vary from a separate internal audit department comprising a considerable staff down to a system entailing no additional staff but consisting only of sets of rules to be followed in all cash dealings, designed to render fraud difficult if not impossible. If the company can support a large organization then the addition of a separate internal audit department of, say, two or three members will not strain the company's finances unduly. This department is placed under the charge of a competent officer, preferably with auditing experience. He is, and must be, absolutely independent of every officer of the company except the members of the board. He may be instructed to report to the managing director, but he should have the right to report direct to the board should he desire to do so. It must not be thought that the appointment of an internal auditor entails the digestion of voluminous and frequent reports. On the contrary, it will be found that a competent internal auditor will not trouble the board if everything is in perfect order. It is only when he has serious matters to disclose that he will make a communication, and on such occasions, of course, the directors must give his papers the fullest consideration, no matter how bulky.

So that an internal audit shall be efficacious it is necessary that its scope shall not be outlined by any officer whose duties it will control. In other words, the instructions to the internal auditor should be framed by an independent person, preferably the company's auditor in collaboration with the board, or it should be framed by the directors and handed to the company's auditor for approval. The director must therefore be acquainted with many matters appertaining to the internal audit in order that he may assure himself that it is efficient.

Schemes of Internal Audit.

There are many accepted schemes of internal audit in use at the present time, all of which agree in principle. With the actual details of these schemes the director need not bother himself, but he should study the following points in order that he may understand the reason for their adoption and press for their introduction in his own company.

(1) It is unwise to allow cheques to be honoured on the signature of one officer only.

(2) All cheques should be signed by at least one

member of the board and countersigned by the secretary, who should produce documentary evidence of their correctness. Long typed lists of cheques do not constitute evidence of the correctness of payments.

(3) All cash received must be banked at once. Petty cash must be drawn from the bank, and not reimbursed from customers' cash payments.

(4) All payments over a small maximum must be made by cheque.

(5) The wages-book clerk and the wages paying-clerk should be different persons.

(6) The duties of the staff should be changed from time to time.

(7) Every member of the staff should be obliged to take his annual holiday.

(8) No cashier should be permitted to make entries in ledgers.

Defalcations usually arise from these sources—

(1) The manipulation of cash receipts from customers.

(2) The diversion of customers' cheques and the closing of their accounts by means of credit notes or transfers to bad debts.

(3) Pilfering petty cash.

(4) The manipulation of wages.

(5) The insertion of fictitious invoices in the books.

It is to these points that the director should give his attention. He himself may assist in the internal audit to a considerable extent by insisting on the production of lists of bad debts to be written off, supported by documentary evidence. The recommendation that all members of the staff should take an annual holiday is not made facetiously; its object is to cause a break in a series of fraud which must be discovered if the perpetrator's duties are taken over by another member during a holiday. Many frauds have been carried out in the past by the " conscientious, tried, and trusted officer " whose enthusiasm for work prevented him from taking respite from his labours for many years. A holiday list should be laid before the board together with a roster of the whole staff. The absence of a member's name from the holiday list will put the director on inquiry.

Work of Internal Audit Department.

The work which may be entrusted to an internal audit department is as follows. This list could be taken as a basis by a director framing instructions or considering a suggested scheme placed before him for approval—

(1) Purchases and expenses should be verified with invoices or other documentary evidence.

(2) Payments should be supported by vouchers.

(3) Sales compared with duplicate invoices.

(4) Purchases, sales and material requisitions verified with stock ledgers.

(5) Stocks on hand verified physically with stock ledger balances.

(6) Cash balances counted or verified with certificates.

(7) Ledger Control or Balancing Accounts checked.

(8) Book debts verified and long credit items inquired into.

(9) Bad debts written off and allowances credited, verified with documentary evidence.

(10) Methods adopted for allocating wages, material and oncost charges in the costing records inquired into.

(11) Costing records thoroughly tested.

The official in charge of the internal audit staff should report any serious discrepancy or inefficient accounting and should put forward suggestions for remedying the matter. His report should always state the ground covered during the audit and the manner in which the accounting is carried out. The directors should compare this report with the programme indicated above and satisfy themselves as to the reasons for the omission of any portion. Every recommendation contained in the report should be carefully considered and definite instructions given thereon.

Common Types of Fraud.

In order to emphasize the importance of the director's duty regarding the internal control of the company's funds, we discuss below the types of fraud which are most commonly encountered whenever the supervision is not so close as it should be.

The principal is the " snowball " fraud. This type of defalcation is marked by the misappropriation of cash—and sometimes cheques—received by a company in its daily post. In order to conceal the misappropriation the perpetrator uses the cash received on the following day to make up the previous day's defalcation, but as he helps himself to an increasing amount as time goes on, the total accumulates in " snowball " fashion until he experiences great difficulty in making up the total deficiency out of the subsequent takings.

Discovery of " Snowball " Frauds.

The discovery of "snowball" frauds usually occurs on the occasion of the annual audit. If the company's cash book is due to be closed on 31st December, the defaulting cashier uses the cash received on 1st and/or 2nd January to make up his deficiency and shows this cash as " effects not yet credited by bank." The auditor, however, can tell from the paying-in book that the effects were not paid in until after 31st December, and this leads, as a rule, to the admission of the fraud. If the auditor actually attends to count the cash balances on hand at the close of business on 31st December, the defalcation is discovered a little earlier. A little reflection serves to show that this type of fraud is rendered difficult if the directors appoint an internal auditor whose duties include the frequent counting of all cash balances in hand.

Sales Ledger Frauds.

The next common type of fraud is the manipulation of accounts in the Sales Ledgers. Payments by selected customers are suppressed, and the debit balances standing against them are closed off by means of fictitious credit notes. In order to prevent this method of defalcation the director should see that no credit notes are allowed unless they are passed and initialed by a senior official of some department other than the counting-house, e.g. the works manager. The system of internal audit should include Rule No. 8, given on page 227, viz. " No cashier should be permitted to make entries in ledgers."

Bought Ledger Frauds.

Bought ledger frauds are slightly more elaborate. They are carried out, as a rule, by passing fictitious invoices into the ledger, the cheques in payment being sent, in the ordinary way, to what is usually an accommodation address of the clerk. The fraud necessitates the printing of account headings and, often, the forging of the signature of the official whose duty it is to pass the bills sent in against the company. The director should observe that whereas collusion between two members of the staff is frequently necessary to carry out Sales Ledger frauds, the payment of fictitious accounts can be arranged single-handed. This point will be clear if we explain that the paying cashier may send out cheques against a false account in all good faith. On the other hand a receiving cashier who suppresses Sales Ledger cash has a difficult task to close off the Sales Ledger Accounts by credit notes without the assistance of the Sales Ledger keeper.

To minimize the risk of Bought Ledger frauds the director should see that the system of passing invoices is sound. The storekeeper should initial the invoices for the quantities of goods received, the prices should be verified by the order office, and the works manager should pass the invoice as correct. The stores system should be well-kept, and kept up to date; the internal auditor should be able to ascertain readily that goods appearing on fictitious invoices have not been entered in the stores records, and therefore not received. Lastly, the director should not be content to sign cheques merely because they appear on a typed list laid before him in support of payments to be made.

Wages Frauds.

Wages frauds may be carried out in a variety of ways, but the more usual form they take is by the inclusion of non-existent workmen in the wages book. The wages of these men are then retained by the cashier who hands out the pay envelopes. To overcome this type of fraud, the paying cashier should not be allowed to make up the wages book. This precaution is generally sufficient, but there is still the possibility of collusion between the wages-book clerk and the paying cashier. It is for this reason, among others, that the duties of the staff should be varied by the directors from time to time.

CHAPTER XXI

THE CONTROL OF BRANCHES ABROAD

IT is not possible to lay down the procedure followed in the direction of every class of foreign or colonial branch business. The technical control must necessarily vary with each particular trade. To a certain extent, however, the principles to be followed in financial control will be found identical in every company trading in foreign countries.

Merchanting and Producing Companies.

A distinction must first be drawn between those companies whose activities abroad consist of buying and selling commodities and those engaged in the production, manufacture, or growing of commodities. In the case of the first it is possible, and usual, to commit the control of the business to a subsidiary company with a local board of directors. In the case of the producing company it is generally sufficient to place the company's interest under the care of a local manager. The principal class of business placed under the control of a local board is that in which the buying or selling is carried out with natives. A board of directors in England cannot, as a rule, appreciate the peculiar requirements and conditions attaching to this class of trade to the extent of being able to change a policy with the rapidity so often demanded by local circumstances. A board of directors resident abroad, on the other hand, is able to exercise local foresight and is less likely to be found unprepared by sudden changes in market conditions, It is not impossible to place this class of trade under the charge of a manager, but whenever that course is adopted it is essential to give the representative almost plenary powers. The company is then committed to the decisions which may be taken from time to time by this one man.

When the branch or station is engaged in producing, it is usual to appoint a manager only and not a local board of directors. The manager is concerned only with such matters as the purchase of raw materials and the engaging of native labour. The English board is not called upon to relinquish its authority or to delegate its power over vital matters of policy. Trade with the customers is carried on by the English office or by the selling agents under the immediate supervision of the home board. Although a local manager is relied upon to carry out a production programme, therefore, and is left to his own resources in that respect, the real responsibility remains with the directors. It must be observed, however, that a local manager controlling a plantation or factory abroad must necessarily have a wider scope of authority than that possessed by the manager of a home factory. His appointment is the subject of great discrimination on the part of those delegated to select him.

Whether the immediate supervision of a foreign branch is in the hands of a local board of directors or a local manager, the same rigid control of finance should be kept in the hands of the principal directors. The methods by which this is accomplished are set out hereunder.

Local Companies.

The board of a local company is responsible for all routine matters connected with their charge, but upon matters of policy and upon all questions which necessitate the outlay of cash by the parent company the local board consults the principal board. Detailed balance sheets and trading accounts should be prepared at frequent intervals and forwarded to the head office. The branch company's accounts should be subjected to audit by a local firm of auditors at quarterly or half-yearly periods, and the half-yearly and annual accounts, at least, should be accompanied by the auditors' detailed report when sent to England.

As the formation of a local board is designed to relieve the home directors of detailed supervision, it is not usually necessary to insist upon reports or returns other than those accompanying the accounts which have been prepared by the local directors and auditors. This is a matter upon which it is not possible to lay down definite rules. The circumstances must be taken into account and rather more latitude allowed to a competent local board than to one composed of members with whose capabilities and failings the parent directors are not entirely familiar.

Local Branches.

Control over foreign branches, as distinct from foreign companies, can be maintained by arranging for complete reports covering the whole of the activities of the branch to be sent to the head office at frequent intervals. The reports fall into two classifications—financial and those relating to production or trading. The financial reports consist of monthly summaries of expenditure analysed to show the outgoings on revenue account and on capital account separately. It is usual to provide that no expenditure of a capital nature shall be incurred without express authority from the parent board. The same rigid control cannot be applied over revenue expenditure. This is a matter in which the discretion and ability of the local manager must be trusted. An efficient check upon revenue expenditure is, however,

provided by the production accounts supplied at
monthly intervals by the branch. These accounts are
made up to a date to coincide with the period covered
by the financial statement and are framed to give
the cost of production or trading over the previous
month.

In the case of branches engaged in plantation work it
is usual to frame the production accounts to give the
cost of production per unit shipped, e.g. per lb. of
rubber, and so on. By means of the information
provided by the two classes of monthly report the
directors can watch the expenditure of cash abroad
and take steps to terminate inefficient management
without loss of time. It may happen that the company's activities abroad are of such importance that
a branch office is required. In such cases the branch
may carry out a considerable amount of the actual
accounting work and assume a position somewhat
similar to that occupied by a local subsidiary company. However much elaboration is introduced, the
principle of responsibility to the main board remains
the same, and the duty of the parent directors to deal
fully with the periodical returns remains constant.

Financing a Branch Abroad.

The first step in the financing of a branch abroad
consists of crediting a local bank with a sum to
cover initial local expenditure on lands and buildings plus normal working capital calculated to meet
immediate requirements. The local manager is given
authority to draw upon this account either upon his
own signature, or upon his own signature countersigned
by the secretary whenever the payment is greater
than the agreed maximum. When production commences, the branch invoices the whole of its output
to the head office at cost price and sends forward the

production in accordance with instructions from the sales manager or the secretary. The head office then acts as selling agent or instructs the usual brokers. It is sometimes provided that the branch manager may hand over the documents relating to shipments to the local bank and draw against their value. In this way the financing of the branch becomes more or less automatic. It is not always possible to follow this procedure, however, for it is occasionally necessary to keep all available funds in England. In such cases the head office remits sums to cover the actual requirements of the branch by telegraphic transfer or exchange draft, and the branch sends the documents relating to shipments direct to the head office. This latter method is also resorted to in order to avoid interest, discount and brokerage. The method to be adopted must necessarily depend upon circumstances and prevailing conditions, among which may be mentioned the variations which occur in rates of exchange between this country and the branch country and the differences in interest charges existing from time to time.

Local Capital Expenditure.

All additional capital expenditure to be incurred by branches abroad should be remitted by the home company and never drawn from a balance of trading capital held by the managers.

Remuneration of Local Managers.

It is customary to remunerate local managers by means of a fixed salary and a percentage calculated either on production or on trading profits. This is calculated to induce the rendering of the manager's best efforts in the interests of the company and is a practice which may be adopted with safety. It should always be arranged, whether the manager is remunerated upon profits or not, that the branch is charged with interest upon the average capital employed abroad. This leads to the remitting to England of all surplus funds without delay and counters frivolous applications for additional capital outlay.

The Local Manager's Returns.

The nature of the information which the director may expect from the managers of branches abroad has been indicated above. It may assist, however, to enumerate the usual periodical returns which should be sent home and laid before the board—

(a) Cash expenditure statement analysed under the headings—

     (1) Raw material.

     (2) Wages.

     (3) Expenses in detail.

     (4) Salaries.

     (5) Capital expenditure as approved.

(b) Branch banking account—giving a summary of the bank transactions since the previous return.

(c) Branch current account, showing the amounts charged to head office for produce shipped and the amounts credited for cash received.

(d) Production account for the period.

(e) Stock account, showing quantities held in stock and the transactions in the commodities produced during the period.

(f) Costing statement, showing the unit cost of production over the period.

(g) Branch trading account and profit and loss account.

The various returns outlined above should be examined immediately upon receipt by the head office officials and then placed before the board. Any

further information required should be called for at
once from the manager presenting the returns. It
is advisable to pass a communication to the manager
upon every set of returns he sends in, even though
this communication may amount to little more than
acknowledgment of receipt. This display of interest
and encouragement assists the interests of the company generally. Any tendency to treat branch returns
with indifference is bound to have an adverse effect
upon the zeal and efficiency of the branch.

Special Taxation Points.

It is well for a director of a company possessing
branches abroad to know that the trading results of
overseas branches of British companies are subject
to British income tax notwithstanding that local
taxation may already have been borne. If the branches
are situated in British Dominions, however, a measure
of relief is provided which has the effect of reducing
the rate of combined tax paid both at home and in the
Dominion to the higher of the two rates in force in
either Great Britain or the Colony.

If the foreign branch is a joint stock company
controlled by a local board, then the profits will not
ordinarily be subject to British income tax. Tax will
be payable upon any dividends received by the parent
company from the subsidiary abroad.

Directors of companies possessing mills and factories
abroad should note that their companies are entitled
to a deduction from the company's profit of a sum
equal to one-sixth of the gross annual value of the
factory calculated in a similar manner to that followed
in England for this purpose. There is a proviso
attaching to this concession, namely, that the buildings
to which it applies must have power-driven plant
installed therein.

Commercial Agency System.

Before leaving the matter of branches abroad reference must be made to a system whereby many companies manage their foreign properties through agents. The method is known as the commercial agency system. It is in common use among rubber, tea, and similar planting companies and consists of committing the destiny of the companies concerned to firms of agents who have a house in London and one in a port abroad.

The system has many advantages and many disadvantages which are admirably set out in a speech made some years ago by Mr. D. F. L. Zorn, a gentleman of great experience with this class of company—

" The system has grown up gradually during the last 30 years and in a great many cases works successfully, but there are certain directions in which it is possible for serious abuses to creep in, partly because there is frequently a stringent agreement under which the planting company is bound to the agents for a fixed term of years. The broad criticisms made against the system are : firstly, there is a tendency for the commercial agents to usurp the functions of the London board of directors and the estate manager. Secondly, that as the agent in the East usually holds full power of attorney, the estate manager is dependent for his position on satisfying, not the owners of the estate, but the agent representing those owners, which is by no means the same thing. Thirdly, it not infrequently happens that gentlemen who are partners in an agency firm acting for a particular company also sit as directors upon the board of that company. Sometimes these agent directors constitute an actual majority of the board."

The director who accepts a seat on the board of this class of company should pay careful heed to these points. The commercial agency system is one by which directors may easily become mere figureheads unless they grasp the real control and retain it firmly. There is no real analogy in any other class of company except perhaps in the shipping industry, in which the control of a line of vessels is committed to a firm of managers. A directorship in this industry calls for equal caution and self-assertion.

CHAPTER XXII

THE PURCHASE OF NEW BUSINESSES

THE negotiations which precede the amalgamation of companies, the absorption of subsidiaries and the complete purchase of ancillary businesses are so involved that their treatment could only be dealt with adequately in a separate volume. The part which directors play in these matters is often less than it might be, rather too much being left to the solicitors and accountants of the respective companies. Though an amalgamation will often be carried through on more advantageous and mutually satisfactory terms if left entirely to the people who understand the principles involved, it should not be thought that it is only the solicitors or accountants who are bound to understand the details of the scheme. The fact that many directors merely grasp the general outline of a suggested purchase, amalgamation or absorption, and give their consent because they are recommended to do so by the company's advisers, is no reason why a practical director should refrain from making himself acquainted with the methods by which such transactions are effected. It is insufficient, for instance, to be content with a hazy idea of the meaning of goodwill in purchase transactions. The director should be acquainted with the methods by which a value is placed upon this and other assets. He will not then be induced to agree to a purchase of a business at a round figure—apparently reasonable—without satisfying himself that value is received for cash paid away for intangible assets.

The Purchase of Small Businesses.

The reader is asked to bear with us awhile in order that we may deal with a matter which affects the small financier who is requested to invest his savings in more or less insignificant concerns in return for employment and a seat on a board. The word "insignificant" is used to denote small businesses which might, from the point of view of capital, be quite conveniently carried on in partnership. It is not used in a slighting manner towards small concerns possessing valuable fields for their particular business and requiring only a little capital to render their success assured. Unfortunately, however, this class of company is made up, to a considerable extent, of risky one-man concerns with little past history capable of courting inquiry, and with small prospects of a successful future.

A good deal has been written concerning this type of concern, but the following summary of advice will bear repetition for the benefit of any reader who is seeking employment for his spare capital and leisure moments, and who is tempted to cast in his lot with such a company—

(*a*) Companies offering a salaried post as director or secretary in return for an investment of a comparatively small sum of money should always be the subject of the closest inquiry.

(*b*) The would-be director is unwise to trust to his own perspicacity in sifting the information given to him by owners of such small concerns.

(*c*) The services of an independent investigator should be employed. He will probably delve for information not readily available and ignore that given gratuitously.

(*d*) A director investing his money in a one-man company recently founded and with no tangible proof of prospects should realize that he is indulging in a speculation and that he has only himself to blame if he loses his money.

Generally speaking, observance of these maxims will lead to the saving of money, and their non-observance will lead to its speedy disappearance. If the concern has been in existence for some time, then an independent investigation and report are absolutely essential. If it is newly founded, then the investor who is offered a seat in return for his money must use his discretion and acquire as much independent advice as he can command. If the company is formed for the exploitation of a new process or patent, technical advice should be sought. If the object of the concern is a business conflicting with the laws of a nation, such as whisky-running to the United States, then the less the investor has to do with the proposal the better. Companies which set out to acquire huge tracts of rich oil-bearing land with the magnificent sum of one thousand pounds or so should be left to their own devices. The oil they promise to raise will speedily place them in funds and render them independent of the small premium they require from an intending director or secretary.

Business Agencies.

Before leaving the subject of small businesses we must mention the existence, in the City, of numerous agencies, for bringing would-be directors into touch with small businesses. Several of these concerns are beyond reproach and are fulfilling a need which should be filled by some well-founded central institution. Others are a snare and a delusion. They should be avoided both by the owner of the small business and by the prospective director. The exorbitant rate of commission they charge cripples the small owner who seeks their aid, and their utter disregard of the proper precautions which they should exercise in advising an

investor mark them down as a danger to the commercial life of the City and indeed of the country.

Absorption of Companies.

The absorption of companies by other companies
may be carried out in many ways, the two chief being—
(1) The complete purchase of the assets.
(2) The purchase of the issued share capital.

The term " complete purchase of the assets " is
used in connection with businesses previously carried
on by a sole trader or a partnership, as well as to companies incorporated under the Companies Acts. In the
case of a sole trader's business, the transaction is
no more than a simple acquisition of a business on
terms agreed to by the vendor and the purchasing
company.

Absorption of companies by purchase of the issued
share capital differs from complete purchase in that
it does not entail the formal liquidation of the vendor
company. The latter continues as a separate constitution, and the effect of the amalgamation is that
its shares have changed hands and the control is transferred to the majority shareholder—the purchasing
company.

If the absorption is carried out by means of an
exchange of shares, the procedure is governed either
by the Memorandum and Articles or by Sec. 234 of the
Companies Act, 1929. Sec. 234 applies to a company
which is, or is proposed to be, in course of voluntary
liquidation. The text is as follows—

SEC. 234.—(1) Where a company is proposed to be, or is in course
of being, wound up altogether voluntarily, and the whole or part of
its business or property is proposed to be transferred or sold to
another company whether a company within the meaning of this
Act or not (in this section called " the transferee company "), the
liquidator of the first-mentioned company (in this section called " the
transferor company ") may, with the sanction of a special resolution
of that company, conferring either a general authority on the

liquidator or an authority in respect of any particular arrangement, receive in compensation or part compensation for the transfer or sale, shares, policies, or other like interests in the transferee company, for distribution among the members of the transferor company, or may enter into any other arrangement whereby the members of the transferor company may, in lieu of receiving cash, shares, policies, or other like interests, or in addition thereto, participate in the profits of or receive any other benefit from the transferee company.

(2) Any sale or arrangement in pursuance of this section shall be binding on the members of the transferor company.

(3) If any member of the transferor company who did not vote in favour of the special resolution expresses his dissent therefrom in writing addressed to the liquidator, and left at the registered office of the company within seven days after the passing of the resolution, he may require the liquidator either to abstain from carrying the resolution into effect, or to purchase his interest at a price to be determined by agreement or by arbitration in manner provided by this section.

(4) If the liquidator elects to purchase the member's interest, the purchase money must be paid before the company is dissolved, and be raised by the liquidator in such manner as may be determined by special resolution.

(5) A special resolution shall not be invalid for the purposes of this section by reason that it is passed before or concurrently with a resolution for voluntary winding-up, or for appointing liquidators, but, if an order is made within a year for winding-up the company by or subject to the supervision of the court, the special resolution shall not be valid unless sanctioned by the court.

(6) For the purposes of an arbitration under this section, the provisions of the Companies Clauses Consolidation Act, 1845, or, in the case of a winding-up in Scotland, the Companies Clauses Consolidation (Scotland) Act, 1845, with respect to the settlement of disputes by arbitration, shall be incorporated with this Act, and in the construction of those provisions this Act shall be deemed to be the special Act, and " the company " shall mean the transferor company, and any appointment by the said incorporated provisions directed to be made under the hand of the secretary or any two of the directors may be made under the hand of the liquidator, or, if there is more than one liquidator, then of any two or more of the liquidators.

It will be seen that this method of purchase for shares is subject to definite rights of dissentient shareholders. Any member—provided he did not vote for the scheme—is entitled to call upon the liquidator to purchase his shares. If the price cannot be agreed upon, then provision is made for the submission of the matter to arbitration.

There are no special points of law connected with the alternative method, viz. the purchase of shares.

It is therefore possible to proceed with the consideration of the practical points involved without reference
to the statutes.

Fixing a Purchase Price.

As soon as tentative proposals for a purchase have·
been made, the two companies concerned instruct
their respective accountants to commence an investigation with a view to recommending a purchase price.
This work is carried out without prejudice to subsequent negotiations and is, of course, only a preliminary
to the real transactions which take place at a later date.
As, however, the recommendations of the accountants
may subsequently be used as a basis for the purchase,
the reports presented to the board must be thoroughly
understood.

Purchase of a Going Concern.

When a company intends to purchase another
going concern outright, it is first necessary to fix a
date upon which the purchase shall take effect.   The
fixing of this date may affect many important aspects
of the transaction.   It may be agreed, for instance, that
all liabilities up to the purchase date shall be satisfied
by the vendors.   Again, it may be agreed that the
purchasing company shall take the benefit of profits
accruing from the agreed date.

The chief points governing the fixing of a purchase
price are four in number, of which two concern the
accountants in the first place, one the valuers and
one the directors.   The final decision rests with the
respective boards.   The points are—

(1) Valuation of the assets other than goodwill.

(2) The investigation into the past profits and the
assessment of goodwill.

(3) The ascertainment of the liabilities

(4) Consideration of the future of the purchased company and the prospects awaiting its products under the new arrangement.

Valuation of Assets.

Fixed assets such as plant, machinery, furniture, fixtures and fittings, are valued by firms of valuers appointed by the two companies. The directors should make it their business to inquire whether obsolete machinery has been excluded and that full regard has been paid to any contemplated change in the nature of the business to be acquired.

Investments in quoted securities may be valued by the accountants from the Stock Exchange Official Lists. Investments in subsidiaries or in private companies, for the shares of which there is no quotation, are usually valued by mutual arrangement between the two firms of accountants engaged, from such data as is available.

The valuation of patent rights, trade marks and similar assets is not governed by any set code of procedure. Full regard must be made to the unexpired terms of all patents, but the value can be agreed upon only by the directors, or by such agents delegated to represent the companies as have complete knowledge of the intentions of the board concerning future policy. No little responsibility rests upon the directors in the valuation of this class of asset, and it is imperative that they should devote as much time and consideration to the question as possible before agreeing to pay any price suggested by the vendors.

Book debts are valued by the accountants in consultation. Reserves for discounts to be allowed on book debts must be taken into account; reserves for bad debts must be deducted, unless the vendor company agrees to the more satisfactory course of guaranteeing the debtors. Stocks on hand should be valued by valuers experienced in the particular class of business concerned. All out-of-date, old, unsaleable or unfashionable stock must be excluded, and for this purpose the directors should ask to see the stock schedules when considering the final proposals.

Past Profits and Goodwill.

The price to be paid for goodwill cannot be fixed by such methods of valuation as are employed for other assets. Goodwill may be defined as the value of a reputation for a class of goods or services built up by means of satisfaction accorded to customers, with the probability that the public will continue to buy those goods if the same methods of manufacture, branding and advertising can be used by the purchasers of the business. There is also a certain class of good-will attaching to the personality of the owner of goods, independent of the quality of his supplies. This goodwill frequently, and quite naturally, disappears when the business changes hands and the personality holding the public's goodwill retires from the scene. Another class of goodwill depends upon position of the place of business. A hotel company may, for example, possess a valuable goodwill from the fact that its property adjoins a railway station. The diverting of the railway or the closure of the hotel lease, causing removal to another site, destroys the goodwill or lessens its value. As distinct from the goodwill attaching to goods, the other two classes will be referred to below as personal goodwill and local goodwill respectively.

Valuation of Goodwill.

It must first be ascertained whether the asset good-will, though an intangible one, is likely to pass to the purchasing company without serious deterioration in value from causes beyond the power of the purchasing board. In order to determine this point the directors must ask themselves the following questions—

(*a*) Is the goodwill dependent upon a patented article, the term of which is practically expired ?

(*b*) Is it dependent upon a craze or caprice of the public which is likely to die out or become unfashionable ?

(*c*) Does it owe its value to a commodity which does not completely fulfil the public requirements, and is it likely to be superseded by improved processes and inventions ?

(*d*) If the goodwill is dependent on personal factors, will the purchasing company be in a position to retain the personal services concerned ?

(*e*) If it relies upon locality and position, can the premises be purchased, or will a favourable lease be transferred ?

According to whether these matters are favourable or not, a valuation based on a number of years' purchase will be fixed. The purchase price usually varies from two to seven years' purchase calculated by multiplying average normal past profits by the agreed number of years.

Average Normal Past Profits.

Average normal past profits are arrived at by ranging in comparative form as many of the profit and loss accounts of the business to be acquired as possible. An investigation—and sometimes an audit —is then carried out with a view to ascertaining the policy adopted in the compilation of the accounts, and the methods followed in the disposition of reserves, creation of funds, depreciation of assets, and securing economy in administration. The profits are then adjusted on the lines adopted for prospectus purposes, i.e. non-recurring charges and profits are eliminated, excessive depreciation is written back, allowances are made for secret reserves, and profits arising from such abnormal circumstances as war contracts are excluded.

When the profit and loss accounts have been re-cast, an average is ascertained and the negotiators agree upon a number by which this average is to be multiplied. It must be remembered that the purchasing of goodwill depletes cash and raises an intangible asset, which becomes worthless if the fortunes of the purchased company do not turn out as satisfactorily as the vendors foretell. The directors should therefore exercise more care in the purchase of this asset than they would in the case of a tangible one. They should be particularly careful in the examination of a proposal to include in goodwill, at an extra price, the benefits of doubtful or new contracts, concessions, or agencies.

It frequently happens that items of this nature account for the whole of the Goodwill, particularly if the purchased company has no past profits upon which to base the asset. This burden upon companies was one frequently encountered during the immediate post-war years and again in the " mad-finance " period of 1928–29. The tendency to pay away cash for concessions, rights, foreign rights, and untried patents upon the slightest representations of the vendors springs up regularly in every boom period. In this connection we may mention the Stock Exchange Rules which are designed to counteract this abuse.

Stock Exchange Rules.

Following on the 1929–30 share market crisis, a special Stock Exchange Committee was appointed to consider what alterations were necessary to the Stock

Exchange Regulations. In its report the Committee dealt with the necessity for " *keeping the shares of immature companies off the market and thus protecting the public from investing their money in concerns which have not at that date the right to command support.*"

In Appendix III to their Report the Special Committee pointed out that—

1. The Committee will, in general, be disinclined to grant permission to deal in the shares of a subsidiary company until after the publication of the first annual report of the parent company, and the fact that the principal asset is a patent, new process, or invention or undeveloped commercial enterprise will weigh largely with the Committee in considering its decision.

2. Where the estimated or actual preliminary expenses, including stamp duties, underwriting, and fees to promoters or others for services rendered form an undue percentage of the capital it is proposed to raise, the Committee will defer consideration of an application for permission to deal until after the publication of the first annual report and accounts.

Payment for Goodwill Otherwise than in Cash.

Unless the circumstances prevent, it is always advisable for directors to stipulate that the purchase price for goodwill, and indeed for as many of the other assets as possible, shall be taken in a form other than cash. If a complete purchase and liquidation of the vendor company is contemplated, then shares in the parent company should be offered to the liquidator. If a liquidation is not to take place, but the subsidiary is to continue, the vendors should be left with shares in the subsidiary company at least to the amount of the intangible assets. This arrangement will not, of course, give the parent company complete control of the subsidiary, and may be a less preferable course than the first alternative. The willingness of vendors to take their consideration in a form other than cash is usually regarded by the public as a measure of the vendors' confidence in the prospects of the business they have sold. The taking of the purchase price wholly in cash may usually be interpreted to indicate less confidence in the property sold than the acceptance of shares. The public cannot be expected to display greater confidence in the assets than that exhibited by vendors who desire to part with them once and for all.

The Ascertainment of Liabilities.

The ascertainment of liabilities is equally important in the case in which the vendor company pays off the creditors as when the transferee assumes the obligation. If the purchasing company assumes the liabilities the assets price must be reduced by the amount of the obligations to be taken over. The method of taking over liabilities is perhaps the more convenient, for the process is a gradual one and less likely to interfere with the future trading. Under the alternative method, in which the vendor pays his own creditors, great care has to be exercised by the purchaser to see that invoices received after the date fixed for purchase do not relate to stock included in the purchase price. This entails considerable detailed stock-keeping and accounting work until the absorption is complete.

In a purchase from a partnership or sole trader provision should be made for guaranteeing the purchasers against undisclosed liabilities. In the case of purchase from a company, arrangements should be made with the liquidator to hold up distribution of funds in his hands until contingencies are remote. These precautions are hardly necessary if the liabilities remain with the vendors, but even then safeguards should be introduced to ensure that they, the vendors, comply with their undertaking.

The Future of the Purchased Business.

The valuation of the assets, including goodwill, and the ascertainment of liabilities provide the directors with the information necessary to decide upon a price, but the future of the purchased business will be the factor governing the execution or the rejection of the contract of sale. The points previously dealt with, such as retention of goodwill dependent upon personality of officers, must be fully weighed. Agreements for service with such officers should be arranged simultaneously with the main contract.

It may happen that the type of product of either the purchased company or the parent company is of a higher grade than that made by the other company. The amalgamation of two such companies has been known to have most serious effects on the trade of the company which had the better class connection before the purchase. This was due to an unfounded fear on the part of the wholesale and retail houses that the inferior goods would be foisted upon them by the controlling company.

It is not possible to formulate exact rules upon this particular portion of the work of valuation. Needless to say, it is a matter in which the ordinary business acumen of directors is called into play. They alone know the general state of trade in their particular business and—more important still—they only are aware of the prospects awaiting such ventures as the absorption of subsidiaries or extension of the parent company's field.

APPENDIX

IMPORTANT SECTIONS OF THE COMPANIES ACT, 1929

REGISTRATION AND FILING OF PROSPECTUSES.

Sec. 34.—(1) A prospectus issued by or on behalf of a company or in relation to an intended company shall be dated, and that date shall, unless the contrary is proved, be taken as the date of publication of the prospectus

(2) A copy of every such prospectus, signed by every person who is named therein as a director or proposed director of the company, or by his agent authorized in writing, shall be delivered to the registrar of companies for registration on or before the date of its publication, and no such prospectus shall be issued until a copy thereof has been so delivered for registration.

(3) The registrar shall not register any prospectus unless it is dated, and the copy thereof signed, in manner required by this section.

(4) Every prospectus shall state on the face of it that a copy has been delivered for registration as required by this section.

(5) If a prospectus is issued without a copy thereof being so delivered, the company, and every person who is knowingly a party to the issue of the prospectus, shall be liable to a fine not exceeding five pounds for every day from the date of the issue of the prospectus until a copy thereof is so delivered.

RESPONSIBILITY OF DIRECTORS AS TO INFORMATION IN PROSPECTUSES.

Sec. 35.—(1) Every prospectus issued by or on behalf of a company, or by or on behalf of any person who is or has been engaged or interested in the formation of the company, must state the matters specified in Part I of the Fourth Schedule to this Act, and set out the reports specified in Part II of that Schedule, and the said Parts I and II shall have effect subject to the provisions contained in Part III of the said Schedule.

(2) A condition requiring or binding an applicant for shares in or debentures of a company to waive compliance with any requirement of this section, or purporting to affect him with notice of any contract, document, or matter not specifically referred to in the prospectus, shall be void.

(3) It shall not be lawful to issue any form of application for shares in or debentures of a company unless the form is issued with a prospectus which complies with the requirements of this section:

Provided that this subsection shall not apply if it is shown that the form of application was issued either—

(a) in connection with a *bona fide* invitation to a person to enter into an underwriting agreement with respect to the shares or debentures; or

(b) in relation to shares or debentures which were not offered to the public.

If any person acts in contravention of the provisions of this sub-section, he shall be liable to a fine not exceeding five hundred pounds.

(4) In the event of non-compliance with or contravention of any of the requirements of this section, a director or other person responsible for the prospectus shall not incur any liability by reason of the non-compliance or contravention, if—

(a) as regards any matter not disclosed, he proves that he was not cognisant thereof; or

(b) he proves that the non-compliance or contravention arose from an honest mistake of fact on his part; or

(c) the non-compliance or contravention was in respect of matters which in the opinion of the court dealing with the case were immaterial or was otherwise such as ought, in the opinion of that court, having regard to all the circumstances of the case, reasonably to be excused:

Provided that, in the event of failure to include in a prospectus a statement with respect to the matter specified in paragraph 15 of Part I of the Fourth Schedule to this Act, no director or other person shall incur any liability in respect of the failure unless it be proved that he had knowledge of the matters not disclosed.

(5) This section shall not apply to the issue to existing members or debenture holders of a company of a prospectus or form of application relating to shares in or debentures of the company, whether an applicant for shares or debentures will or will not have the right to renounce in favour of other persons, but subject as aforesaid, this section shall apply to a prospectus or a form of application whether issued on or with reference to the formation of a company or subsequently.

(6) Nothing in this section shall limit or diminish any liability which any person may incur under the general law or this Act apart from this section.

DIRECTORS AND MISREPRESENTATION IN PROSPECTUSES.

Sec. 37.—(1) Where a prospectus invites persons to subscribe for shares in or debentures of a company—

(a) every person who is a director of the company at the time of the issue of the prospectus; and

(b) every person who has authorized himself to be named and is named in the prospectus as a director or as having agreed to become a director either immediately or after an interval of time; and

(c) every person being a promoter of the company; and

(d) every person who has authorized the issue of the prospectus, shall be liable to pay compensation to all persons who subscribe for any shares or debentures on the faith of the prospectus for the loss or damage they may have sustained by reason of any untrue statement therein, or in any report or memorandum appearing on the face thereof, or by reference incorporated therein or issued therewith, unless it is proved—

(i) that having consented to become a director of the company he withdrew his consent before the issue of the prospectus, and that it was issued without his authority or consent; or

(ii) that the prospectus was issued without his knowledge or consent, and that on becoming aware of its issue he forthwith gave reasonable public notice that it was issued without his knowledge or consent; or

(iii) that after the issue of the prospectus and before allotment thereunder, he, on becoming aware of any untrue statement therein, withdrew his consent thereto, and gave reasonable public notice of the withdrawal, and of the reason therefor; or

(iv) that—

(a) as regards every untrue statement not purporting to be made on the authority of an expert or of a public official document or statement, he had reasonable ground to believe, and did up to the time of the allotment of the shares or debentures, as the case may be, believe, that the statement was true; and

(b) as regards every untrue statement purporting to be a statement by an expert or contained in what purports to be a copy of or extract from a report or valuation of an expert, it fairly represented the statement, or was a correct and fair copy of or extract from the report or valuation; and

(c) as regards every untrue statement purporting to be a statement made by an official person or contained in what purports to be a copy of or extract from a public official document, it was a correct and fair representation of the statement or copy of or extract from the document:

Provided that a person shall be liable to pay compensation as aforesaid if it is proved that he had no reasonable ground to believe that the person making any such statement, report or valuation as is mentioned in paragraph (iv) (b) of this subsection was competent to make it.

(2) Where the prospectus contains the name of a person as a director of the company, or as having agreed to become a director thereof, and he has not consented to become a director, or has withdrawn his consent before the issue of the prospectus, and has not authorized or consented to the issue thereof, the directors of the company, except any without whose knowledge or consent the prospectus was issued, and any other person who authorized the issue thereof, shall be liable to indemnify the person named as aforesaid against all damages, costs, and expenses to which he may be made liable by reason of his name having been inserted in the prospectus, or in defending himself against any action or legal proceedings brought against him in respect thereof.

(3) Every person who, by reason of his being a director or named as a director or as having agreed to become a director, or of his having authorized the issue of the prospectus, becomes liable to make any payment under this section may recover contribution, as in cases of contract, from any other person who, if sued separately, would have been liable to make the same payment, unless the person who has become so liable was, and that other person was not, guilty of fraudulent misrepresentation.

(4) For the purposes of this section—

The expression "promoter" means a promoter who was a party to the preparation of the prospectus, or of the portion thereof containing the untrue statement, but does not include any person by reason of his acting in a professional capacity for persons engaged in procuring the formation of the company:

The expression "expert" includes engineer, valuer, accountant, and any other person whose profession gives authority to a statement made by him.

Directors and Payment of Interest Out of Capital.

Sec. 54.—(1) Where any shares of a company are issued for the purpose of raising money to defray the expenses of the construction of any works or buildings or the provision of any plant which cannot be made profitable for a lengthened period, the company may pay interest on so much of that share capital as is for the time being paid up for the period and subject to the conditions and restrictions in this section mentioned, and may charge the sum so paid by way of interest to capital as part of the cost of construction of the work or building, or the provision of plant :
Provided that—

(a) No such payment shall be made unless it is authorized by the articles or by special resolution :

(b) No such payment, whether authorized by the articles or by special resolution, shall be made without the previous sanction of the Board of Trade :

(c) Before sanctioning any such payment the Board of Trade may, at the expense of the company, appoint a person to inquire and report to them as to the circumstances of the case, and may, before making the appointment, require the company to give security for the payment of the costs of the inquiry :

(d) The payment shall be made only for such period as may be determined by the Board of Trade, and that period shall in no case extend beyond the close of the half year next after the half year during which the works or buildings have been actually completed or the plant provided :

(e) The rate of interest shall in no case exceed four per cent per annum or such other rate as may for the time being be prescribed by Order in Council :

(f) The payment of the interest shall not operate as a reduction of the amount paid up on the shares in respect of which it is paid :

(g) The accounts of the company shall show the share capital on which, and the rate at which, interest has been paid out of capital during the period to which the accounts relate :

(h) Nothing in this section shall affect any company to which the Indian Railways Act, 1894, as amended by any subsequent enactment, applies.

(2) If default is made in complying with proviso (g) to subsection (1) of this section, the company and every officer of the company who is in default shall be liable to a fine not exceeding fifty pounds.

Companies Must File an Annual Return.

Sec. 108.—(1) Every company having a share capital shall once at least in every year make a return containing a list of all persons who, on the fourteenth day after the first or only ordinary general meeting in the year, are members of the company, and of all persons who have ceased to be members since the date of the last return or in the case of the first return, of the incorporation of the company.

(2) The list must state the names, addresses, and occupations of

all the past and present members therein mentioned, and the number of shares held by each of the existing members at the date of the return, specifying shares transferred since the date of the last return or, in the case of the first return, of the incorporation of the company by persons who are still members and have ceased to be members respectively and the dates of registration of the transfers, and, if the names therein are not arranged in alphabetical order, must have annexed to it an index sufficient to enable the name of any person in the list to be readily found:

Provided that, where the company has converted any of its shares into stock and given notice of the conversion to the registrar of companies, the list must state the amount of stock held by each of the existing members instead of the amount of shares and the particulars relating to shares hereinbefore required.

(3) The return must also state the address of the registered office of the company and must contain a summary distinguishing between shares issued for cash and shares issued as fully or partly paid up otherwise than in cash, and specifying the following particulars—

(a) The amount of the share capital of the company, and the number of the shares into which it is divided;

(b) The number of shares taken from the commencement of the company up to the date of the return;

(c) The amount called up on each share;

(d) The total amount of calls received;

(e) The total amount of calls unpaid;

(f) The total amount of the sums, if any, paid by way of commission in respect of any shares or debentures;

(g) Particulars of the discount allowed on the issue of any shares issued at a discount, or of so much of that discount as has not been written off at the date on which the return is made;

(h) The total amount of the sums, if any, allowed by way of discount in respect of any debentures, since the date of the last return;

(i) The total number of shares forfeited;

(k) The total amount of shares for which share warrants are outstanding at the date of the return;

(l) The total amount of share warrants issued and surrendered respectively since the date of the last return;

(m) The number of shares comprised in each share warrant;

(n) All such particulars with respect to the persons who at the date of the return are the directors of the company as are by this Act required to be contained with respect to directors in the register of the directors of a company;

(o) The total amount of indebtedness of the company in respect of all mortgages and charges which are required (or, in the case of a company registered in Scotland which, if the company had been registered in England, would be required) to be registered with the registrar of companies under this Act, or which would have been required so to be registered if created after the first day of July nineteen hundred and eight.

(4) The return shall be in accordance with the form set out in the Sixth Schedule to this Act, or as near thereto as circumstances admit.

(5) In the case of a company keeping a Dominion register, the particulars of the entries in that register shall, so far as they relate to matters which are required to be stated in the return, be included in the return made next after copies of those entries are received at the registered office of the company.

Sec. 109.—(1) Every company not having a share capital shall once at least in every calendar year make a return stating—

(a) the address of the registered office of the company;

(b) all such particulars with respect of the persons who at the date of the return are the directors of the company as are by this Act required to be contained with respect to directors in the register of directors of a company.

(2) There shall be annexed to the return a statement containing particulars of the total amount of the indebtedness of the company in respect of all mortgages and charges which are required (or, in the case of a company registered in Scotland, which, if the company had been registered in England, would be required) to be registered with the registrar of companies under this Act, or which would have been required so to be registered if created after the first day of July, nineteen hundred and eight.

Sec. 110.—(1) The annual return must be contained in a separate part of the register of members, and must be completed within twenty-eight days after the first or only general meeting in the year, and the company must forthwith forward to the registrar of companies a copy signed by a director or by the manager or by the secretary of the company.

(2) Section ninety-eight of this Act shall apply to the annual return as it applies to the register of members.

(3) Except where the company is a private company, or is an assurance company which has complied with the provisions of sub-section (4) of section seven of the Assurance Companies Act, 1909, the annual return shall include a written copy, certified by a director or the manager or secretary of the company to be a true copy, of the last balance sheet which has been audited by the company's auditors, including every document required by law to be annexed thereto, together with a copy of the report of the auditors thereon certified as aforesaid, and if any such balance sheet is in a foreign language there shall also be annexed to it a translation thereof in English, certified in the prescribed manner to be a correct translation:

Provided that, if the said balance sheet did not comply with the requirements of the law as in force at the date of the audit with respect to the form of balance sheets there shall be made such additions to and corrections in the said copy as would have been required to be made in the said balance sheet in order to make it comply with the said requirements and the fact that the said copy has been so amended shall be stated thereon.

(4) If a company fails to comply with this section or either of the two last foregoing sections of this Act the company and every officer of the company who is in default shall be liable to a default fine.

(5) For the purposes of subsection (4) of this section the expression " officer," and for the purposes of the two last foregoing sections of this Act the expression " director," shall include any person in accordance with whose directions or instructions the directors of the company are accustomed to act.

DIRECTOR'S CONSENT TO ACT.

Sec. 140.—(1) A person shall not be capable of being appointed director of a company by the articles, and shall not be named as a director or proposed director of a company in a prospectus issued by or on behalf of the company, or as proposed director of an intended company in a prospectus issued in relation to that intended company, or in a statement in lieu of prospectus delivered to the registrar by or on behalf of a company, unless, before the registration of the articles or the publication of the prospectus, or the delivery of the statement in lieu of prospectus, as the case may be, he has by himself or by his agent authorized in writing—

(a) signed and delivered to the registrar of companies for registration a consent in writing to act as such director; and

(b) either—

(i) signed the memorandum for a number of shares not less than his qualification, if any; or

(ii) taken from the company and paid or agreed to pay for his qualification shares, if any; or

(iii) signed and delivered to the registrar for registration an undertaking in writing to take from the company and pay for his qualification shares, if any; or

(iv) made and delivered to the registrar for registration a statutory declaration to the effect that a number of shares, not less than his qualification, if any, are registered in his name.

(2) Where a person has signed and delivered as aforesaid an undertaking to take and pay for his qualification shares, he shall, as regards those shares, be in the same position as if he had signed the memorandum for that number of shares.

(3) On the application for registration of the memorandum and articles of a company the applicant shall deliver to the registrar a list of the persons who have consented to be directors of the company, and, if this list contains the name of any person who has not so consented, the applicant shall be liable to a fine not exceeding fifty pounds.

(4) This section shall not apply to—

(a) A company not having a share capital; or

(b) a private company; or

(c) a company which was a private company before becoming a public company; or

(d) a prospectus issued by or on behalf of a company after the expiration of one year from the date on which the company was entitled to commence business.

Sec. 141.—(1) Without prejudice to the restrictions imposed by the last foregoing section, it shall be the duty of every director who is by the articles of the company required to hold a specified share qualification, and who is not already qualified, to obtain his qualification within two months after his appointment, or such shorter time as may be fixed by the articles.

(2) For the purpose of any provision in the articles requiring a director or manager to hold a specified share qualification, the bearer of a share warrant shall not be deemed to be the holder of the shares specified in the warrant.

(3) The office of director of a company shall be vacated if the

director does not within two months from the date of his appointment, or within such shorter time as may be fixed by the articles, obtain his qualification, or if after the expiration of the said period or shorter time he ceases at any time to hold his qualification.

(4) A person vacating office under this section shall be incapable of being re-appointed director of the company until he has obtained his qualification.

(5) If after the expiration of the said period or shorter time any unqualified person acts as a director of the company, he shall be liable to a fine not exceeding five pounds for every day between the expiration of the said period or shorter time or the day on which he ceased to be qualified, as the case may be, and the last day on which it is proved that he acted as a director.

Regulations as to Bankrupt Directors.

Sec. 142.—(1) If any person being an undischarged bankrupt acts as director of, or directly or indirectly takes part in or is concerned in the management of, any company except with the leave of the court by which he was adjudged bankrupt, he shall be liable on conviction on indictment to imprisonment for a term not exceeding two years, or on summary conviction to imprisonment for a term not exceeding six months or to a fine not exceeding five hundred pounds, or to both such imprisonment and fine:

Provided that a person shall not be guilty of an offence under this section by reason that he, being an undischarged bankrupt, has acted as director of, or taken part or been concerned in the management of, a company, if he was on the third day of August, nineteen hundred and twenty-eight, acting as director of, or taking part or being concerned in the management of, that company and has continuously so acted, taken part, or been concerned since that date and the bankruptcy was prior to that date.

(2) In England the leave of the court for the purposes of this section shall not be given unless notice of intention to apply therefor has been served on the official receiver and it shall be the duty of the official receiver, if he is of opinion that it is contrary to the public interest that any such application should be granted, to attend on the hearing of and oppose the granting of the application.

(3) In this section the expression " company " includes an unregistered company and a company incorporated outside Great Britain which has an established place of business within Great Britain, and the expression " official receiver " means the official receiver in bankruptcy.

(4) Subsection (1) of this section in its application to Scotland shall have effect as if the words " sequestration of his estates was awarded " were substituted for the words " he was adjudged bankrupt."

Transfers of Assets to Another Company.

Sec. 234.—(1) Where a company is proposed to be, or is in course of being, wound up altogether voluntarily, and the whole or part of its business or property is proposed to be transferred or sold to another company, whether a company within the meaning of this Act or not (in this section called " the transferee company ") the liquidator of the first-mentioned company (in this section called " the transferor company ") may, with the sanction of a special resolution of that company, conferring either a general authority on the liquidator or an authority in respect of any particular arrangement, receive in compensation or part compensation for the transfer or sale, shares, policies, or other like interests in the transferee company, for distribution among the members of the transferor company, or may enter into any other arrangement whereby the members of the transferor company may, in lieu of receiving cash, shares, policies, or other like interests, or in addition thereto, participate in the profits of or receive any other benefit from the transferee company.

(2) Any sale or arrangement in pursuance of this section shall be binding on the members of the transferor company.

(3) If any member of the transferor company who did not vote in favour of the special resolution expresses his dissent therefrom in writing addressed to the liquidator, and left at the registered office of the company within seven days after the passing of the resolution, he may require the liquidator either to abstain from carrying the resolution into effect, or to purchase his interest at a price to be determined by agreement or by arbitration in manner provided by this section.

(4) If the liquidator elects to purchase the member's interest, the purchase money must be paid before the company is dissolved, and be raised by the liquidator in such manner as may be determined by special resolution.

(5) A special resolution shall not be invalid for the purposes of this section by reason that it is passed before or concurrently with a resolution for voluntary winding up or for appointing liquidators, but, if an order is made within a year for winding up the company by or subject to the supervision of the court, the special resolution shall not be valid unless sanctioned by the court.

(6) For the purposes of an arbitration under this section, the provisions of the Companies Clauses Consolidation Act, 1845, or, in the case of a winding-up in Scotland, the Companies Clauses Consolidation (Scotland) Act, 1845, with respect to the settlement of disputes by arbitration, shall be incorporated with this Act, and in the construction of those provisions this Act shall be deemed to be the special Act, and " the company " shall mean the transferor company, and any appointment by the said incorporated provisions directed to be made under the hand of the secretary, or any two of the directors, may be made under the hand of the liquidator, or, if there is more than one liquidator, then of any two or more of the liquidators.

Directors and Misfeasance.

Sec. 277.—(1) If it appears to the court in the course of a winding up by, or subject to the supervision of, the court that any past or present director, manager or other officer, or any member, of the company has been guilty of any offence in relation to the company for which he is criminally liable, the court may, either on the application of any person interested in the winding up or of its own motion, direct the liquidator—

(a) in the case of a winding up in England either himself to prosecute the offender or to refer the matter to the Director of Public Prosecutions ;

(b) in the case of a winding up in Scotland to refer the matter to the Lord Advocate.

(2) If it appears to the liquidator in the course of a voluntary winding up that any past or present director, manager or other officer, or any member, of the company has been guilty of any offence in relation to the company for which he is criminally liable, he shall forthwith report the matter, in the case of a winding up in England, to the Director of Public Prosecutions, and, in the case of a winding up in Scotland, to the Lord Advocate, and shall furnish to the Director or Lord Advocate, as the case may be, such information and give to him such access to and facilities for inspecting and taking copies of any documents, being information or documents in the possession or under the control of the liquidator and relating to the matter in question, as they respectively may require.

(3) Where any report is made under the last foregoing subsection to the Director of Public Prosecutions or Lord Advocate, he may, if he thinks fit, refer the matter to the Board of Trade for further inquiry, and the Board shall thereupon investigate the matter and may if they think it expedient, apply to the court for an order conferring on the Board or any person designated by the Board for the purpose with respect to the company concerned all such powers of investigating the affairs of the company as are provided by this Act in the case of a winding up by the court.

(4) If on any report to the Director of Public Prosecutions under subsection (2) of this section it appears to him that the case is not one in which proceedings ought to be taken by him, he shall inform the liquidator accordingly, and thereupon, subject to the previous sanction of the court, the liquidator may himself take proceedings against the offender.

(5) If it appears to the court in the course of a voluntary winding up that any past or present director, manager or other officer, or any member, of the company has been guilty as aforesaid, and that no report with respect to the matter has been made by the liquidator to the Director of Public Prosecutions or the Lord Advocate under subsection (2) of this section, the court may, on the application of any person interested in the winding up or of its own motion, direct the liquidator to make such a report, and on a report being made accordingly the provisions of this section shall have effect as though the report had been made in pursuance of the provisions of subsection (2) of this section.

(6) If, where any matter is reported or referred to the Director of Public Prosecutions or Lord Advocate under this section, he considers that the case is one in which a prosecution ought to be instituted and, further, that it is desirable in the public interest that the proceedings in the prosecution should be conducted by him, he shall institute proceedings accordingly, and it shall be the duty of the liquidator and of every officer and agent of the company past and present (other than the defendant in the proceedings) to give him all assistance in connection with the prosecution which he is reasonably able to give.

For the purposes of this subsection, the expression " agent " in relation to a company shall be deemed to include any banker or solicitor of the company and any person employed by the company as auditor, whether that person is or is not an officer of the company.

(7) If any person fails or neglects to give assistance in manner required by subsection (6) of this section, the court may, on the application of the Director of Public Prosecutions or Lord Advocate, as the case may be, direct that person to comply with the requirements of the said subsection, and where any such application is made with respect to a liquidator the court may, unless it appears that the failure or neglect to comply was due to the liquidator not having in his hands sufficient assets of the company to enable him so to do, direct that the costs of the application shall be borne by the liquidator personally.

(8) The Board of Trade, with the consent of the Treasury, may direct that the whole or any part of any costs and expenses properly incurred by the liquidator in proceedings duly brought by him under this section shall be defrayed as expenses incurred by the Board under this Act in relation to the winding up of companies in England and subsection (3) of section thirteen of the Economy (Miscellaneous Provisions) Act, 1926, shall apply accordingly.

Subject to any direction under this subsection and to any mortgages or charges on the assets of the company and any debts to which priority is given by section two hundred and sixty-four of this Act, all such costs and expenses as aforesaid shall be payable out of those assets in priority to all other liabilities payable thereout.

INTERPRETATION OF TERMS.

Sec. 380.—(1) In this Act, unless the context otherwise requires, the following expressions have the meanings hereby assigned to them (that is to say)—

" Annual return " means the return required to be made, in the case of a company having a share capital, under section one hundred and eight, and, in the case of a company not having a share capital, under section one hundred and nine, of this Act;

" Articles " means the articles of association of a company, as originally framed or as altered by special resolution, including, so far as they apply to the company, the regulations contained (as the case may be) in Table B in the Schedule annexed to the Joint Stock Companies Act, 1856, or in Table A in the First Schedule annexed to the Companies Act, 1862, or in that Table as altered in pursuance of section seventy-one of the last-mentioned Act, or in Table A in the First Schedule to the Companies (Consolidation) Act, 1908, or in that Table as altered in pursuance of section one hundred and eighteen of the last mentioned Act, or in Table A in the First Schedule to this Act;

" Book and paper " and " book or paper " include accounts, deeds, writings, and documents;

" Company " means a company formed and registered under this Act or an existing company;

" Existing company " means a company formed and registered under the Joint Stock Companies Acts, the Companies Act, 1862, or the Companies (Consolidation) Act, 1908, but does not include a company registered under the said enactments in Northern Ireland or the Irish Free State;

" Company within the stannaries " means a company engaged in or formed for working mines within the stannaries;

" The court " used in relation to a company means the court having jurisdiction to wind up the company;

" The court exercising the stannaries jurisdiction " used in relation to any proceedings means the county court in which the jurisdiction formerly exercised by the court of the vice-warden of the stannaries in respect of those proceedings is for the time being vested;

" Debenture " includes debenture stock, bonds and any other securities of a company whether constituting a charge on the assets of the company or not;

" Director " includes any person occupying the position of director by whatever name called;

" Document " includes summons, notice, order, and other legal process, and registers;

" The Gazette " means, as respects companies registered in England, the *London Gazette*, and as respects companies registered in Scotland, the *Edinburgh Gazette* ;

" General rules " means general rules made under section three hundred and five of this Act, and includes forms;

" Joint Stock Companies Acts " means the Joint Stock Companies Act, 1856, the Joint Stock Companies Acts, 1856, 1857, the Joint Stock Banking Companies Act, 1857, and the Act to enable Joint Stock Banking Companies to be formed on the principle of limited liability, or any one or more of those Acts, as the case may require; but does not include the Act passed in the eighth year of the reign of Her Majesty Queen Victoria, chapter one hundred and ten, intituled An Act for the Registration, Incorporation, and Regulation of Joint Stock Companies;

" Memorandum " means the memorandum of association of a company, as originally framed or as altered in pursuance of any enactment;

" Prescribed " means as respects the provisions of this Act relating to the winding up of companies, prescribed by general rules, and as respects the other provisions of this Act, prescribed by the Board of Trade;

" Prospectus " means any prospectus, notice, circular, advertisement, or other invitation, offering to the public for subscription or purchase any shares or debentures of a company;

" Real and personal," as respects Scotland, means heritable and moveable;

" The registrar of companies," or, when used in relation to registration of companies, " the registrar," means the registrar or other officer performing under this Act the duty of registration of companies in England or Scotland, or in the stannaries, as the case requires;

" Share " means share in the share capital of a company, and includes stock, except where a distinction between stock and shares is expressed or implied;

" Table A " means Table A in the First Schedule to this Act.

(2) A person shall not be deemed to be within the meaning of any provision in this Act a person in accordance with whose directions or instructions the directors of a company are accustomed to act, by reason only that the directors of the company act on advice given by him in a professional capacity.

INDEX

Fraud, common types of, 229
Frauds, bought ledger, 230
——, sales ledger, 230
——, "snowball," 229
——, wages, 231
"Frozen" position, 86, 87
Funds, nature of, 159
—— to meet liabilities, 159
—— to replace assets, 163

GENERAL manager, 40
Giants of finance, 5
Gift shares, 11, 15
Goodwill, 248
——, payment for, otherwise
than in cash, 251
*Greymouth Point Elizabeth and
Coal Co.*, 1904, 168
"Guinea-pig" director, vi, 3

HOLDEN, Sir Edward, 17

INCOME tax, 66, 105, 106
"Indemnification" clause illegal,
2
Inland Revenue, 105
Inter-subsidiary trading and
taxation, 193
Interest on advances to subsidi-
aries, 106
—— out of capital, 78
Internal audit, 29, 225
Investment companies, 40
Issuing houses, 3, 220

Johnson v. *Chestergate Hat Manufacturing Co.*, 67

*Kindersley V. C. New Brunswick
and Canada Rail Co.* v. *Muggeridge*, 1859, 213
Kingston Cotton Mills Co., 1896,
28

Lagunas Nitrate Co. v. *Lagunas
Syndicate*, 1899, 5
Leasehold redemption fund, 164
Leases, 57
Ledger, nominal, 139
——, purchase, 139
——, sales, 139
Liabilities, ascertainment of, 252
——, classification of, 84
——, treatment of, 148

"Liquid" position, 86
Loan redemption fund, 159
Local board, 233
—— companies, 233
—— Government Act, 1929,
195
—— manager, 233
Lopes, Mr. Justice, 28
Losses, concealment of, 158
—— of subsidiaries, 108, 150

MACHINERY, 58
Majority of shareholders, 26, 27
Management committees, 38
Managers, remuneration of local,
236
——, returns of, 237
Managing director, 37
Manufacturing account, 62
Material, 120, 122
——, contracts for, 122, 123
Meeting, board, 166, 167
——, extraordinary, 170
——, ordinary general, 171
——, statutory, 169
Memorandum of association, 36
Methods of financing subsidi-
aries, 102
Minimum subscription, 207
Minority's interest, 26, 27
Minutes, 34
—— and absent director, 35
——, directors', 168
——, draft copies of, 35
——, filing of, 36
Misrepresentation, 212
Monopoly commodities, 134
Multiple directorships, 8

Newton v. *B.S.A., Ltd.*, 31
Nominal ledger, 139
Normandy & Co. v. *Ind, Coope
& Co.*, 1908, 173
Notice of meeting, 173, 174

OBSOLESCENCE, 57
Offers for sale, 220
Officers, election of, 182
"Official Intelligence," 9
Oncost, 120, 122, 124
One-man control, 8
Orders, outstanding, 135
——, shortage of, 113, 114
——, treatment of, 20, 21

PRINTED IN GREAT BRITAIN AT THE PITMAN PRESS, BATH
C1—(1641)

PITMAN'S
BUSINESS HANDBOOKS

*An Abridged List of Practical Guides for
Business Men and Advanced Students*

The Prices contained in this book apply only to Great Britain

Complete List of Commercial Books Post Free on Application

BOOK-KEEPING AND ACCOUNTS

ADVANCED ACCOUNTS. Edited by ROGER N. CARTER, M.Com., F.C.A.
In demy 8vo, cloth 1058 pp. **7s. 6d.** net.
KEY. By R. A. GOODMAN. In demy 8vo, cloth, 924 pp. **20s.** Second
Edition.

THE PRINCIPLES OF AUDITING. By F. R. M. DE PAULA, O.B.E., F.C.A.
Fifth Edition. In demy 8vo, cloth gilt, 242 pp. **7s. 6d.** net.

PRACTICAL AUDITING. By E. E. SPICER, F.C.A., and E. C. PEGLER, F.C.A.
Fifth Edition. Size 10 in. by 6 in. Cloth gilt, 815 pp. **21s.** net.

AUDIT PROGRAMMES. By the same Authors. In demy 8vo, cloth gilt,
124 pp. **4s. 6d.** net. Eighth Edition.

SHARE TRANSFER AUDITS. By R. A. DAVIES, A.C.I.S. In crown 8vo,
cloth gilt, 96 pp. **3s. 6d.** net.

COST ACCOUNTING. By W. B. LAWRENCE, C.P.A., *Professor of Accounting,
De Paul University.* In demy 8vo, cloth gilt, 543 pp. **21s.** net.

STORES ACCOUNTS AND STORES CONTROL. By J. H. BURTON. In
demy 8vo, cloth gilt, 154 pp. **5s.** net. Second Edition.

CLUB ACCOUNTS. By C. A. HOLLIDAY, A.S.A.A. In demy 8vo, cloth, 80 pp.
3s. 6d. net.

RAILWAY ACCOUNTS. By C. H. NEWTON, F.A.A., *Chief Accountant,
London and North Eastern Railway.* In demy 8vo, cloth gilt, 256 pp.
10s. 6d. net.

COST ACCOUNTS IN PRINCIPLE AND PRACTICE. By A. CLIFFORD
RIDGWAY, F.C.A. In demy 8vo, cloth gilt, 120 pp. **5s.** net.

COST ACCOUNTS FOR THE METAL INDUSTRY. By H. E. PARKES,
M.Com., A.C.W.A. In demy 8vo, cloth gilt, 156 pp. **10s. 6d.** net.

C 1—4

DOCUMENTS OF COMMERCE. By F. A. WILLMAN, Cert. A.I.B. In demy 8vo, cloth gilt, 288 pp. **7s. 6d.** net.

COSTS FOR MANUFACTURERS. By C. SMITH. In demy 8vo, cloth gilt, 100 pp. **5s.** net.

PRIMER OF COSTING. By R. J. H. RYALL. In demy 8vo, cloth, 115 pp. **5s.** net.

DICTIONARY OF COSTING. By the same Author. In demy 8vo, cloth gilt, 390 pp. **10s. 6d.** net.

THEORY AND PRACTICE OF COSTING. By E. W. NEWMAN, F.C.A. In demy 8vo, cloth gilt, 203 pp. **8s. 6d.** net.

COSTING AND PRICE-FIXING. By J. M. SCOTT MAXWELL, B.Sc., F.C.W.A. In demy 8vo, cloth gilt, 223 pp. **6s.** net. Second Edition.

ESTIMATING. By T. H. HARGRAVE. Second Edition. In demy 8vo, cloth gilt, 128 pp. **7s. 6d.** net.

COSTING ORGANIZATION FOR ENGINEERS. By E. W. WORKMAN, B.Sc., A.M.I.E.E., A.L.A.A., A.C.W.A. Second Edition. In demy 8vo, cloth, 96 pp. **3s. 6d.** net.

MANUAL OF COST ACCOUNTS. By JULIUS LUNT, F.C.A. (Hons.), F.C.I.S., F.C.W.A. Fifth Edition. In demy 8vo, cloth gilt, 238 pp. **7s. 6d.** net.

MANUFACTURING BOOK-KEEPING AND COSTS. By GEORGE JOHNSON, F.C.I.S. In demy 8vo, cloth gilt, 120 pp. **3s. 6d.** net.

COMPANY ACCOUNTS. By ARTHUR COLES. Fourth Edition. Revised by W. CECIL WOOD, A.C.I.S. In demy 8vo. cloth gilt, 408 pp. **7s. 6d.** net.

HOLDING COMPANIES. By A. J. SIMONS, A.C.A. (Hons.). In demy 8vo, cloth gilt, 198 pp. **10s. 6d.** net.

DICTIONARY OF BOOK-KEEPING. By R. J. PORTERS, F.C.R.A. Second Edition. In demy 8vo, 780 pp. **7s. 6d.** net.

THE BOOK-KEEPER'S VADE MECUM. By S. HOWARD WITHEY, F.C.I., A.L.A.A. In crown 8vo, 150 pp. **3s. 6d.** net.

INVESTIGATIONS: ACCOUNTANCY AND FINANCIAL. By J. H. BURTON. In demy 8vo, cloth, 172 pp. **5s.** net.

SECRETARIAL BOOK-KEEPING AND ACCOUNTS. By H. E. COLESWORTHY, A.S.A.A. In demy 8vo, cloth gilt, 364 pp. **7s. 6d.** net.

THE ACCOUNTANT'S DICTIONARY. Edited by F. W. PIXLEY, F.C.A., *Barrister-at-Law*. Third Edition. In two vols., crown 4to, half leather, 1100 pp. **£3 7s. 6d.** net.

BOOK-KEEPING AND ACCOUNTS. By E. E. SPICER, F.C.A., and E. C. PEGLER, F.C.A. Eighth Edition. In crown 4to, cloth gilt, 507 pp. **20s.** net.

EXECUTORSHIP ACCOUNTS. By C. TOWNSEND, *Incorporated Accountant*. In demy 8vo, cloth, 116 pp. **5s.** net.

THE ACCOUNTS OF EXECUTORS, ADMINISTRATORS, AND TRUSTEES. By WILLIAM B. PHILLIPS, F.C.A., A.C.I.S. Sixth Edition. In demy 8vo, cloth gilt, 176 pp. **5s.** net.

APPORTIONMENT IN RELATION TO TRUST ACCOUNTS. By ALAN F. CHICK, *Incorporated Accountant*. In demy 8vo, cloth, 160 pp. **6s.** net.

BUSINESS BALANCE SHEETS. By F. R. STEAD. In demy 8vo, cloth gilt, 160 pp. **10s. 6d.** net.

BALANCE SHEETS. HOW TO READ AND UNDERSTAND THEM. By PHILIP TOVEY, F.C.I.S. In demy 8vo, cloth, 110 pp. **3s. 6d.** net. Third Edition.

MODERN METHODS OF BOOK-KEEPING. By R. H. EPPS, *Chartered Accountant*. In demy 8vo, cloth, 343 pp. **4s.** net.

A COURSE IN BOOK-KEEPING. By R. W. HOLLAND, O.B.E., M.A., M.Sc., LL.D. In demy 8vo, cloth, 290 pp. **4s.** net.

DEPRECIATION AND WASTING ASSETS, and Their Treatment in Computing Annual Profit and Loss. By P. D. LEAKE, F.C.A. Fourth Edition. In demy 8vo, cloth gilt, 257 pp. **15s.** net.

COMMERCIAL GOODWILL. Its History, Value, and Treatment in Accounts. By the same Author. Second Edition. In demy 8vo, cloth gilt, 284 pp. **15s.** net.

SINKING FUNDS, RESERVE FUNDS, AND DEPRECIATION. By J. H. BURTON, *Incorporated Accountant*. Second Edition. In demy 8vo, 140 pp. **3s. 6d.** net.

CONSIGNMENTS, ACCOUNT SALES, AND ACCOUNTS CURRENT. By E. J. HAMMOND. In demy 8vo, cloth, 160 pp. **5s.** net.

FOREIGN CURRENCIES IN ACCOUNTS. By A. E. HALLS. In demy 8vo, cloth, 156 pp. **5s.** net.

CURRENCY ACCOUNTS IN STERLING BOOKS. By C. RALPH CURTIS, *Chief Accountant of the British and Continental Banking Co., Ltd., Fellow of the Institute of Bankers*. In demy 8vo, cloth gilt, 120 pp. **5s.** net.

BRANCH ACCOUNTS. By P. TAGGART, A.S.A.A. In demy 8vo, 87 pp. **3s.** net.

BUILDERS' ACCOUNTS AND COSTS. By ROBERT G. LEGGE. In demy 8vo, cloth gilt, 130 pp. **3s. 6d.** net.

HOSPITAL ACCOUNTS AND FINANCIAL CONTROL. By J. E. STONE, *Incorporated Accountant*. In crown 4to, cloth gilt, 160 pp. **21s.** net.

COMMERCE

THE THEORY AND PRACTICE OF COMMERCE. Edited by F. HEELIS, F.C.I.S., assisted by Specialist Contributors. In demy 8vo, cloth gilt, 620 pp., with many facsimile forms. **7s. 6d.** net.

QUESTIONS AND ANSWERS ON BUSINESS PRACTICE. By E. J. HAMMOND. In demy 8vo, cloth, 140 pp. **5s.** net.

THE PRINCIPLES AND PRACTICE OF COMMERCE. By JAMES STEPHENSON, M.A., M.Com., D.Sc. In demy 8vo, cloth gilt, 650 pp., with many facsimile forms. **8s. 6d.** net.

THE PRINCIPLES AND PRACTICE OF COMMERCIAL CORRESPONDENCE. By the same Author. In demy 8vo, 308 pp. **7s. 6d.** net.

THE PRINCIPLES OF COMMERCIAL HISTORY. By James Stephenson, M.A., M.Com., D.Sc. In demy 8vo, 279 pp. **7s. 6d.** net.

THE PRINCIPLES AND-PRACTICE OF COMMERCIAL ARITHMETIC. By P. W. Norris, M.A., B.Sc. (Hons.). In demy 8vo, 452 pp. **7s. 6d.** net.

MODERN BUSINESS AND ITS METHODS. By W. Campbell, *Chartered Secretary.* In crown 8vo, cloth, 493 pp. **7s. 6d.** net.

THE PRINCIPLES OF BUSINESS. By C. W. Gerstenberg, Ph.B., J.D. Fourth Edition. Size 5½ in. by 8 in., cloth, 821 pp. **16s.** net.

WHOLESALE AND RETAIL TRADE. By William Campbell, *Chartered Secretary.* In demy 8vo, cloth gilt, 248 pp. **5s.** net.

THE BEDROCK OF MODERN BUSINESS. Edited by James Stephenson, M.A., M.Com., D.Sc. In medium 8vo, cloth gilt, 840 pp. **15s.** net.

INSURANCE

THE PRINCIPLES OF INSURANCE AND THEIR APPLICATION. By J. Alfred Eke. In demy 8vo, cloth, 186 pp. **5s.** net.

INSURANCE. By T. E. Young, B.A., F.I.A., F.R.A.S. Fourth Edition, Revised and Enlarged. In demy 8vo, cloth gilt, 460 pp. **10s. 6d.** net.

INSURANCE OFFICE ORGANIZATION AND ROUTINE. By J. B. Welson, LL.M., F.C.I.I., F.C.I.S., *of Gray's Inn, Barrister-at-Law,* and F. H. Sherriff, F.I.A. Second Edition. In demy 8vo, cloth gilt, 292 pp. **7s. 6d.** net.

INSURANCE PRINCIPLES AND PRACTICES. By R. Riegel and H. J. Loman. Size 6 in. by 9 in., cloth, 450 pp. **16s.** net.

THE PRINCIPLES OF COMPOUND INTEREST. By H. H. Edwards, F.I.A. In demy 8vo, cloth gilt, 135 pp. **5s.** net.

THE ELEMENTS OF ACTUARIAL SCIENCE. By R. E. Underwood, M.B.E., F.I.A. Second Edition. In crown 8vo, cloth, 164 pp. **5s.** net.

BUILDING CONSTRUCTION, PLAN DRAWING, AND SURVEYING IN RELATION TO FIRE INSURANCE. By D. W. Wood, M.B.E. In demy 8vo, cloth gilt, 164 pp. **6s.** net.

FIRE WASTE (LOSS OF PROPERTY BY FIRE). By G. E. Keay, F.C.I.I., F.R.S.A. In crown 8vo, cloth gilt, 60 pp. **2s. 6d.** net.

AVERAGE CLAUSES AND FIRE-LOSS APPORTIONMENTS. By E. H. Minnion, F.C.I.I. In demy 8vo, cloth gilt, 286 pp. **8s. 6d.** net.

THE PRINCIPLES AND PRACTICE OF FIRE INSURANCE. By Frank Godwin. Third Edition. In demy 8vo, cloth gilt, 150 pp. **5s.** net.

THE LAW OF FIRE INSURANCE. By John Rowlatt, B.A., *Barrister-at-Law.* In demy 8vo, cloth gilt, 208 pp. **7s. 6d.** net.

THE COMMON HAZARDS OF FIRE INSURANCE. By W. G. Kubler Ridley, F.C.I.I. Second Edition. In demy 8vo, cloth gilt, 92 pp. **5s.** net.

FIRE POLICY DRAFTING AND ENDORSEMENTS. By W. C. H. Darley. In demy 8vo, cloth gilt, 204 pp. **7s. 6d.** net.

FIRE EXTINGUISHMENT AND FIRE ALARM SYSTEMS. By R. Northwood. In demy 8vo, cloth gilt, 224 pp. **7s. 6d.** net.

DICTIONARY OF FIRE INSURANCE. Edited by B. C. Remington, F.C.I.I. In crown 4to, half-leather gilt, 480 pp. **30s.** net.

THE LAW AND PRACTICE AS TO FIDELITY GUARANTEES. By C. Evans, *Barrister-at-Law*, and F. H. Jones. Second Edition. In demy 8vo, cloth gilt, 167 pp. **6s.** net.

INSURANCE AS A CAREER. By F. H. Sherriff, F.I.A. In crown 8vo, cloth, 196 pp. **3s. 6d.** net.

INSURANCE OF PUBLIC LIABILITY RISKS. By S. V. Kirkpatrick, F.C.I.I. Second Edition. In demy 8vo, cloth gilt, 152 pp. **5s.** net.

BURGLARY RISKS. By E. H. Grout, B.Sc., A.C.I.I. In demy 8vo, cloth gilt, 326 pp. **10s. 6d.** net.

LAW OF NEGLIGENCE. By J. B. Welson, LL.M., F.C.I.I., F.C.I.S. In demy 8vo, cloth, 122 pp. **5s.** net.

WORKMEN'S COMPENSATION INSURANCE. By C. E. Golding, LL.D., F.C.I.I., F.S.S. Second Edition. In demy 8vo, cloth, 112 pp. **5s.** net.

MOTOR INSURANCE. By W. F. Todd. In demy 8vo, cloth gilt, 176 pp. **6s.** net.

THE MARINE INSURANCE OF GOODS. By F. W. S. Poole. Second Edition. In demy 8vo, cloth gilt, 440 pp. **15s.** net.

GUIDE TO MARINE INSURANCE. By H. Keate. Seventh Edition. In crown 8vo, cloth, 255 pp. **3s. 6d.** net.

GUIDE TO LIFE ASSURANCE. By S. G. Leigh, *Fellow of the Institute of Actuaries*. Third Edition. In crown 8vo, cloth, 192 pp. **5s.** net.

LIFE ASSURANCE FROM PROPOSAL TO POLICY. By H. Hosking Tayler, F.I.A., A.C.I.I., and V. W. Tyler, F.I.A. In demy 8vo, cloth gilt, 198 pp. **6s.** net.

DICTIONARY OF LIFE ASSURANCE. Edited by G. W. Richmond, F.I.A., and F. H. Sherriff, F.I.A. In crown 4to, half-leather gilt, 598 pp. **50s.** net.

THE PRINCIPLES AND PRACTICE OF PERSONAL ACCIDENT, DISEASE, AND SICKNESS INSURANCE. By J. B. Welson, LL.M. In demy 8vo, cloth gilt, 133 pp. **5s.** net.

DICTIONARY OF ACCIDENT INSURANCE. Edited by J. B. Welson, LL.M., F.C.I.I., F.C.I.S. In crown 4to, half-leather gilt, 814 pp. **60s.** net.

LAW OF ACCIDENT AND CONTINGENCY INSURANCE. By F. H. Jones, *Solicitor*. In demy 8vo, cloth gilt, 290 pp. **7s. 6d.** net.

PHYSIOLOGY AND ANATOMY. By H. Gardiner, M.S. (Lond.), F.R.C.S. (Eng.). In demy 8vo, cloth gilt, 428 pp. **10s. 6d.** net.

CASUALTY INSURANCE. By Clyde J. Crobaugh, M.A., and Amos E. Redding, B.S. In medium 8vo, cloth gilt, 788 pp. **25s.** net.

TALKS ON INSURANCE LAW. By Jos. A. Watson, LL.B., B.Sc. In crown 8vo, cloth, 140 pp. **3s. 6d.** net.

PENSION AND SUPERANNUATION FUNDS. Their Formation and Administration Explained. By Bernard Robertson, F.I.A., and H. Samuels. *Barrister-at-Law*. Second Edition. In demy 8vo, cloth gilt, 158 pp. **5s.** net,

PENSION, ENDOWMENT, LIFE ASSURANCE, AND OTHER SCHEMES FOR COMMERCIAL COMPANIES. By HAROLD DOUGHARTY, F.C.I.I. Second Edition. In demy 8vo, cloth gilt, 144 pp. **6s.** net.

COMMERCIAL CREDIT RISKS. By A. H. SWAIN. In demy 8vo, 148 pp. **5s.** net.

THE PRINCIPLES AND PRACTICE OF ACCIDENT INSURANCE. By G. E. BANFIELD, A.C.I.I., *of the Middle Temple, Barrister-at-Law*. In demy 8vo, cloth gilt, 200 pp. **6s.** net.

INSURANCE OF PROFITS. By A. G. MACKEN. Second Edition. In demy 8vo, cloth gilt, 136 pp. **5s.** net.

THE SUCCESSFUL INSURANCE AGENT. By J. J. BISGOOD, B.A. In crown 8vo, cloth, 135 pp. **2s. 6d.** net. Second Edition.

THE BUSINESS MAN'S GUIDE TO INSURANCE. By A. PHILPOTT. In crown 8vo, cloth, 183 pp. **3s. 6d.** net.

ORGANIZATION AND MANAGEMENT

OFFICE ORGANIZATION AND MANAGEMENT. Including Secretarial Work. By LAWRENCE R. DICKSEE, M.Com., F.C.A., and Sir H. E. BLAIN, C.B.E. Ninth Edition, Revised. In demy 8vo, cloth gilt, 300 pp. **7s. 6d.** net.

COUNTING HOUSE AND FACTORY ORGANIZATION. By J. GILMOUR WILLIAMSON. In demy 8vo, cloth gilt, 182 pp. **7s. 6d.** net.

FILING SYSTEMS. Their Principles and their Application to Modern Office Requirements. By EDWARD A. COPE. In crown 8vo, cloth gilt, 200 pp., with illustrations. **3s. 6d.** net.

SOLICITOR'S OFFICE ORGANIZATION, MANAGEMENT, AND ACCOUNTS. By E. A. COPE and H. W. H. ROBINS. In demy 8vo, cloth gilt, 176 pp., with numerous forms. **6s.** net.

COLLIERY OFFICE ORGANIZATION AND ACCOUNTS. By J. W. INNES, F.C.A., and T. COLIN CAMPBELL, F.C.I. In demy 8vo. **7s. 6d.** net.

BUSINESS LEADERSHIP. Edited by HENRY C. METCALF, Ph.D. In demy 8vo, cloth gilt, 368 pp. **10s. 6d.** net.

BUSINESS OWNERSHIP ORGANIZATION. By A. H. STOCKDER, M.A. In demy 8vo, cloth, 630 pp. **10s. 6d.** net.

COMMERCIAL MANAGEMENT. By CUNLIFFE L. BOLLING. Second Edition. In demy 8vo, cloth gilt, 435 pp. **10s. 6d.** net.

BUSINESS MANAGEMENT. By PERCIVAL WHITE. In demy 8vo, cloth gilt, 740 pp. **15s.** net.

BUILDERS' BUSINESS MANAGEMENT. By J. H. BENNETTS, A.I.O.B. In demy 8vo, cloth gilt, 240 pp. **10s. 6d.** net.

ORGANIZATION AND MANAGEMENT IN THE FLOUR-MILLING INDUS-TRY. By E. LEIGH PEARSON, M.Sc.(Tech.), A.I.C. In demy 8vo, cloth gilt, 254 pp. **12s. 6d.** net.

ORGANIZATION, MANAGEMENT, AND TECHNOLOGY IN THE MANU-FACTURE OF MEN'S CLOTHING. By MARTIN E. POPKIN. In medium 8vo, cloth gilt, 416 pp. **25s.** net.

GROCERY BUSINESS ORGANIZATION AND MANAGEMENT. By C. L. T. BEECHING, O.B.E. With Chapters on Buying a Business, Grocers' Office Work and Book-keeping, etc., by J. A. SMART. Third Edition. In demy 8vo, cloth, 183 pp. **6s.** net.

HOW TO MANAGE A PRIVATE HOTEL. By P. HOBBS. In demy 8vo, cloth gilt, 80 pp. **3s. 6d.** net.

HOTEL ORGANIZATION, MANAGEMENT, AND ACCOUNTANCY. By G. DE BONI and F. F. SHARLES. In demy 8vo, cloth gilt, 215 pp. **10s. 6d.** net.

CLUBS AND THEIR MANAGEMENT. By F. W. PIXLEY. Second Edition. In demy 8vo, cloth. 252 pp. **10s. 6d.** net.

THE STOCKBROKER'S OFFICE. Organization, Management, and Accounts. By JULIUS E. DAY. In demy 8vo, cloth gilt, 250 pp. **7s. 6d.** net.

THE HISTORY, LAW, AND PRACTICE OF THE STOCK EXCHANGE. By A. P. POLEY, B.A., *Barrister-at-Law.* Fourth Edition, Revised. In demy 8vo, cloth gilt, 428 pp. **7s. 6d.** net.

SELF-ORGANIZATION FOR BUSINESS MEN. By MORLEY DAINOW, B.Sc. (Hons.). Second Edition. In demy 8vo, cloth gilt, 154 pp. **5s.** net.

THE ORGANIZATION OF A SMALL BUSINESS. By WM. A. SMITH, A.C.W.A. Second Edition. In crown 8vo, cloth, 120 pp. **2s. 6d.** net.

MULTIPLE SHOP ORGANIZATION. By A. E. HAMMOND. In demy 8vo, cloth, 152 pp. **6s.** net.

MODERN OFFICE MANAGEMENT. By H. W. SIMPSON, F.C.I.S. In demy 8vo, cloth gilt, 330 pp. **7s. 6d.** net.

INDUSTRIAL ADMINISTRATION

THE PHILOSOPHY OF MANAGEMENT. By OLIVER SHELDON, B.A. In demy 8vo, cloth gilt, 310 pp. **10s. 6d.** net.

EMPLOYMENT MANAGEMENT. Compiled and edited by DANIEL BLOOMFIELD. In demy 8vo, 507 pp. **8s. 6d.** net.

LABOUR PROBLEMS. By GORDON S. WATKINS, Ph.D. In demy 8vo, cloth gilt, 742 pp. **15s.** net.

PROBLEMS OF LABOUR. Compiled and Edited by DANIEL BLOOMFIELD. In demy 8vo, cloth gilt, 434 pp. **8s. 6d.** net.

LABOUR ORGANIZATION. By J. CUNNISON, M.A. In demy 8vo, cloth gilt, 280 pp. **7s. 6d.** net.

MODERN INDUSTRIAL MOVEMENTS. Compiled and Edited by DANIEL BLOOMFIELD. In demy 8vo, cloth gilt, 380 pp. **10s. 6d.** net.

A MERCHANT'S HORIZON. By A. L. FILENE and BURTON KLEINE. In demy 8vo, cloth gilt, 272 pp. **10s. 6d.** net.

NEW LEADERSHIP IN INDUSTRY. By SAM. A. LEWISOHN. Second Edition. In demy 8vo, cloth gilt, 224 pp. **7s. 6d.** net.

LECTURES ON INDUSTRIAL ADMINISTRATION. Edited by B. MUSCIO, M.A. In crown 8vo, cloth, 276 pp. **6s.** net.

OUTLINES OF INDUSTRIAL ADMINISTRATION. By R. O. HERFORD, H. T. HILDAGE, and H. G. JENKINS. In demy 8vo, cloth gilt, 124 pp. **6s. net.**

ENGINEERING FACTORY SUPPLIES. By W. J. HISCOX. In demy 8vo, cloth gilt, 184 pp. **5s. net.**

FACTORY LAY-OUT, PLANNING, AND PROGRESS. By W. J. HISCOX. In demy 8vo, cloth gilt, 200 pp. **7s. 6d. net.**

FACTORY ADMINISTRATION IN PRACTICE. By W. J. HISCOX. In demy 8vo, cloth gilt, 224 pp. **8s. 6d. net.**

FACTORY ORGANIZATION. By C. H. NORTHCOTT, M.A., Ph.D.; O. SHELDON, B.A.; J. W. WARDROPPER, B.Sc., B.Com., A.C.W.A.; and L. URWICK, M.A. In demy 8vo, cloth gilt, 264 pp. **7s. 6d. net.**

MANAGEMENT. By J. LEE, C.B.E., M.A., M.Com.Sc. In demy 8vo, cloth gilt, 133 pp. **5s. net.**

AN INTRODUCTION TO INDUSTRIAL ADMINISTRATION. By JOHN LEE, C.B.E., M.A., M.Com.Sc. In demy 8vo, cloth gilt, 200 pp. **5s. net.**

DICTIONARY OF INDUSTRIAL ADMINISTRATION. Edited by JOHN LEE, C.B.E., M.A., M.Com.Sc. Assisted by eminent specialists. In Two Volumes, crown 4to, bound in buckram, 1166 pp. **63s. net.**

INDUSTRIAL ORGANIZATION. By JOHN LEE, C.B.E., M.A., M.Com.Sc. In demy 8vo, cloth gilt, 130 pp. **5s. net.**

THE PRINCIPLES OF INDUSTRIAL WELFARE. By JOHN LEE, C.B.E., M.A., M.Com.Sc. In demy 8vo, cloth, 103 pp. **5s. net.**

THE EVOLUTION OF INDUSTRIAL ORGANIZATION. By B. F. SHIELDS, M.A., *Professor of Commerce and Dean of the Faculty of Commerce, University College, Dublin.* Second Edition. In demy 8vo, cloth gilt, 429 pp. **10s. 6d. net.**

WELFARE WORK IN INDUSTRY. By members of the Institute of Industrial Welfare Workers. Edited by ELEANOR T. KELLY. In demy 8vo, cloth, 128 pp. **5s. net.**

TIME STANDARDIZATION OF WORKSHOP OPERATIONS. By T. PILKINGTON, M.I.Mech.E. In demy 8vo, cloth gilt, 263 pp. **16s. net.**

WORKSHOP COMMITTEES. By C. G. RENOLD. In demy 8vo, 52 pp. **1s. net.**

INTRODUCTION TO THE PRINCIPLES OF INDUSTRIAL ADMINISTRATION. By A. P. M. FLEMING and H. J. BROCKLEHURST, M.Eng., A.M.I.E.E. In demy 8vo, 140 pp. **3s. 6d. net.**

SHARING PROFITS WITH EMPLOYEES. By J. A. BOWIE, M.A., D.Litt. Second Edition. In demy 8vo, cloth gilt, 230 pp. **10s. 6d. net.**

RATIONALIZATION. By the same Author. In demy 8vo, 36 pp. **1s. net.**

PRACTICAL ADVICE TO INVENTORS AND PATENTEES. By C. M. LINLEY. In crown 8vo, cloth, 134 pp. **3s. 6d.** net.

PATENTS FOR INVENTIONS. By J. EWART WALKER, B.A., *Barrister-at-Law,* and R. BRUCE FOSTER, B.Sc., *Barrister-at-Law.* In demy 8vo, cloth gilt, 390 pp. **21s.** net.

TRANSPORT

PRACTICAL TRANSPORT MANAGEMENT. By ANDREW HASTIE. In demy 8vo, cloth gilt, 190 pp. **10s. 6d.** net.

INDUSTRIAL TRAFFIC MANAGEMENT. By GEO. B. LISSENDEN, M.Inst.T. Third Edition. In demy 8vo, cloth gilt, 422 pp. **25s.** net.

COMMERCIAL AIR TRANSPORT. By LIEUT.-COL. IVO EDWARDS, C.M.G., and F. TYMMS, A.F.R.Ae.S. In demy 8vo, cloth, 178 pp. **7s. 6d.** net.

HOW TO MAKE THE BRITISH RAILWAYS PAY. By M. F. FARRAR. In demy 8vo, cloth gilt, 96 pp. **3s. 6d.** net.

RAILWAY RATES, PRINCIPLES, AND PROBLEMS. By PHILIP BURTT, M.Inst.T. In demy 8vo, cloth gilt, 174 pp. **6s.** net.

RAILWAY STATISTICS: THEIR COMPILATION AND USE. By A. E. KIRKUS, O.B.E., M.Inst.T. In demy 8vo, cloth gilt, 146 pp. **5s.** net.

MODERN RAILWAY OPERATION. By D. R. LAMB, M.Inst.T. In demy 8vo, cloth gilt, 183 pp. **7s. 6d.** net.

RAILWAY ELECTRIFICATION AND TRAFFIC PROBLEMS. By PHILIP BURTT, M.Inst.T. In demy 8vo, cloth gilt, 210 pp. **10s. 6d.** net.

MOTOR ROAD TRANSPORT FOR COMMERCIAL PURPOSES. By JOHN PHILLIMORE. With an Introduction by Sir H. P. MAYBURY, K.C.M.G., C.B. Second Edition. In demy 8vo, cloth gilt, 233 pp. **10s. 6d.** net.

THE HISTORY AND DEVELOPMENT OF ROAD TRANSPORT. By J. PATERSON, M.C., M.Inst.T. In demy 8vo, cloth gilt, 128 pp. **6s.** net.

THE HISTORY AND ECONOMICS OF TRANSPORT. By ADAM W. KIRKALDY, M.A., B.Litt. (Oxon), M.Com. (B'ham.), and ALFRED DUDLEY EVANS. Fourth Edition. In demy 8vo, cloth gilt, 438 pp. **16s.** net.

THE RIGHTS AND DUTIES OF TRANSPORT UNDERTAKINGS. By H. BARRS DAVIES, M.A. In demy 8vo, cloth, 135 pp. **5s.** net.

ROAD MAKING AND ROAD USING. By T. SALKIELD, M.Inst.C.E., M.Inst.T. In demy 8vo, cloth gilt, 180 pp. **7s. 6d.** net.

PORT ECONOMICS. By B. CUNNINGHAM, D.Sc., B.E., F.R.S.E., M.Inst.C.E. In demy 8vo, cloth gilt, 144 pp. **6s.** net.

MODERN DOCK OPERATION. By D. ROSS-JOHNSON, C.B.E., V.D., M.Inst.T. In demy 8vo, cloth gilt, 113 pp., illustrated. **6s.** net.

ROAD TRANSPORT OPERATION—PASSENGER. By R. STUART PILCHER, F.R.S.E., M.Inst.T. In demy 8vo, cloth gilt, 220 pp. **10s. 6d.** net.

CANALS AND INLAND WATERWAYS. By GEORGE CADBURY, *Managing Director of Messrs. Cadbury Bros., Ltd., Chairman of the Severn and Canal Carrying Co., Ltd.; and* S. P. DOBBS, B.A. In demy 8vo, cloth gilt, 176 pp. **7s. 6d.** net.

2

SHIPPING

SHIPPING OFFICE ORGANIZATION, MANAGEMENT, AND ACCOUNTS. By ALFRED CALVERT. In demy 8vo, cloth gilt, 203 pp. **6s.** net.

THE SHIPPING WORLD, Afloat and Ashore. Compiled and Edited by J. A. TODD, M.A., B.L. In crown 8vo, cloth gilt, 306 pp. **7s. 6d.** net.

SHIPPING TERMS AND PHRASES. Compiled by JAMES A. DUNNAGE, F.S.S., F.C.I., A.M.Inst.T. In crown 8vo, cloth, 102 pp. **2s. 6d.** net.

THE EXPORTER'S HANDBOOK AND GLOSSARY. By F. M. DUDENEY. In demy 8vo, cloth gilt, 254 pp. **7s. 6d.** net.

THE IMPORTER'S HANDBOOK. By J. A. DUNNAGE. In demy 8vo, cloth gilt, 382 pp. **10s. 6d.** net.

HOW TO EXPORT GOODS. By F. M. DUDENEY. In crown 8vo, cloth, 112 pp. **2s.** net.

MANUAL OF EXPORTING. By J. A. DUNNAGE. In demy 8vo, cloth gilt, 392 pp. **10s. 6d.** net.

HOW TO IMPORT GOODS. By J. A. DUNNAGE. Second Edition. In crown 8vo, cloth, 128 pp. **2s.** net.

CASE AND FREIGHT COSTS. By A. W. E. CROSFIELD. In crown 8vo, cloth, 62 pp. **2s.** net.

INTRODUCTION TO SHIPBROKING. By C. D. MACMURRAY and M. M. CREE. Second Edition. In demy 8vo, cloth, 115 pp. **3s. 6d.** net.

SHIPPING AND SHIPBROKING. By the same Authors. Second Edition. In demy 8vo, cloth gilt, 543 pp. **15s.** net.

SHIPPING BUSINESS METHODS. By R. B. PAUL. Second Edition. In demy 8vo, cloth gilt, 104 pp. **5s.** net.

SHIPPING FINANCE AND ACCOUNTS. By the same Author. In demy 8vo, cloth gilt, 74 pp. **2s. 6d.** net.

BANKING AND FINANCE

THE MONEY MACHINE. By FRANCIS WHITMORE, B.Com. In demy 8vo, cloth gilt, 144 pp. **5s.** net.

MONEY, EXCHANGE, AND BANKING, in their Practical, Theoretical, and Legal Aspects. By H. T. EASTON, *Associate of the Institute of Bankers.* Third Edition. In demy 8vo, cloth gilt, 331 pp. **6s.** net.

THE THEORY AND PRINCIPLES OF CENTRAL BANKING. By WILLIAM A. SHAW, Litt.D. In demy 8vo, cloth gilt, 262 pp. **12s. 6d.** net.

AN OUTLINE OF ENGLISH BANKING ADMINISTRATION. By JOSEPH SYKES, B.A. (Hons.) In crown 8vo, cloth, 96 pp. **2s. 6d.** net.

ENGLISH BANKING METHODS. By LEONARD LE MARCHANT MINTY, Ph.D., B.Sc. (Econ.), B.Com., LL.B. Fourth Edition. In demy 8vo, cloth gilt, 552 pp. **15s.** net.

BANKING FOR ADVANCED STUDENTS. By PERCY G. H. WOODRUFF, Cert. A.I.B. In demy 8vo, cloth, 248 pp. **7s. 6d.** net.

ENGLISH PUBLIC FINANCE. With Chapters on the Bank of England. By HARVEY E. FISK. In demy 8vo, cloth gilt, 215 pp. **7s. 6d.** net.

THEORY AND PRACTICE OF FINANCE. By W. COLLIN BROOKS. Second Edition. In demy 8vo, 440 pp. **10s. 6d.** net.

MODERN FINANCE AND INDUSTRY. By A. S. WADE. Second Edition. In demy 8vo, cloth gilt, 136 pp. **5s.** net.

THE ARITHMETIC AND PRACTICE OF THE FOREIGN EXCHANGES. By A. G. SUGG, Cert. A.I.B. In demy 8vo, cloth gilt, 144 pp. **3s. 6d.** net. Second Edition.

FOREIGN EXCHANGE ACCOUNTING. By C. DJÖRUP, B.C.S., C.P.A. Size 6 in. by 9 in., cloth gilt, 420 pp. **15s.** net.

FOREIGN BANKING SYSTEMS. Edited by H. P. WILLIS and B. H. BECKHART. In demy 8vo, cloth, 1300 pp. **21s.** net.

FOREIGN EXCHANGE AND FOREIGN BILLS IN THEORY AND IN PRACTICE. By W. F. SPALDING, *Fellow and Member of the Council of the London Institute of Bankers.* Seventh Edition. In demy 8vo, 320 pp. **7s. 6d.** net.

EASTERN EXCHANGE, CURRENCY, AND FINANCE. By the same Author. Fourth Edition. In demy 8vo, cloth, 485 pp., illustrated. **15s.** net.

FOREIGN EXCHANGE, A PRIMER OF. By the same Author. Second Edition. In demy 8vo, cloth, 124 pp. **3s. 6d.** net.

THE FINANCE OF FOREIGN TRADE. By the same Author. In demy 8vo, cloth gilt, 190 pp. **7s. 6d.** net.

DICTIONARY OF THE WORLD'S CURRENCIES AND FOREIGN EXCHANGES. By the same Author. In crown 4to, half-leather gilt, 208 pp. **30s.** net.

BANKERS' CREDITS AND ALL THAT APPERTAINS TO THEM IN THEIR PRACTICAL, LEGAL, AND EVERYDAY ASPECTS. By the same Author. Third Edition. In demy 8vo, cloth gilt, 170 pp. **10s. 6d.** net.

THE FUNCTIONS OF MONEY. By the same Author. In demy 8vo, cloth gilt, 179 pp. **7s. 6d.** net.

THE LONDON MONEY MARKET. By the same Author. Fourth Edition. In demy 8vo, cloth gilt, 264 pp. **10s. 6d.** net.

THE BANKER'S PLACE IN COMMERCE. By the same Author. In demy 8vo, cloth, 80 pp. **3s. 6d.** net.

THE DISCOUNT MARKET IN LONDON. Its Organization and Recent Development. By H. W. GREENGRASS. In demy 8vo, cloth gilt, 194 pp. **6s.** net.

PRINCIPLES OF BANKING, CURRENCY, AND FOREIGN EXCHANGE. By R. H. KING, *Certificated Associate of the Institute of Bankers.* In crown 8vo, cloth gilt. **5s.** net.

PRACTICAL BANKING. By J. F. G. BAGSHAW. With chapters on " The Principles of Currency," by C. F. HANNAFORD ; and " Bank Book-keeping," by W. H. PEARD. Revised Edition. In demy 8vo, cloth gilt, 448 pp. **7s. 6d.** net.

THE SECURITIES CLERK IN A BRANCH BANK. By F. J. Lewcock, Cert. A.I.B., A.C.I.S. In demy 8vo, cloth gilt, 228 pp. **7s. 6d.** net.

BANK ORGANIZATION, MANAGEMENT, AND ACCOUNTS. By J. F. Davis, D.Lit., M.A., LL.B. Second Edition. In demy 8vo, cloth gilt, 175 pp. **6s.** net.

CHEQUES: THEIR ORIGIN AND DEVELOPMENT, AND HOW THEY ARE HANDLED BY AN ENGLISH BANK. By C. F. Hannaford. Edited by Sir John Paget, K.C. In demy 8vo, cloth gilt, 195 pp. **6s.** net.

BILLS, CHEQUES, AND NOTES. By J. A. Slater, B.A., LL.B. (Lond.). Fourth Edition. In demy 8vo, cloth gilt, 214 pp. **6s.** net.

THE BILLS OF EXCHANGE ACT, 1882. By M. H. Megrah, B.Com. (Lond.), Cert. A.I.B. In demy 8vo, cloth gilt, 195 pp. **6s.** net.

A PRACTICAL EXAMINATION OF THE BILLS OF EXCHANGE ACTS. By C. H. Fennell. Second Edition. In medium 8vo, cloth gilt, 168 pp. **7s. 6d.** net.

THE BANKERS' CLEARING HOUSE. What it is and what it does. By P. W. Matthews. In demy 8vo, cloth gilt, 175 pp. **7s. 6d.** net.

TITLE DEEDS OLD AND NEW. By Francis R. Stead. In demy 8vo, cloth gilt, 192 pp. **5s.** net.

THE BANKER AS A LENDER. By F. E. Steele. In demy 8vo, cloth gilt, 150 pp. **5s.** net.

HOW TO SUCCEED IN A BANK. By the same Author. In crown 8vo, cloth, 156 pp. **3s. 6d.** net.

BANKING AS A CAREER. By F. A. Willman, *Certificated Associate of the Institute of Bankers.* In demy 8vo, cloth gilt, 144 pp. **3s. 6d.** net.

TALKS ON BANKING TO BANK CLERKS. By Harold E. Evans, *Fellow of the Institute of Bankers.* In crown 8vo, cloth, 152 pp. **2s. 6d.** net.

ANSWERS TO QUESTIONS SET AT THE EXAMINATIONS OF THE INSTITUTE OF BANKERS. By L. L. M. Minty, Ph.D., B.Sc. (Econ.), B.Com. **Foreign Exchange,** Parts I and II. Each **3s. 6d.** net. **Economics,** Parts I and II. Each **5s.** net. **English Grammar and Composition,** Part I. **3s. 6d.** net. Part II, **5s.** net.

BANKERS AND THE PROPERTY STATUTES OF 1925 AND 1926. By R. W. Jones, *Certificated Associate of the Institute of Bankers.* Second Edition. In demy 8vo, cloth gilt, 200 pp. **6s.** net.

BANKERS' ADVANCES. By F. R. Stead. Third Edition by C. R. W. Cuckson, B.A., LL.B. In demy 8vo, cloth gilt, 150 pp. **6s.** net.

BANKERS' TESTS. By F. R. Stead. In demy 8vo, cloth gilt, 144 pp. **10s. 6d.** net.

BANKERS' ADVANCES AGAINST PRODUCE. By A. Williams. In demy 8vo, cloth gilt, 147 pp. **6s.** net.

ENGLISH COMPOSITION AND BANKING CORRESPONDENCE. By L. E. W. O. FULLBROOK-LEGGATT, M.C., B.A. In demy 8vo, cloth gilt, 300 pp. **5s.** net.

DICTIONARY OF BANKING. A Complete Encyclopaedia of Banking Law and Practice. By W. THOMSON, *Bank Inspector.* Seventh Edition. In crown 4to, half-leather gilt, 754 pp. **30s.** net.

A COMPLETE DICTIONARY OF BANKING TERMS IN THREE LANGUAGES (ENGLISH–FRENCH–GERMAN). By L. HERENDI, *Managing Clerk, Hungarian General Credit-Bank.* Size 9½ in. by 6¼ in., cloth gilt, 566 pp. **21s.** net.

SECRETARIAL WORK, ETC.

ENGLISH FOR SECRETARIAL STUDENTS. By WALTER SHAWCROSS, B.A. In demy 8vo, cloth gilt. (*In the Press.*)

THE COMPANY SECRETARY'S VADE MECUM. Edited by PHILIP TOVEY, F.C.I.S. Fourth Edition, Revised by C. W. ADAMS, A.C.I.S. In foolscap 8vo, cloth, 170 pp. **3s. 6d.** net.

COMPANY SECRETARIAL WORK. By ERNEST MARTIN, F.C.I.S. Second Edition. In crown 8vo, cloth, 154 pp. **2s.** net.

SECRETARY'S HANDBOOK. Edited by Sir H. E. BLAIN, C.B.E. Second Edition. In demy 8vo, cloth gilt, 168 pp. **5s.** net.

GUIDE FOR THE COMPANY SECRETARY. By ARTHUR COLES. Third Edition, Revised by W. CECIL WOOD, A.C.I.S. In demy 8vo, cloth gilt, 512 pp. **6s.** net.

PRACTICAL SECRETARIAL WORK. By HENRY I. LEE, A.I.S.A., and WILLIAM N. BARR. In demy 8vo, cloth gilt, 406 pp. **7s. 6d.** net.

HOW TO BECOME A PRIVATE SECRETARY. By J. E. McLACHLAN, F.I.P.S. (Hons.). In crown 8vo, cloth, 120 pp. **3s. 6d.** net.

GUIDE TO COMPANY SECRETARIAL WORK. By O. OLDHAM, A.C.I.S. Fifth Edition, Revised by G. K. BUCKNALL, A.C.I.S. (Hons.). In crown 8vo, cloth gilt, 256 pp. **3s. 6d.** net.

DICTIONARY OF SECRETARIAL LAW AND PRACTICE. Edited by PHILIP TOVEY, F.C.I.S., assisted by specialist contributors. Fourth Edition. In crown 4to, half-leather gilt, 1040 pp. **50s.** net.

HONORARY SECRETARYSHIP. By W. B. THORNE. In crown 8vo, cloth, 81 pp. **2s. 6d.** net.

THE TRANSFER OF STOCKS, SHARES, AND OTHER MARKETABLE SECURITIES. A Manual of the Law and Practice. By F. D. HEAD, B.A. (Oxon), *Barrister-at-Law.* Fourth Edition. In demy 8vo, cloth gilt, 204 pp. **7s. 6d.** net.

FORMATION AND MANAGEMENT OF A PRIVATE COMPANY. By the same Author. In demy 8vo, cloth, 245 pp. **7s. 6d.** net.

THE COMPANY REGISTRAR'S MANUAL. By J. J. QUINLIVAN. Second Edition. In demy 8vo, cloth gilt, 360 pp. **10s. 6d.** net.

MEETINGS. By F. D. HEAD, B.A. (Oxon), *of Lincoln's Inn, Barrister-at-Law.* Third Edition. In demy 8vo, cloth gilt, 262 pp. **5s.** net.

a

THE CHAIRMAN'S MANUAL. By GURDON PALIN, *Barrister-at-Law*, and ERNEST MARTIN, F.C.I.S. Second Edition. In crown 8vo, cloth gilt, 174 pp. **5s.** net.

HOW TO TAKE MINUTES. Edited by ERNEST MARTIN, F.C.I.S. Fourth Edition. In demy 8vo, cloth gilt, 144 pp. **2s. 6d.** net.

PROSPECTUSES: HOW TO READ AND UNDERSTAND THEM. By PHILIP TOVEY, F.C.I.S., and H. LAMBERT SMITH, B.Sc. Second Edition. In demy 8vo, cloth gilt, 109 pp. **5s.** net.

PRACTICAL SHARE TRANSFER WORK. By F. W. LIDINGTON. In crown 8vo, 123 pp. **3s. 6d.** net.

QUESTIONS AND ANSWERS ON SECRETARIAL PRACTICE. By E. J. HAMMOND. Third Edition. Revised by G. K. BUCKNALL, A.C.I.S. (Hons.). In demy 8vo, cloth gilt, 250 pp. **7s. 6d.** net.

EXAMINATION NOTES ON SECRETARIAL PRACTICE. By C. W. ADAMS, A.C.I.S. Second Edition. In crown 8vo, cloth, 80 pp. **2s. 6d.** net.

INCOME TAX

DICTIONARY OF INCOME TAX AND SUR-TAX PRACTICE. By W. E. SNELLING. Eighth Edition. In demy 8vo, half leather gilt, 732 pp. **25s.** net.

INTRODUCTION TO INCOME TAX. By E. D. FRYER, A.L.A.A. In crown 8vo, cloth, 100 pp. **2s. 6d.** net.

DOUBLE INCOME TAX RELIEF. By H. E. SEED and A. W. RAWLINSON. In crown 8vo, cloth gilt, 136 pp. **10s. 6d.** net.

INCOME TAX RELIEFS. By A. W. RAWLINSON, A.C.A. In demy 8vo, cloth gilt, 422 pp. **20s.** net.

INCOME TAX, SUPER-TAX, AND SURTAX. By V. WALTON, F.C.A., F.R.S., F.R.Econ.S. In demy 8vo, cloth, 240 pp. **7s. 6d.** net.

SNELLING'S PRACTICAL INCOME TAX. In crown 8vo, cloth, 181 pp. **3s. 6d.** net. Tenth Edition revised in accordance with the Finance Act, 1930.

NOTES ON INCOME TAX. By W. S. CARRINGTON, *Chartered Accountant.* In crown 8vo, cloth, 88 pp. **3s. 6d.** net.

INCOME TAX HANDBOOK FOR COMPANY SECRETARIES. By C. W. CHIVERS. In demy 8vo, cloth gilt. **5s.** net.

ECONOMICS

ECONOMICS OF THE ENGLISH BANKING SYSTEM. By W. J. WESTON, M.A., B.Sc., *of Gray's Inn, Barrister-at-Law.* In demy 8vo, cloth gilt, 136 pp. **5s.** net.

DICTIONARY OF ECONOMIC AND BANKING TERMS. By W. J. WESTON. M.A., B.Sc.; and A. CREW, *Barrister-at-Law.* In crown 8vo, cloth, 185 pp. **5s.** net. Second Edition.

ECONOMIC GEOGRAPHY. By J. McFARLANE, M.A., M.Com. Third Edition. In demy 8vo, cloth gilt, 656 pp. **10s. 6d.** net.

THE PRINCIPLES OF ECONOMIC GEOGRAPHY. By R. N. RUDMOSE BROWN, D.Sc., *Lecturer in Geography in the University of Sheffield.* Second Edition. In demy 8vo, cloth gilt, 223 pp. **6s.** net.

ECONOMIC RESOURCES OF THE EMPIRE. Edited by T. WORSWICK, O.B.E., M.Sc. In crown 8vo, cloth gilt, 172 pp. **5s.** net.

THE HISTORY OF COMMERCE. By T. G. WILLIAMS, M.A., F.R.Hist.S., F.R.Econ.S. In demy 8vo, cloth gilt, 343 pp. **5s.** net.

HISTORY OF AGRICULTURE IN EUROPE AND AMERICA. By N. S. B. GRAS. In demy 8vo, cloth gilt, 472 pp. **15s.** net.

OUTLINES OF THE ECONOMIC HISTORY OF ENGLAND. By H. O. MEREDITH, M.A., M.Com. Second Edition. In demy 8vo, cloth gilt, 430 pp. **7s. 6d.** net.

ECONOMIC HISTORY OF THE UNITED STATES. By T. W. V. METRE. In demy 8vo, cloth, 680 pp. **10s. 6d.** net.

NEW GOVERNMENTS OF EASTERN EUROPE. By M. W. GRAHAM, Junr. In demy 8vo, cloth gilt, 836 pp. **21s.** net.

INTERNATIONAL RELATIONS. By R. L. BUELL. In demy 8vo, cloth gilt, 784 pp. **21s.** net.

MAIN CURRENTS OF SOCIAL AND INDUSTRIAL CHANGE. By T. G. WILLIAMS, M.A., F.R.Hist.S., F.R.Econ.S. In crown 8vo, cloth gilt, 320 pp. **5s.** net.

AN INTRODUCTION TO SOCIOLOGY AND SOCIAL PROBLEMS. By W. G. BEACH. In demy 8vo, cloth gilt, 383 pp. **6s.** net.

THE PRINCIPLES OF BUSINESS ECONOMICS. By JAS. STEPHENSON, M.A., M.Com., D.Sc. In demy 8vo. cloth gilt, 504 pp. **10s. 6d.** net.

ECONOMICS OF THE MANUFACTURING BUSINESS. By W. A. STEWART JONES, F.C.W.A., F.S.S. In demy 8vo, cloth, 160 pp. **3s. 6d.**

ECONOMICS FOR BUSINESS MEN. By W. J. WESTON, M.A., B.Sc. In crown 8vo, cloth gilt, 265 pp. **3s. 6d.** net.

PRINCIPLES OF ECONOMICS. By L. A. RUFENER, Ph.D. In medium 8vo, cloth gilt, 862 pp. **16s.** net.

A TEXTBOOK OF ECONOMICS. By W. J. WESTON, M.A., B.Sc. In demy 8vo, cloth gilt, 460 pp. **10s. 6d.** net.

ECONOMIC PRINCIPLES FOR INDIAN READERS. By Dr. P. BASU, Principal of the Holkar College, Indore. In demy 8vo, cloth, 356 pp. **7s. 6d.** net.

ECONOMICS OF INSTALMENT TRADING AND HIRE PURCHASE. By W. F. CRICK. In demy 8vo, cloth gilt, 126 pp. **5s.** net.

LABOUR ECONOMICS. By SOLOMON BLUM. In demy 8vo, cloth gilt, 590 pp. **12s. 6d.** net.

THIS AGE OF PLENTY. By C. M. HATTERSLEY, M.A., LL.B. Second Edition. In crown 8vo, 348 pp., paper, **3s. 6d.** net; cloth, **6s.** net.

A FAIR WAGE. By EDWARD BATTEN, M.I.Mech.E. 100 pp. **2s. 6d.** net.

INTERNATIONAL MIGRATIONS (STATISTICS). Compiled on behalf of the International Labour Office, Geneva, by IMRE FERENCZI. Edited by WALTER F. WILCOX. In medium 8vo, cloth gilt, 1112 pp. **42s.** net.

NATIONAL ECONOMICS. By EDWARD BATTEN. In demy 8vo, cloth, 229 pp. **5s.** net.

THE SUBSTANCE OF ECONOMICS. By H. A. Silverman, B.A. (Econ.) Sixth Edition. In crown 8vo, cloth gilt, 370 pp. 6s. net.

ECONOMICS OF PRIVATE ENTERPRISE, THE. By J. H. Jones, M.A., *Professor of Economics, University of Leeds.* In demy 8vo, cloth gilt, 456 pp. 7s. 6d. net.

INDUSTRIAL COMBINATION IN ENGLAND. By Patrick Fitzgerald, D.Sc. (Econ.), *Acting Editor* "The Statist." Second Edition. In demy 8vo, cloth gilt, 248 pp. 10s. 6d. net.

ECONOMICS OF THE WHOLESALE AND RETAIL TRADE. By James Stephenson, M.A., M.Com., D.Sc. In demy 8vo, cloth, 292 pp. 5s.

ECONOMICS OF THE IMPORT AND EXPORT TRADE. By Hiromu Nagaoka. In demy 8vo, cloth, 235 pp. 5s.

ECONOMICS EDUCATOR. Edited by Professor J. H. Jones, M.A. In three volumes. Crown 4to, cloth gilt, 1450 pp. 63s. net.

ENGINEERING ECONOMICS. By T. H. Burnham, B.Sc., Hons., B.Com. (Lond.), A.M.I.Mech.E. Second Edition. In demy 8vo, cloth gilt, 392 pp. 10s. 6d. net.

A THEORY OF CONSUMPTION. By Hazel Kyrk, Ph.D. In demy 8vo, cloth, 312 pp. 10s. 6d. net.

MUNICIPAL WORK

COSTING SCHEMES FOR LOCAL AUTHORITIES. By J. H. Burton. In demy 8vo, 144 pp. 5s. net.

LOANS AND BORROWING POWERS OF LOCAL AUTHORITIES. By J. H. Burton. In demy 8vo, cloth gilt, 228 pp. 7s. 6d. net.

LOCAL GOVERNMENT OF THE UNITED KINGDOM AND THE IRISH FREE STATE. By J. J. Clarke, M.A., F.S.S., *of Gray's Inn, Barrister-at-Law.* Sixth Edition. In crown 8vo, cloth gilt, 835 pp. 12s. 6d. net.

RATES AND RATING. By Albert Crew, *Barrister-at-Law*, and W. T. Creswell. Sixth Edition (England and Wales). In crown 8vo, cloth gilt, 526 pp. 12s. 6d. net.

MUNICIPAL BOOK-KEEPING. By J. H. McCall, F.S.A.A. Third Edition. In demy 8vo, cloth gilt, 130 pp. 7s. 6d. net.

MUNICIPAL AUDIT PROGRAMMES. By S. Whitehead, A.S.A.A. In demy 8vo, cloth gilt. 116 pp. 3s. 6d. net.

MUNICIPAL ACCOUNTING SYSTEMS. By the same Author. Second Edition. In demy 8vo, cloth gilt, 168 pp. 5s. net.

MUNICIPAL STUDENT'S EXAMINATION NOTEBOOK. By S. Whitehead. In crown 8vo, cloth, 220 pp. 7s. 6d. net.

AMERICAN CITY GOVERNMENT. By W. Anderson, Ph.D. In demy 8vo, cloth gilt, 686 pp. 21s. net.

MUNICIPAL SERIES. The Organization and Administration of the Various Departments of a Municipal Office. Edited by W. BATESON, A.C.A., F.S.A.A.—

> **PRINCIPLES OF ORGANIZATION.** By WILLIAM BATESON, A.C.A., F.S.A.A. In demy 8vo, cloth gilt, 92 pp. **3s. 6d.** net.
>
> **FINANCE DEPARTMENT.** By WILLIAM BATESON, A.C.A., F.S.A.A. In demy 8vo, cloth gilt, 274 pp. **7s. 6d.** net.
>
> **TRAMWAYS DEPARTMENT.** By S. B. NORMAN MARSH, *Accountant to the Birmingham Corporation Tramways.* In demy 8vo, cloth gilt, 170 pp. **6s.** net.
>
> **ELECTRICITY UNDERTAKING.** By C. L. E. STEWART, M.I.E.E. In demy 8vo, cloth gilt, 180 pp. **6s.** net.
>
> **GAS UNDERTAKING.** By EDWIN UPTON, F.S.A.A. In demy 8vo, cloth gilt, 130 pp. **5s.** net.
>
> **TOWN CLERK'S DEPARTMENT AND THE JUSTICES' CLERK'S DEPARTMENT.** By A. S. WRIGHT and E. H. SINGLETON. In demy 8vo, cloth gilt, 268 pp. **7s. 6d.** net.
>
> **WATERWORKS UNDERTAKING.** By FREDERICK J. ALBAN, F.S.A.A., F.I.M.T.A., A.C.I.S. In demy 8vo, cloth gilt, 314 pp. **10s. 6d.** net.
>
> **EDUCATION DEPARTMENT.** By ALFRED E. IKIN, B.Sc., LL.D. In demy 8vo, cloth gilt, 251 pp. **7s. 6d.** net.
>
> **PUBLIC HEALTH DEPARTMENT.** By W. A. LEONARD, *Chief Clerk and Statistician in the Public Health Department, Birmingham.* In demy 8vo, cloth gilt, 155 pp. **6s. net.**
>
> **MUNICIPAL ENGINEER AND SURVEYOR'S DEPARTMENT.** By E. J. ELFORD, *Engineer, Architect and Surveyor to the Metropolitan Borough of Wandsworth.* In demy 8vo, cloth gilt, 245 pp. **10s. 6d.** net.
>
> **RATING DEPARTMENT.** By A. H. PEACOCK, M.A., A.S.A.A., *Incorporated Accountant.* In demy 8vo, cloth gilt, 96 pp. **5s.** net.

ADVERTISING AND SALESMANSHIP

THE DICTIONARY OF ADVERTISING AND PRINTING. In crown 4to, half leather gilt, 460 pp. **42s.** net.

MODERN ADVERTISING. In two volumes, 11 in. by 8½ in., bound in buckram, with gilt lettering. **63s.** net.

ADVERTISING TO WOMEN. By CARL A. NAETHER, M.A. Size 9 in. by 6 in., cloth gilt, 356 pp. **21s.** net.

STORECRAFT. By S. A. WILLIAMS, M.A. In crown 8vo, cloth, 143 pp. **3s. 6d.** net.

PRINCIPLES OF RETAILING. By N. A. BRISCO, Ph.D. In demy 8vo, cloth gilt, 336 pp. **16s.** net.

SUCCESSFUL RETAILING. By E. N. SIMONS. In demy 8vo, cloth gilt, 210 pp. **5s.** net.

THE CRAFT OF SILENT SALESMANSHIP. A Guide to Advertisement Construction. By C. Maxwell Tregurtha and J. W. Frings. Size 6¼ in. by 9¼ in., cloth, 98 pp., with illustrations. 5s. net.

PERSONAL SALESMANSHIP. By R. Simmat, M.A. In demy 8vo, cloth gilt, 108 pp. 5s. net.

SALESMANSHIP. By William Maxwell. In crown 8vo, cloth gilt, 238 pp. 5s. net.

SALESMANSHIP. By W. A. Corbion and G. E. Grimsdale. In crown 8vo, cloth, 168 pp. 3s. 6d. net.

SALESMANSHIP. By C. H. Fernald, M.B.A. In medium 8vo, cloth, 491 pp. 18s. net.

TRAINING FOR MORE SALES. By C. C. Knights. In demy 8vo, cloth, 240 pp. 5s. net.

AN OUTLINE OF SALES MANAGEMENT. By the same Author. In demy 8vo, cloth gilt, 196 pp. 5s. net.

TECHNIQUE OF SALESMANSHIP. By the same Author. In demy 8vo, cloth gilt, 249 pp. 5s. net.

BUILDING RETAIL SALES. By the same Author. In demy 8vo, cloth gilt, 230 pp. 5s. net.

MORE SALES THROUGH THE WINDOW. By the same Author. In demy 8vo, cloth gilt, 170 pp. 5s. net.

PRACTICAL SALESMANSHIP. By N. C. Fowler, Junr. In crown 8vo, 337 pp. 7s. 6d. net.

SALES MANAGEMENT. By Cunliffe L. Bolling. In demy 8vo, cloth gilt, 320 pp. 10s. 6d. net.

RETAIL SALESMANSHIP. By Cunliffe L. Bolling. Second Edition. In demy 8vo, cloth gilt, 284 pp. 7s. 6d. net.

HIRE PURCHASE TRADING. By Cunliffe L. Bolling. Second Edition. In crown 8vo, cloth. 276 pp. 10s. 6d. net.

SALESMEN'S AGREEMENTS. Compiled from the proceedings of a special Conference of the Incorporated Association of Sales Managers of Great Britain. In demy 8vo, cloth gilt, 84 pp. 5s. net.

PSYCHOLOGY AS A SALES FACTOR. By A. J. Greenly. Second Edition. In demy 8vo, cloth gilt, 224 pp. 10s. 6d. net.

MODERN SALES CORRESPONDENCE. By D. M. Wilson. In demy 8vo, cloth gilt, 80 pp. 5s. net.

COMMERCIAL TRAVELLING. By Albert E. Bull. In crown 8vo, cloth gilt, 174 pp. 3s. 6d. net.

TRAINING FOR TRAVELLING SALESMEN. By Frank W. Shrubsall. In crown 8vo, cloth gilt, 90 pp. 2s. 6d. net.

THE BUSINESS MAN'S GUIDE TO ADVERTISING. By A. E. Bull. In crown 8vo, cloth, 127 pp. 3s. 6d. net.

ADVERTISING AND THE SHOPKEEPER. By Harold W. Eley. In crown 8vo, 160 pp. 3s. 6d. net.

ADVERTISING PROCEDURE. By O. Kleppner. In demy 8vo, cloth gilt, 555 pp. 21s. net.

THE LANGUAGE OF ADVERTISING. By J. B. OPDYCKE. Size 9¼ in. by 6¾ in., cloth, 506 pp. **15s.** net.

LAY-OUTS FOR ADVERTISING. By JOHN DELL. In crown 8vo, cloth gilt, 176 pp. **12s. 6d.** net.

ADVERTISEMENT LAY-OUT AND COPY-WRITING. By A. J. WATKINS. In crown 4to, cloth, 130 pp. **15s.** net.

PRACTICAL TYPOGRAPHY AND COPY WRITING. By COURTNEY D. FARMER, *Lecturer and Instructor to the Municipal College of Technology, Manchester.* In demy 8vo, cloth gilt, 110 pp. **5s.** net.

THE PRINCIPLES OF PRACTICAL PUBLICITY. By TRUMAN A. DE WEESE. In large crown 8vo, cloth, 266 pp., with 43 illustrations. **10s. 6d.** net.

BUSINESS LETTER PRACTICE. By J. B. OPDYCKE. In demy 8vo, cloth gilt, 602 pp. **7s. 6d.** net.

EFFECTIVE POSTAL PUBLICITY. By MAX RITTENBERG. Size 6½ in. by 9¼ in., cloth, 167 pp. **7s. 6d.** net.

PRACTICAL POINTS IN POSTAL PUBLICITY. By MAX RITTENBERG. Size, 6½ in. by 9¼ in., cloth, 128 pp. **7s. 6d.** net.

MAIL ORDER AND INSTALMENT TRADING. By A. E. BULL. In demy 8vo, cloth gilt, 356 pp. **7s. 6d.** net.

MAIL ORDER ORGANIZATION. By P. E. WILSON. In crown 8vo, cloth gilt, 127 pp. **3s. 6d.** net.

THE OUTDOOR SALES FORCE. By P. E. WILSON. In crown 8vo, cloth, 146 pp. **3s. 6d.** net.

SUCCESSFUL BUYING. By E. N. SIMONS. In demy 8vo, cloth gilt, 291 pp. **10s. 6d.** net.

MODERN PUBLICITY. By A. W. DEAN. In crown 8vo, cloth, 70 pp. **2s. 6d.** net.

ADVERTISING AND SELLING. By 150 Advertising and Sales Executives. Edited by NOBLE T. PRAIGG. In demy 8vo, cloth, 495 pp. **10s. 6d.** net.

PRACTICAL AIDS TO RETAIL SELLING. By A. EDWARD HAMMOND. In demy 8vo, cloth gilt, 180 pp. 128 pp. **7s. 6d.** net.

SELLING POLICIES. By PAUL D. CONVERSE. In demy 8vo, cloth gilt, 714 pp. **21s.** net.

MODERN METHODS IN SELLING. By L. J. HOENIG. In large crown 8vo, cloth gilt, 310 pp. **10s. 6d.** net.

EXPORT ADVERTISING PRACTICE. By C. F. PROPSON. Size 6 in. by 9 in., cloth gilt, 284 pp. **16s.** net.

ADVERTISING THROUGH THE PRESS. By N. HUNTER. In demy 8vo, cloth, 146 pp. **5s.** net.

PRACTICAL PRESS PUBLICITY. By A. L. CULYER. In demy 8vo, cloth, 95 pp. **3s. 6d.** net.

SHOP FITTINGS AND DISPLAY. By A. E. HAMMOND. In demy 8vo, cloth, 142 pp. **5s.** net.

WINDOW DRESSING. By G. L. TIMMINS. In crown 8vo, cloth, 85 pp. **2s.** net.

COMMERCIAL PHOTOGRAPHY. By D. CHARLES. In demy 8vo, cloth gilt, 156 pp. **5s.** net.

HINTS AND TIPS FOR COMMERCIAL ARTISTS. By BERNARD J. PALMER. In crown 8vo, 112 pp. **5s.** net.

TRAINING IN COMMERCIAL ART. By V. L. DANVERS. In crown 4to. **21s.** net.

TICKET AND SHOW CARD DESIGNING. By F. A. PEARSON. In foolscap, 180 pp. 4to, cloth. **3s. 6d.** net.

PLAIN AND ORNAMENTAL LETTERING. By E. G. FOOKS. Size, 9¼ in. by 6¾ in., 94 pp. **3s. 6d.** net.

DECORATIVE WRITING AND ARRANGEMENT OF LETTERING. By Prof. A. ERDMANN and A. A. BRAUN. Size 9½ in. by 6½ in., 134 pp. **10s. 6d.** net. Second Edition.

TYPES AND TYPE FACES. (From *Modern Advertising*.) By C. M. TREGURTHA. In crown 4to, quarter cloth, 48 pp. **2s. 6d.** net.

PRINTING. By H. A. MADDOX. In demy 8vo, cloth, 159 pp. **5s.** net.

CONTEMPORARY ART APPLIED TO THE STORE. By FREDERICK KIESLER. Size 11 in. by 8 in., 158 pp., with over 150 photographic reproductions. **30s.** net.

JOURNALISM

MODERN JOURNALISM. By C. F. CARR and F. E. STEVENS. In demy 8vo, cloth gilt, 252 pp. **10s. 6d.** net.

JOURNALISM AS A CAREER. Edited by W. T. CRANFIELD. In demy 8vo, cloth, 108 pp. **5s.** net.

AUTHORSHIP AND JOURNALISM. By ALBERT E. BULL. In crown 8vo, cloth, 170 pp. **3s. 6d.** net.

POPULAR GUIDE TO JOURNALISM. By ALFRED KINGSTON. Fourth Edition. In crown 8vo, cloth, 124 pp. **2s. 6d.** net.

PITMAN'S PRACTICAL JOURNALISM. By ALFRED BAKER. Second Edition, Revised by E. A. COPE. In crown 8vo, cloth, 180 pp. **3s. 6d.** net.

SHORT STORY WRITING AND FREE-LANCE JOURNALISM. By SYDNEY A. MOSELEY. Second Edition. In demy 8vo, cloth gilt, 241 pp. **7s. 6d.** net.

LAW

ELEMENTARY LAW. By E. A. COPE. In crown 8vo, cloth, 224 pp., with specimen legal forms. **4s.** net. Second Edition, Revised by A. H. COSWAY.

MERCANTILE LAW. By J. A. SLATER, B.A., LL.B. Sixth Edition. Revised by R. W. HOLLAND, O.B.E., M.A., M.Sc., LL.D., *of the Middle Temple, Barrister-at-Law*. In demy 8vo, cloth gilt, 474 pp. **7s. 6d.** net.

INTRODUCTION TO COMMERCIAL LAW. By NORMAN A. WEBB, B.Sc. In demy 8vo, cloth, 175 pp. **5s.**

COMPANIES AND COMPANY LAW. Together with the Companies Act, 1929. By A. C. CONNELL, LL.B. (Lond.), *of the Middle Temple, Barrister-at-Law*. Fourth Edition, Revised by W. E. WILKINSON, LL.D. In demy 8vo, cloth gilt, 422 pp. **6s.** net.

MANUAL OF COMPANY LAW AND PRACTICE. By LESLIE MADDOCK, *of the Inner Temple and the Midland Circuit, Barrister-at-Law*. In demy 8vo, cloth gilt, 437 pp. **10s. 6d.** net.

COMPANY LAW. By D. F. DE L'HOSTE RANKING, M.A., LL.D., and E. E. SPICER, F.C.A. Fifth Edition. In demy 8vo, cloth gilt, 404 pp. **10s. net.**

THE LAW OF JOINT STOCK COMPANIES. By W. J. WESTON, M.A., B.Sc., *of Gray's Inn, Barrister-at-Law.* In demy 8vo, 308 pp. **7s. 6d.** net.

LAW OF CARRIAGE BY RAILWAY. By L. R. LIPSETT, M.A., LL.D., and T. J. D. ATKINSON, M.A. Size 6 in. by 9 in., cloth gilt, 966 pp. **50s.** net.

THE LAW RELATING TO SECRET COMMISSIONS AND BRIBES. By ALBERT CREW, *Barrister-at-Law, of Gray's Inn.* Second Edition, Revised and Enlarged. In demy 8vo, cloth gilt, 252 pp. **10s. 6d.** net.

RIGHTS AND DUTIES OF LIQUIDATORS, TRUSTEES, AND RECEIVERS. By D. F. DE L'HOSTE RANKING, M.A., LL.D., E. E. SPICER, F.C.A., and E. C. PEGLER, F.C.A. Size 9¾ in. by 7 in., cloth gilt, 398 pp. **15s.** net. Seventeenth Edition.

LIQUIDATOR'S INDEX AND SUMMARY OF THE COMPANIES ACT AND WINDING-UP RULES, 1929. By JOHN H. SENIOR, F.C.A., and H. M. PRATT. In foolscap folio, buckram, 96 pp. **15s.** net.

GUIDE TO BANKRUPTCY LAW AND WINDING UP OF COMPANIES. By F. PORTER FAUSSET, M.A., *Barrister-at-Law.* Second Edition. In crown 8vo, cloth gilt, 216 pp. **5s.** net.

BANKRUPTCY, DEEDS OF ARRANGEMENT, AND BILLS OF SALE. By W. VALENTINE BALL, M.A., *Barrister-at-Law.* Fourth Edition. Revised in accordance with the Bankruptcy and the Deeds of Arrangement Acts, 1914. In demy 8vo, 394 pp. **12s. 6d.** net.

NOTES ON BANKRUPTCY LAW. By V. R. ANDERSON, A.C.A. In crown 8vo, cloth, 86 pp. **2s. 6d.** net.

PRINCIPLES OF MARINE LAW. By LAWRENCE DUCKWORTH, *Barrister-at-Law.* Fourth Edition, Revised by WM. MARSHALL FREEMAN, *Barrister-at-Law.* In demy 8vo, 400 pp. **7s. 6d.** net.

LAW FOR JOURNALISTS. By CHARLES PILLEY, *Barrister-at-Law, of Gray's Inn and the Western Circuit.* In demy 8vo, cloth, 170 pp. **5s.** net.

THE LAW RELATING TO BANKING AND FOREIGN EXCHANGE. By L. LE M. MINTY, Ph.D., B.Sc. (Econ.), B.Com., LL.B., Cert. A.I.B., *of Gray's Inn and the South-Eastern Circuit, Barrister-at-Law.* In crown 4to, cloth gilt. **30s.** net.

PARTNERSHIP LAW. By D. F. DE L'HOSTE RANKING, M.A., LL.D., E. E. SPICER, F.C.A., and E. C. PEGLER, F.C.A. Fourth Edition. In medium 8vo, cloth, 167 pp. **7s. 6d.** net.

PARTNERSHIP LAW AND ACCOUNTS. By R. W. HOLLAND, O.B.E., M.A., M.Sc., LL.D., *Barrister-at-Law.* In demy 8vo, 174 pp. **6s.** net.

THE LAW OF CONTRACT. By the same Author. Revised and Enlarged Edition. In demy 8vo, cloth, 123 pp. **5s.** net.

TRUSTS. By C. KELLY and J. COLE-HAMILTON, *Chartered Accountants.* In demy 8vo, cloth gilt, 418 pp. **15s.** net.

EXECUTORSHIP LAW AND ACCOUNTS. By D. F. DE L'HOSTE RANKING, M.A., LL.D., E. E. SPICER, F.C.A., and E. C. PEGLER, F.C.A. Size 10 in. by 7½ in., cloth gilt, 370 pp. **15s.** net. Ninth Edition.

WILLS. A Complete Guide for Testators, Executors, and Trustees. With a Chapter on Intestacy. By R. W. HOLLAND, O.B.E., M.A., M.Sc., LL.D., *of the Middle Temple, Barrister-at-Law.* In foolscap 8vo, cloth, 122 pp. **2s. 6d.** net. Third Edition.

SOLICITOR'S CLERK'S GUIDE. By EDWARD A. COPE. Revised by FRED G. W. LESTER. In crown 8vo, cloth gilt, 214 pp. **4s.** net.

MUNICIPAL AND LOCAL GOVERNMENT LAW. By H. EMERSON SMITH, LL.B. (Lond.). Second Edition. In demy 8vo, cloth gilt, 272 pp. **10s. 6d.** net.

LAW FOR THE HOUSE OWNER. By A. H. COSWAY. Second Edition. 128 pp. In crown 8vo, cloth. **2s. 6d.** net.

THE BUSINESS TENANT. By E. S. COX-SINCLAIR, *Barrister-at-Law*, and T. HYNES, *Barrister-at-Law*, LL.B. In crown 8vo, cloth, 263 pp. **7s. 6d.** net.

THE LAW RELATING TO BUILDING AND BUILDING CONTRACTS. By W. T. CRESWELL, Hon. A.R.I.B.A., F.R.San.Inst., *of Gray's Inn, Barrister-at-Law.* Second Edition. In demy 8vo, cloth, 372 pp. **12s. 6d.** net.

LEGAL TERMS, PHRASES, AND ABBREVIATIONS. By E. A. COPE. In crown 8vo, cloth gilt, 216 pp. **3s.** net. Third Edition, Revised.

COPYRIGHT IN INDUSTRIAL DESIGNS. By A. D. RUSSELL-CLARKE, *of the Inner Temple, Barrister-at-Law.* In demy 8vo, cloth, 212 pp. **10s. 6d.** net.

THE LAW OF EVIDENCE. By W. NEMBHARD HIBBERT, LL.D., *Barrister-at-Law.* Fifth Edition, Revised. In crown 8vo, 132 pp. **7s. 6d.** net.

THE LAW OF PROCEDURE. By the same Author. Third Edition. In demy 8vo, cloth gilt, 133 pp. **7s. 6d.** net.

THE LAW OF MASTER AND SERVANT. By FRANCIS RALEIGH BATT, LL.M., *of Gray's Inn, Barrister-at-Law, Professor of Commercial Law in the University of Liverpool.* In demy 8vo, cloth gilt, 410 pp. **10s. 6d.** net.

TRADE MARK LAW AND PRACTICE. By A. W. GRIFFITHS, B.Sc. (Eng.), Lond., *Barrister-at-Law.* In demy 8vo, cloth gilt, 268 pp. **10s. 6d.** net.

THE LAW RELATING TO ADVERTISING. By E. LING-MALLISON, B.Sc. (Lille), *of the Midland Circuit, the Central Criminal Court, North London Sessions, and the Middle Temple, Barrister-at-Law.* In crown 8vo, cloth gilt, 234 pp. **7s. 6d.** net.

THE LAW RELATING TO INDUSTRY. By H. SAMUELS, M.A., *of the Middle Temple, Barrister-at-Law.* In demy 8vo, cloth gilt, 258 pp. **15s.** net.

THE HISTORY, LAW, AND PRACTICE OF THE STOCK EXCHANGE. By A. P. POLEY, B.A., *Barrister-at-Law.* In demy 8vo, cloth gilt, 428 pp. **7s. 6d.** net. Fourth Edition.

BUSINESS REFERENCE BOOKS

BUSINESS MAN'S ENCYCLOPAEDIA AND DICTIONARY OF COMMERCE.
A reliable and comprehensive work of reference on all commercial subjects.
Fourth Edition. Edited by FRANK HEYWOOD, F.C.I.S. Assisted by up-
wards of 50 specialists as contributors. In 2 vols., large crown 4to, cloth
gilt, 1926 pp. £2 7s. 6d. net.

BUSINESS BUILDING. A complete guide for the wholesaler, retailer,
manufacturer, agent, etc. Edited by F. F. SHARLES, F.S.A.A. (Gold
Medallist), F.C.I.S. In 2 vols., crown 4to, cloth gilt, 1167 pp. complete,
42s. net. Second Edition.

PSYCHOLOGY IN MODERN BUSINESS. By H. W. HEPNER. In medium
8vo, cloth gilt, 743 pp. 21s. net.

BUSINESS TERMS, PHRASES, AND ABBREVIATIONS. In crown 8vo,
cloth, 280 pp. 3s. 6d. net. Fifth Edition. With equivalents in French,
German, Spanish, and Italian; and facsimile documents.

MERCANTILE TERMS AND ABBREVIATIONS. Size 3 in. by 4¾ in., cloth,
126 pp. 1s. 6d. net. Containing over 1,000 terms and 500 abbreviations
with definitions.

BUSINESS FORECASTING AND ITS PRACTICAL APPLICATION. By W.
WALLACE, M.Com. (Lond.). Second Edition. In demy 8vo, cloth gilt,
140 pp. 7s. 6d. net.

BOOK-KEEPING AND OFFICE WORK. By R. J. PORTERS, F.C.R.A. In
two volumes. Crown 4to, 728 pp. 30s. net.

PRACTICAL BUSINESS FORECASTING. By D. F. JORDAN. Size 6 in. by
9 in., cloth, 270 pp. 16s. net.

BUSINESS CHARTS. By T. G. ROSE, A.M.I.Mech.E. In demy 8vo, cloth
gilt, 104 pp. 10s. 6d. net.

COMMERCIAL ARBITRATIONS. By E. J. PARRY, B.Sc., F.I.C., F.C.S.
In crown 8vo, cloth gilt, 105 pp. 3s. 6d. net.

COMMERCIAL CONTRACTS. By the same Author. A Guide for Business
Men. In crown 8vo, cloth, 200 pp. 5s. net.

FINANCIAL ORGANIZATION AND MANAGEMENT. By C. W. GERSTENBERG,
Professor of Finance at New York University. Size 6 in. by 9 in., cloth
gilt, 739 pp. 25s. net.

MONEY MAKING IN STOCKS AND SHARES. By SYDNEY A. MOSELEY.
In demy 8vo, cloth gilt, 252 pp. 7s. 6d. net. Third Edition.

HOW THE STOCK MARKET REALLY WORKS. By W. COLLIN BROOKS.
In demy 8vo, cloth gilt, 160 pp. 5s. net.

MARKETS OF LONDON. By CUTHBERT MAUGHAN. In demy 8vo, cloth gilt,
218 pp. 6s. net.

THE SHAREHOLDER'S MANUAL. By H. H. BASSETT. In crown 8vo, cloth gilt, 140 pp. **3s. 6d.** net.

THE SMALL INVESTOR'S GUIDE. By SYDNEY A. MOSELEY. In demy 8vo, cloth, 160 pp. **5s.** net.

THE ROOT PRINCIPLES OF INVESTMENT. By H. COPE WEST. In demy 8vo, cloth, 232 pp. **15s.** net.

TYPES OF BUSINESS ENTERPRISE. By M. C. CROSS, LL.B., Ph.D. In medium 8vo, cloth gilt, 348 pp. **21s.** net.

HOW TO USE A BANKING ACCOUNT. By C. BIDWELL. In crown 8vo, cloth, 116 pp. **3s. 6d.** net.

DUPLICATING AND COPYING PROCESSES. By W. DESBOROUGH, O.B.E. In demy 8vo, cloth gilt, 146 pp. **5s.** net.

BUSINESS CYCLES. The Problem and its Setting. By W. C. MITCHELL. Size 6 in. by 9 in., cloth gilt, 511 pp. **30s.** net.

STATISTICAL METHODS. By F. C. MILLS, *Associate Professor of Business Statistics, Columbia University.* In demy 8vo, cloth gilt, 620 pp. **15s.** net.

STATISTICS. By WILLIAM VERNON LOVITT, Ph.D., *Professor of Mathematics, Colorado College;* and HENRY F. HOLTZCLAW, Ph.D., *Professor of Commerce, University of Kansas.* In medium 8vo, cloth gilt, 304 pp. **15s.** net.

BUSINESS STATISTICS, THEIR PREPARATION, COMPILATION, AND PRESENTATION. By R. W. HOLLAND, O.B.E., M.A., M.Sc., LL.D. Second Edition. In crown 8vo, cloth, 108 pp. **3s. 6d.** net.

STATISTICS AND THEIR APPLICATION TO COMMERCE. By A. L. BODDINGTON, *Fellow of the Royal Statistical and Economic Societies.* Fourth Edition. In medium 8vo, cloth gilt, 340 pp. **12s. 6d.** net.

A MANUAL OF CHARTING. Size 6 in. by 9 in., cloth gilt, 116 pp. **6s.** net.

PITMAN'S BOOK OF SYNONYMS AND ANTONYMS. In crown 8vo, cloth, 140 pp. **2s. 6d.** net.

PITMAN'S OFFICE DESK BOOK. In crown 8vo, 320 pp., cloth. **2s. 6d.** net.

MODERN DEBATE PRACTICE. By WALDO O. WILLHOFT. In crown 8vo, cloth, 339 pp. **5s.** net.

REPORT WRITING. By CARL G. GAUM, M.E., and HAROLD F. GRAVES, M.A. In medium 8vo, cloth gilt, 322 pp. **12s. 6d.** net.

THE ESSENTIALS OF PUBLIC SPEAKING. By W. C. DUBOIS, A.M., LL.B. In large crown 8vo, cloth, 276 pp. **8s. 6d.** net.

SPEAKING IN PUBLIC. By ARLEIGH B. WILLIAMSON, M.A., *Associate Professor of Public Speaking, Washington Square College, New York University.* In medium 8vo, cloth gilt, 430 pp. **15s.** net.

HOW TO SPEAK IN PUBLIC. By C. F. CARR and F. E. STEVENS. Second Edition. In crown 8vo, cloth, 128 pp. **3s. 6d.** net.

DICTIONARY OF THE WORLD'S COMMERCIAL PRODUCTS. By J. H. VANSTONE, F.R.G.S. With French, German, and Spanish equivalents for the names of the products. In demy 8vo, cloth, 170 pp. **5s.** net. Third Edition.

RAW MATERIALS OF COMMERCE. Edited by J. H. VANSTONE, F.R.G.S. In two volumes, demy 4to, cloth gilt, 793 pp. Complete, **40s.** net.

COMMERCIAL COMMODITIES. By F. W. MATTHEWS, B.Sc., A.I.C., F.C.S. In demy 8vo, cloth gilt, 326 pp. **12s. 6d.** net.

THE COTTON WORLD. Compiled and Edited by J. A. TODD, M.A., B.L. In crown 8vo, cloth, 246 pp. **5s.** net.

FRUIT AND THE FRUIT TRADE. By FORD FAIRFORD. In demy 8vo, cloth, 162 pp. **6s.** net.

TEA AND TEA DEALING. By F. W. S. STAVEACRE. In demy 8vo, cloth gilt, 150 pp. **7s. 6d.** net.

THE COCOA AND CHOCOLATE INDUSTRY. By A. W. KNAPP, M.Sc., F.I.C. In demy 8vo, cloth gilt, 200 pp. **7s. 6d.** net. Second Edition.

THE FURNITURE STYLES. By H. E. BINSTEAD. Size 9½ in. by 6½ in., cloth, 208 pp., illustrated. **10s. 6d.** net. Second Edition.

BUYING AND SELLING A BUSINESS. By A. H. COSWAY. In crown 8vo, cloth, 110 pp. **3s. 6d.** net.

HOW TO COLLECT ACCOUNTS BY LETTER. By C. HANNEFORD-SMITH, F.C.W.A. In crown 8vo, cloth gilt, 94 pp. **3s. 6d.** net.

LETTERS THAT COLLECT. By JOHN WHYTE, Ph.D., and F. R. OTTER, B.A. In medium 8vo, cloth gilt, 435 pp. **15s.** net.

HOW TO GRANT CREDIT. By CUTHBERT GREIG, *Secretary, London Association for Protection of Trade, Ltd.* In crown 8vo, cloth, 102 pp. **3s. 6d.** net.

HOW TO APPEAL AGAINST YOUR RATES. By A. STANLEY EAMER, F.S.I., *Rating Surveyor to the Metropolitan Borough of Lambeth.* In two volumes, in crown 8vo, cloth. Vol. I (without the Metropolis), **5s.** net. Vol. II (within the Metropolis), **3s. 6d.** net.

A HANDBOOK ON WILLS. By A. H. COSWAY. In crown 8vo, cloth, 123 pp. **2s. 6d.** net.

TRADERS' RAIL CHARGES UP TO DATE. By J. W. PARKER, A.M.Inst.T. In crown 8vo, cloth, 135 pp. **3s. 6d.** net.

GUIDE TO COUNTY COURT PROCEDURE. Being the Second Edition of *The Traders' Guide to County Court Procedure.* By F. H. B. CHAPMAN. Revised by B. S. HILLS. In crown 8vo, cloth, 104 pp. **2s. 6d.** net.

COMMERCIAL ATLAS OF THE WORLD. In crown 4to, cloth, 140 pp. **5s.** net.

STATISTICAL ATLAS OF THE WORLD. By J. STEPHENSON, M.A., M.Com., D.Sc. In foolscap folio, cloth, 146 pp. **7s. 6d.** net.

THE CABLE AND WIRELESS COMMUNICATIONS OF THE WORLD. By F. J. BROWN, C.B., C.B.E., M.A., B.Sc. (Lond.). Second Edition. In demy 8vo, cloth gilt, 162 pp. **7s. 6d.** net.

THE FUTURE OF EMPIRE TRADE. By J. E. RAY. With a Foreword by The Rt. Hon. L. S. AMERY. In crown 8vo, paper, 128 pp. **2s.** net.

26 # 26 PITMAN'S BUSINESS HANDBOOKS

FOREIGN LANGUAGE DICTIONARIES

DICTIONARY OF COMMERCIAL CORRESPONDENCE IN SEVEN LANGUAGES: ENGLISH, FRENCH, GERMAN, SPANISH, ITALIAN, PORTUGUESE: AND RUSSIAN. In demy 8vo, cloth, 718 pp. 12s. 6d. net. Third Edition.

ENGLISH-FRENCH AND FRENCH-ENGLISH DICTIONARY OF BUSINESS WORDS AND TERMS. Size 2 in. by 6 in., cloth, rounded corners, 540 pp. 5s. net.

FRENCH-ENGLISH AND ENGLISH-FRENCH COMMERCIAL DICTIONARY of the Words and Terms used in Commercial Correspondence. By F. W. SMITH. Second Edition. In crown 8vo, cloth, 576 pp. 7s. 6d. net.

GERMAN-ENGLISH AND ENGLISH-GERMAN COMMERCIAL DICTIONARY. By J. BITHELL, M.A. In crown 8vo, cloth gilt. Second Edition, 992 pp. 16s. net.

A NEW GERMAN-ENGLISH DICTIONARY FOR GENERAL USE. By F. C. HEBERT and L. HIRSCH. In crown 8vo, cloth gilt, 1769 pp. 15s. net.

ENGLISH-GERMAN AND GERMAN-ENGLISH DICTIONARY OF BUSINESS WORDS AND TERMS. Size 2 in. by 6 in., rounded corners, 440 pp., cloth. 5s. net.

SPANISH-ENGLISH AND ENGLISH-SPANISH COMMERCIAL DICTIONARY of the Words and Terms used in Commercial Correspondence. By G. R. MACDONALD. In crown 8vo, cloth gilt. Third Edition, 833 pp. 12s. 6d. net.

ITALIAN-ENGLISH AND ENGLISH-ITALIAN COMMERCIAL DICTIONARY. By G. R. MACDONALD. In crown 8vo, cloth gilt, 1166 pp. 30s. net.

BARETTI'S ITALIAN AND ENGLISH DICTIONARY. Compiled by GUGLIELMO COMELATI and J. DAVENPORT. In two volumes, cloth gilt, Vol. I, 796 pp.; Vol. II, 752 pp. 25s. net. (Reprinted.)

PORTUGUESE-ENGLISH AND ENGLISH-PORTUGUESE COMMERCIAL DICTIONARY. By F. W. SMITH. In crown 8vo, cloth gilt, 486 pp. 16s. net.

A NEW DICTIONARY OF THE PORTUGUESE AND ENGLISH LANGUAGES. Based on a manuscript of Julius Cornet. By H. MICHAELIS. In two volumes, demy 8vo, cloth gilt. Vol. I, Portuguese-English, 736 pp.; Vol. II, English-Portuguese, 742 pp. Each 21s. net. Abridged Edition, 783 pp. 25s. net.

TECHNICAL DICTIONARY OF ENGINEERING AND INDUSTRIAL SCIENCE IN SEVEN LANGUAGES—ENGLISH, FRENCH, SPANISH, ITALIAN, PORTUGUESE, RUSSIAN, AND GERMAN. Compiled by ERNEST SLATER, M.I.E.E., M.I.Mech.E., in collaboration with leading Authorities. In four volumes. Each in crown 4to, buckram gilt, £8 8s. net complete. (Complete index for each language in preparation.)

PITMAN'S
BUSINESS LIBRARY

THIS series of handy volumes consists of the most important sections which originally appeared in *Business Building*. These have been thoroughly revised and brought up to date. They provide a really interesting and practical treatment of the business man's peculiar problems and difficulties, showing how they may be mastered, avoiding mere theorizing, but plainly setting forth directions for the practice of the most modern methods. The authors are leading men in the particular sphere of business activity about which they write.

1. **THE RETAIL SHOP—Its Organization, Management, and Routine.**
   By C. L. T. BEECHING, O.B.E., F.G.I.

2. **SELLING BY POST—Practical Suggestions for Mail-order Traders.**
   By HAROLD W. ELEY, *Author of "Advertising and the Shopkeeper."*

3. **BUSINESS ORGANIZATION AND ROUTINE.**
   By W. CAMPBELL, *Chartered Secretary.*

4. **BUSINESS ACCOUNTS AND FINANCE.**
   By W. CAMPBELL, *Chartered Secretary.*

5. **LETTER WRITING—A Guide to Business Correspondence.**
   By G. K. BUCKNALL, A.C.I.S. (Hons.).

6. **COMPANY SECRETARIAL ROUTINE.**
   By C. C. WALFORD, A.S.A.A., A.C.I.S.

7. **HIRE PURCHASE.**
   By HAROLD W. ELEY. With a Section on **Hire-purchase Accounts** by S. HOWARD WITHEY.

Each foolscap 8vo, leatherette, 64 pp. **1s.** net.
Other volumes in preparation.

COMMON COMMODITIES
AND INDUSTRIES SERIES

In each of the handbooks in this series a particular product or industry is treated by an expert writer and practical man of business. Beginning with the life history of the plant, or other natural product, he follows its development until it becomes a commercial commodity, and so on through the various phases of its sale in the market and its purchase by the consumer. Industries are treated in a similar manner.

Each book in crown 8vo, illustrated. 3s. net.

Acids and Alkalis
Aluminium
Asbestos
Bookbinding Craft and Industry, The
Books from the MS. to the Bookseller
Boot and Shoe Industry
Bread Making
Brush Making
Butter and Cheese
Button Industry, The
Carpets
Clays
Clocks and Watches
Cloth and the Cloth Trade
Clothing Trades Industry
Coal
Coal Tar
Coffee
Cold Storage and Ice Making
Concrete and Reinforced Concrete
Copper
Cordage and Cordage Hemp and Fibres
Corn Trade, The British
Cotton

Cotton Spinning
Drugs in Commerce
Dyes
Electricity
Engraving
Explosives, Modern
Fertilizers
Fishing Industry, The
Furniture
Furs
Gas and Gas Making
Glass
Gloves and the Glove Trade
Gold
Gums and Resins
Ink
Iron and Steel
Ironfounding
Jute
Knitted Fabrics
Lead
Leather
Linen
Locks and Lockmaking
Match Industry
Meat
Oils
Paints and Varnishes

Paper
Perfumery
Photography
Platinum Metals
Pottery
Rice
Rubber
Salt
Silk
Soap
Sponges
Starch
Stones and Quarries
Sugar
Sulphur
Tea
Telegraphy, Telephony, and Wireless
Textile Bleaching
Timber
Tin and the Tin Industry
Tobacco
Weaving
Wheat
Wine and the Wine Trade
Wool
Worsted
Zinc

PITMAN'S SHORTHAND
INVALUABLE FOR ALL BUSINESS AND PROFESSIONAL MEN

The following Catalogues will be sent, post free, on application—
EDUCATIONAL, TECHNICAL, SHORTHAND, FOREIGN LANGUAGE, AND ART

LONDON: SIR ISAAC PITMAN & SONS, LTD., PARKER ST., KINGSWAY, W.C.2

PRINTED IN GREAT BRITAIN AT THE PITMAN PRESS, BATH
(1285w)